THE JUMP

THE JUMP

Sebastian Telfair
and the High Stakes Business of High School Ball

IAN O'CONNOR

RODALE

Mention of specific companies, organizations, or authorities in this book does not imply endorsement by the author or publisher, nor does mention of specific companies, organizations, or authorities imply that they endorse this book, its author, or the publisher.

© 2005 by Ian O'Connor

Printed in the United States of America
Rodale Inc. makes every effort to use acid-free ♾, recycled paper ♻.

Book design by Christopher Rhoads

Library of Congress Cataloging-in-Publication Data

O'Connor, Ian.
    The jump : Sebastian Telfair and the high stakes business of high school ball / Ian O'Connor.
        p.   cm.
    ISBN-13 978-1-59486-107-9 hardcover
    ISBN-10 1-59486-107-2 hardcover
    1. Telfair, Sebastian.   2. Basketball players—United States—Biography.   3. High school athletes—United States—Biography.   4. Basketball—Social aspects—United States.   I. Title.
GV884.T44O36   2005
796.323'092—dc22   2004026366

Distributed to the trade by Holtzbrinck Publishers

2   4   6   8   10   9   7   5   3   1   hardcover

We inspire and enable people to improve their lives and the world around them

For more of our products visit **rodalestore.com** or call 800-848-4735

To Tracey, the forever love of my life.
To Kyle, the best teammate a father could ever have.
To Mr. O, for showing me how to fight.

To the combat veterans of Vietnam who, like Otis Telfair, deserved much better than they got when they returned home.

CONTENTS

ACKNOWLEDGMENTS

I would like to extend my sincerest thanks to Sebastian Telfair and his family for their cooperation, as this book would not have been possible without it. I'd also like to thank Renan Ebeid, Dwayne Morton, Danny Turner, Rasheem Barker, Bobby Hartstein, Corinne Heslin, and all the Abraham Lincoln players, coaches, and staff members for welcoming me into their world.

Andy Miller, Rick Pitino, Sonny Vaccaro, John Nash, and Thomas Sicignano were among the many basketball figures who granted the access necessary to bring this idea to life; I'm indebted to them all. The Los Angeles Clippers of Elgin Baylor, Mike Dunleavy, Barry Hecker, Gary Sacks, and Evan Pickman allowed me into their private predraft sanctuary, and their trust and professionalism were greatly appreciated.

My bosses and colleagues at the *Journal News* and *USA Today*, including Henry Freeman, Mark Leary, Zana Varner, Monte Lorell, Reid Cherner, Christine Brennan, and Chris Lawlor, offered the support I so desperately needed. My agent, David Black, believed in me even when I didn't; David showed great understanding while I put him through an interminable wait. My editor at Rodale, Jeremy Katz, showed a true scout's eye for shaping the narrative when I lost my way.

Friends and colleagues who offered invaluable aid and guidance included Dan Wetzel, John Canzano, Buster Olney, Dan Martin, Tim Layden, Dan Le Batard, Pat Forde, Fran Fraschilla, Mark Heisler, John Lopez, Sam Smith, Rosalyn Bayer, and Gerard Dietz.

Finally, I'd like to thank a man I've never met, Darcy Frey, for providing such a vivid roadmap of Coney Island in *The Last Shot*.

PROLOGUE

The gates swung wide in Harlem, and two of the most prominent figures in American entertainment came rolling on through, strutting to that exclusive beat of fame, fortune, and youth. LeBron James had just agreed to a Nike deal worth more than $100 million, and Jay-Z had already sold 30 million records. So on this close June night, the fans who had assembled across the river from Yankee Stadium made the kind of ballpark sound once reserved for the Babe and Joe D., a sound that would have signaled unmitigated love if not for one undeniable truth.

The fans were cheering just as loudly for someone else.

Sebastian Telfair swore he was 6 feet tall, but as I watched him enter Holcombe Rucker Park with James on one side and Jay-Z on the other, with the certain first pick in the NBA draft and the undisputed king of hip-hop acting as surrogate bodyguards, the kid had 5-foot-11 stitched to him like an Adidas label. His one extraordinary feature was his ordinariness. Telfair wasn't just a baby-faced point guard from the Coney Island projects with legs skinnier than a Nathan's frank; he was a ballplayer without any physical attribute to suggest he was LeBron's personal choice as his heir, and among the most publicized talents in the fabulously rich history of New York City ball.

Well, he did have big hands, hands of a 6-foot-5 forward. But Telfair could barely dunk. He wasn't heavily muscled about the torso and, in the new-age sports vernacular, he wasn't particularly long, either. But if Telfair could loom as figuratively large as that old Power Memorial center, Lew Alcindor, who were Jay-Z and LeBron but animate props on the point guard's stage?

"Bassy . . . Bassy," they shouted in honor of the jazzed-up version of Telfair's given name. The word had gotten out: LeBron wasn't going to play and risk injury just 72 hours before his local NBA team, the Cleveland Cavaliers, would make the chiseled 6-foot-8 son of Akron and St. Vincent-St. Mary High School graduate the number one pick. Jay-Z? This wasn't some concert at the Garden.

With the Yankees on the road and the Mets locked inside their usual catatonic state, this was the biggest game in town. This was a game at a basketball shrine like no other, a shrine amid the Polo Grounds projects worthy of the hundreds of pilgrims who pressed against the courtside railings, and the hundreds of pilgrims cursing the early birds in vain while pinned behind the blue police barricades outside the park's fence.

Nobody was giving up a seat at the Rucker. You didn't make it there, you didn't make it anywhere. Wilt Chamberlain played the Rucker. So did Kareem Abdul-Jabbar, Julius Erving, Earl "The Pearl" Monroe, and Kobe Bryant. All of the great playground legends who never made it to the league—Earl "The Goat" Manigault, Herman "Helicopter" Knowings, and Joe "The Destroyer" Hammond—made their names dunking and plucking quarters from backboard tops at the Rucker.

It was a rite of passage, a basketball baptism by fire. This was Telfair's night to be christened, right smack in the teeming public square at 155th Street and Frederick Douglass Boulevard.

Jay-Z and LeBron assumed the roles of godparents. Born Shawn Carter, Jay-Z was CEO of a team named for his S. Carter sneaker line that emerged from his unprecedented contract with Reebok; no other rapper had closed such a deal. Jay-Z had his ballers meet at his studio. The rapper rented a luxury bus for the occasion, somehow managed to secure a police escort for the ride, and then made Telfair his team's starting point guard in the Rucker's signature event, the Entertainers Basketball Classic.

LeBron was Telfair's personal coach and psychologist, his Tony Robbins for the evening.

At 18, Telfair had never dribbled across the Rucker court. He had played there only in his midsummer night's dream, slicing his way toward the basket and into an indelible corner of Harlem lore.

Truth was, the playground had never seen a kid quite like this. Telfair had been covered in newspapers and magazines before his freshman year at Brooklyn's Abraham Lincoln High School. He appeared in a 12-page fashion spread in the magazine *Dime*, with lingerie models draped all over his underaged limbs. He seized top billing ahead of his good friend LeBron on the cover of the hip-hop basketball bible *Slam*, with the headline screaming: "Sebastian Telfair and LeBron James are about to rule the world. Imagine that."

Imagine that Telfair was declared the country's best player in the Class of 2004 while in fourth grade. Imagine that he was staring at a chance to become the first public school star in New York history to win city titles in 3 consecutive years. Imagine that hundreds of Division I college coaches would trade in their annuities and courtesy cars to sign Telfair, if only the NBA scouts and sneaker reps trailing him stopped obstructing their views.

Imagine that Telfair would say he rejected illicit offers worth hundreds of thousands of dollars while playing ball at Lincoln High.

"He's got the game, the smile, and a name that rolls right off your tongue," said Sonny Vaccaro, America's most recognizable sneaker rep. Yes, Sebastian Telfair was a living, breathing study in hype.

Only hype never counted at the Rucker. Street punks were treated like millionaires, and millionaires like street punks. The Indiana Pacers' Ron Artest, a millionaire street punk, would make that point. Playing in the undercard game on Telfair's big night, Artest chopped away at every poor soul driving for a layup, inspiring an opposing coach named Mousey Carela— "He's the Phil Jackson of this shit," one Rucker regular explained—to race off his bench and into Artest's face to scream, "We're going to fuck you up."

No blood, no technical. At the Rucker, fans were never alone in demanding their own SportsCenter dunks; on-court announcers provided running commentary encouraging a player to either embarrass his opponent or be embarrassed over the mike.

Despite the chaos and the presence of NBA players such as Artest and Lamar Odom, Telfair wouldn't merely be the youngest and best player in either game; he would be the most poised. The gene pool was tilted in his favor. Telfair was a cousin of Stephon Marbury, and the extended Marbury family was to Brooklyn basketball what the Kennedys were to Massachusetts politics.

Five Marbury boys played Division I ball, and so expectation followed Telfair like a blanket out of the crib. But even Jay-Z wasn't sure how the kid's game would play at the Rucker; he'd expressed some reservations on the ride over. "This is like the Apollo," one of the on-court announcers warned the players. "If you don't show up, you will get booed." These announcers sized up the worthy players and granted them nicknames that would live in perpetuity, like "The Bone Collector" and "Half-Man, Half-Amazing."

Jay-Z didn't want Sebastian Telfair to leave the park still known as Sebastian Telfair. By night's end, Jay-Z was comforted by the fact Telfair would forever be known in Harlem as "2 Fast 2 Furious."

With the crowd so close to the action it formed the sidelines, Telfair ignored the NBA TV cameras and the pleas to deliver the kind of bounce-the-ball-off-your-opponent's-forehead game popularized by that rebel sneaker brand, And 1, and those streetball shows thriving on cable.

If Telfair showed Allen Iverson speed, he also showed John Stockton savvy. Every pass was a bounce pass. Every shot was a good shot. Every individual move was made with a team goal in mind.

The one and only time Telfair answered the crowd's calls for more came on his better-than-Iverson double crossover that nearly broke both ankles owned by "The Director," former St. John's guard and Knicks hopeful David Cain, whom Pat Riley called one of the toughest players he ever had to cut.

This move freed Telfair to suspend his twirling body in midair, draw a foul at the basket, propel the crowd into a near-religious experience, and send LeBron racing onto the court.

Telfair calmly made his free throws before the fans and LeBron settled down. He finished with 24 points and, if anyone cared to count, a dozen or so assists. His one turnover came on a bounce pass. His selfless and disciplined play didn't jibe with family tradition, but his high lift on jump shots did carry the Marbury signature.

All in all, the boy wonder appeared to be precisely what Tiger Woods's college coach had once called his own prodigy—half-Mozart, half-Magic Johnson. Telfair figured out his symphony in the middle of the fast break. Of most consequence, Telfair's team won the game. That's how point guards and quarterbacks were judged.

When the show was complete, fans poured onto the court as if they were students out of some nowhere college celebrating their long-shot bid to the NCAA Tournament. Carmelo Anthony, who had been sitting in the stands dressed in his Tom Seaver retro jersey, had already left the park. So had Dwayne "Tiny" Morton, the head coach at Lincoln and among the few high school coaches in America who would show up at a game wearing his star player's jersey. Morton was last seen in his purple Telfair jersey and backward-turned Yankees cap heading for the Jay-Z bus in the game's final minutes, fleeing the postgame madness to come.

Jay-Z, LeBron, Telfair, and a couple of hired hands who looked like NFL noseguards cut through the crowd. Telfair had assistance from the rear. The man was tall, lean, and weathered; he looked like some old-school boxing trainer. He had his right hand on Telfair's left shoulder, escorting him through the hustle and bustle, when I asked for a minute. The old man responded by yanking the player's top and demanding that he oblige.

When Sylvester "Otis" Telfair was his son's age, he was almost on his way to the killing fields of Vietnam. That was then, this was now. It was closing on midnight, and Otis's son was standing near a park bench in an unlit corner of Harlem. Sebastian was standing at the four-way, big-business intersection connecting the NBA, major college sports, sneaker-backed tournaments, and high-profile high school basketball.

He was standing at the very point where tens of millions could be made or squandered. So Sebastian talked about learning from the cautionary tales embodied by his backup point guard for the night, Omar Cook, and his friend Lenny Cooke, minor league nomads who cost themselves millions by leaving school early to play in an NBA that wasn't ready to receive them.

"You definitely look at the negative things that happened to people," Sebastian said, "and then you go in a different direction."

A different direction? Telfair had been pulled in so many directions, his head spun faster than the world-famous Cyclone roller coaster that still raged off the Atlantic Ocean, one bounce pass away from his Coney Island home.

On this night, Telfair was being pulled only in the direction of the bus. LeBron was shouting for him to come. It was a night to light candles to that holy trinity of fame, fortune, and youth. It was a night to party at Jay-Z's new club, 40/40, where a Telfair friend would introduce the point guard to Britney Spears.

Telfair wanted to be half-Britney, half-LeBron. He wanted his own coast-to-coast tour, and he wanted his games on national TV. Telfair had poured so much blood, sweat, and tears into this moment in time. He had studied NBA game tapes. He had run a million miles in the beach sand a block from his housing authority home. He had risen at 5:00 A.M., day after day, starting his morning just when the dealers were finishing their night, so he could do situps and pushups in his apartment, race up and down the stairs in his 15-story building, jump rope in the lobby, and shoot solitary jump shots in the Lincoln High gym.

Would Telfair ignore conventional wisdom and follow LeBron into the pros? Would he become the first point guard to jump straight from high school to the NBA?

What would he do with his senior season, his one last season by the sea?

Telfair knew only that he would do something people wouldn't forget. You see, kids used to make fun of his name. If Sebastian Telfair had the ring of nobility to it, or sounded like some Evelyn Waugh character out of *Brideshead Revisited*, the name didn't charm the boys in the 'hood.

But there came this seminal moment in the life of Brooklyn's latest, greatest basketball prince. "I decided I liked my name," the point guard said. "Sebastian Telfair. It's a name people are going to remember."

One way or the other.

1

This was the night sure to change everyone's lives. This was a rags-to-riches, American dream kind of night, because David Stern was calling out all those first-round names and Jamel Thomas was certain to be among them.

Jamel was 3 when his mother was murdered. Erica Telfair already had a full house in her project apartment, but she took in Jamel and his 1-year-old brother, Deon, because that's what the good people inside Surf-side Gardens did. They took care of their own. Lord knew nobody was about to do it for them.

Thomas wasn't easy to raise. As a teen, his nickname was "Five Thirty"—that's when he'd come in from the streets and call it a morning. But Thomas and Stephon Marbury were two ballers who would show up in Bobby Hartstein's gym at Abraham Lincoln High as eighth grade prospects determined to someday take the Railsplitters to Madison Square Garden and the city crown.

Hartstein knew Marbury. Everyone in Coney Island knew Marbury. He was the wonderchild, the younger brother coming behind Eric, Donnie, and Norman, Lincoln stars all. So no, Hartstein didn't ask Marbury to identify himself. The coach wanted to know a little about his taller friend.

"Who's that?" Hartstein asked.

"My cousin Jamel," Marbury answered.

"How does he do in school?"

"He doesn't go to school, Coach."

"What do you mean he doesn't go to school?"

"Well, he doesn't go every day."

"Where does he think he's going to high school?"

"Right here, Coach."

"Well, he's going to school every single day if he thinks he's going to play basketball for Lincoln."

Thomas didn't go to school every single day, but he developed into a representative—if withdrawn—student. He was always good in math, but as a freshman, he'd refuse to complete the essay portion of a test simply because he didn't believe he could write one. This inspired Lenore Braverman, English teacher, to make an offer. Braverman asked Thomas if he wanted to live with her and her husband in their upper-middle-class home.

Hartstein thought it was a terrific idea, but he had to run it by the Telfair and Marbury families. "They didn't know Mrs. Braverman from a hole in the wall," Hartstein said. "They were wondering, 'Why is this white Jewish woman going to bring a black kid into her house, because she thinks she's going to cash in on him someday?'" The coach vouched for Braverman, and Stephon did the same.

Thomas would stay with the Bravermans during the week and return to the projects for the weekends. Early on, he struggled with the discipline. No kid nicknamed "Five Thirty" could embrace a 10:00 P.M. bedtime.

Ultimately, the Bravermans helped him turn around his life. Thomas went from a kid who wouldn't write an essay to one who scored high enough on his SAT—in the 800s, Hartstein said—to win a scholarship to Providence College.

Thomas earned that scholarship by being 6-foot-5, and by playing Pippen to Marbury's Jordan. But he was lucky to have had any major Division I possibilities at all. Providence and Rutgers wanted him; all the true powerhouse programs were busy with Marbury, the best prep guard in America.

The Thomas and Marbury home recruiting visits were set up for the same night, with heavyweights such as Syracuse and UCLA making their pitches in Marbury's fourth-floor apartment while Providence set its sights one floor below, literally and figuratively. Bobby Gonzalez, the Providence assistant, worked Thomas hard, believing he had a steal.

But by becoming active participants in the Thomas recruitment, the Marburys nearly blew the best scholarship offer Jamel had. Pete Gillen, the Providence coach, made the home visit with his aide, Louis Orr, while Hartstein was in Lutheran Hospital with a bleeding ulcer and other stomach problems. Gerard Bell, Hartstein's assistant, sat in for his boss. Gillen brought Orr to the meeting instead of Gonzalez because he figured the former Syracuse star and Knicks forward would make a lasting impression.

The Marburys were the ones who made the lasting impression, shuttling between Stephon's meetings and Jamel's. Given their experience with college coaches, the Marburys appointed themselves Jamel's recruiting coordinators. Don Marbury and his sons Donnie and Eric sat in on the Providence home visit. During that visit, Orr emerged from a separate conference with Marbury family members to tell Gillen there was a major problem.

Gillen ended the visit, picked up Gonzalez, and arrived in Hartstein's hospital room. The Lincoln coach had IV tubes running into his arms. He was expecting a courtesy visit but instead got an earful of bad news.

"Bobby H," Gillen said. "I think we've got to back off of this one. You know we love Jamel. He's a great kid. But it's too crazy up there, and I don't think we can get involved with this one."

"Pete," Hartstein said, "let me handle it. As soon as I get this IV out of my arm, I'll straighten it out."

Hartstein immediately called Don Marbury, the patriarch, and one of his older sons to the hospital. "I laid into them," Hartstein said. "I said, 'Are you out of your mind?' They said, 'Coach, but we didn't mean anything.' I said, 'Listen, do what I tell you and keep your mouth shut. Do you want to ruin everything for Jamel?' And they said, 'No, no, no.'"

Gillen would agree to continue recruiting Thomas only if Hartstein gained control of the process. "There were a lot of crazy things in the recruiting process," Gillen said. "I said, 'Bobby, if things are going to be off-kilter and not according to the rules, we're out. We didn't cheat at Xavier to get 6-foot-9 guys who were lottery picks, Brian Grant and Tyrone Hill, so we're not going to cheat for a 6-foot-5 excellent player.'

"We just heard rumors. (Jamel) never asked for any money. We just had to watch it and be careful. We heard people were asking for money, and if that happens, we're out. We're not going to give a kid a gun and let him shoot us with it. (Hartstein) got involved because some people weren't doing the right thing on the periphery."

Asked directly if anyone in the Marbury family had requested money in exchange for Thomas's commitment to Providence, Gillen said, "I've got no comment. I don't want to talk about that."

Bell, the Lincoln assistant who attended the meeting in Hartstein's place, said that if any demand was made, he didn't hear it. Don and Donnie Marbury vehemently denied asking any coach for money. "We knew the rules," Donnie said, "and we definitely followed those rules. We never asked anybody for anything."

Thomas signed with Providence and developed into a Big East star. During his sophomore season, he helped the Friars get to the Elite Eight round of the NCAA Tournament, beating Mike Krzyzewski's Duke team along the way. Before that Duke victory, Thomas threatened to boycott the game unless the Friars staff came up with tickets "for a wave of Marburys who came in from Coney Island unannounced," one Providence coach said. "Thomas demanded tickets for a sold-out tournament game, and we were all going nuts trying to find some."

They found some, and Thomas delivered a big game against the Blue Devils.

"Jamel was a great player with a tremendous heart," Gillen said. "A heart of gold." The coach recalled Thomas sending his basketball shoes and meal money back to the Telfairs, his way of saying thanks. "He didn't talk about what happened to (his mother), and we didn't ask him much about it," Gillen said. "But there was a culture shock coming from Coney Island to this small Catholic school in Rhode Island. There weren't a lot of African-American students there. And Jamel didn't trust people. You really had to earn Jamel's trust. He wasn't your typical student. In the end, without the Bravermans, he would've dropped out his junior year in high school. He'd be nowhere in Coney Island today, just hanging on the corners and getting in trouble."

Lenore Braverman would say only that Jamel "was a gem, a wonderful young man," before declining further comment.

"Jamel is so shy and reserved," said Hartstein, who thought Thomas debunked "the stereotype of what these kids are supposed to be." Thomas was also a better-than-advertised ballplayer. He led the Big East in scoring as a senior, this after nearly declaring for the NBA draft the year before. Gillen had left to go to Virginia, and Thomas had come to see him as a father figure. But Jamel's decision to stay and play for the new coach, Tim Welsh, proved to be a wise one.

"He could take over a game any time he wanted to on the college level," Welsh said. "The guy was the leading scorer in the Big East. You figured he had to get drafted."

The family that took in Thomas as a child figured much the same. The Telfairs read the magazines and listened to the draft experts. Mid- to late first round, they heard from many sources. That meant big money, guaranteed money. That meant the first real chance to escape the crime and poverty that were as much a part of everyday life at Surf-side Gardens as the seagulls hovering over the boardwalk across the street.

True believers all, the Telfairs gathered in their apartment for a draft night feast. Otis and Erica were there with their children, including 14-year-old Sebastian, the sibling who never left Jamel's side.

Erica had been talking up the new home Thomas might buy for her. Stephon Marbury had just finished his third season in the NBA; he'd left Georgia Tech for the draft after his freshman season. The Marburys had moved out of their fourth-floor apartment and on to a new and prosperous life, leaving the Telfairs behind in their third-floor unit, waiting for the same kind of break.

Only Thomas wasn't Marbury, maybe the most talented guard ever to come out of New York. Thomas was known as a tweener—a player a little too short for the forward position and a little too rough around the ballhandling edges for the guard position.

NBA scouts didn't question Jamel's ability to score but did question his commitment to defense. "So I was worried for him," Gonzalez recalled.

"But I was still confident he would at least get drafted in the second round."

The Telfairs didn't want to hear anything about the second round. Only first-round picks got guaranteed contracts and salaries that could forever alter a family's life.

After dinner, the TV went on and the NBA's annual beauty contest began. Sebastian had told friends he was sure Thomas would go in the top 20, and the Telfairs would have been just fine with that. So when David Stern announced the first five picks and called out the names of Elton Brand, Steve Francis, Baron Davis, Lamar Odom, and Jonathan Bender, nobody was alarmed.

But by the end of the first round, people started breaking down. Twenty-nine players were called, players from high school, community college, the Big East, France, and Russia. The guaranteed cash was going, going, gone.

Thomas figured he'd at least get plucked in the second round by a general manager who would discover in training camp that he'd found the steal of the draft. Only that didn't happen, either. Utah selected Eddie Lucas of Virginia Tech with the 58th and final pick.

The Telfairs came unglued. They felt like they'd been had.

"The only ones who didn't cry were me and Jamel," Otis said. "I didn't cry because I'm the head of the family, and I had to hold it in. I told Jamel, 'This ain't the end,' but Sebastian cried like a baby, and it just killed my wife."

The Telfairs feared that Jamel represented their last hope. They figured that getting shut out on draft night meant being locked inside the projects forever. Sebastian? At 14, he was very much a phenom; in fact, he was considered the best eighth-grade basketball player in all of America.

But Erica couldn't look at her short, skin-and-bones son and see anything but another practical joke, a cruel hoax perpetrated by someone fixing to dupe her—like Lucy pulling away the ball from Charlie Brown—when it was time to cash in. "When Jamel was supposed to get drafted, honest to God, we didn't know anything about Sebastian," Erica would say. "Honest. We didn't pay this kid no attention. We had no idea the kid could really play."

"That's true," her husband would say. "We never dreamed anything would happen to Sebastian. After Jamel failed, we felt like we gave it a good try.

"But man, I'll never forget it as long as I live. You want to talk about the worst day of my life."

The worst day of his life? For Otis, that was saying a mouthful.

As a young soldier, he had lived the horrors of the Vietnam bush. As the angry victim of an all-American mugging, he had killed a man on a Coney Island street.

o   o   o   o   o

Talking about Coney Island, circa 1988, was much like talking about Vietnam, circa 1968.

"Brooklyn was the killing fields back then," said Sari Kolatch, a white-collar criminal defense attorney in the New York firm of Cohen, Tauber, Spievack, and Wagner, LLP, and the woman who put Otis Telfair in jail.

Kolatch was familiar with Stephon Marbury, the Knicks' new point guard, and vaguely familiar with his 18-year-old cousin, Sebastian Telfair, the star at Lincoln High. But 16 years after the fact, Kolatch couldn't remember the Otis Telfair manslaughter case. Brooklyn was a depressing blur of murder and mayhem back then, a nonstop procession of Otis Telfairs being spit out of a revolving door.

She was an assistant district attorney under Brooklyn District Attorney Elizabeth Holtzman then, and prosecutors were just changing their computer programs to substitute the word "crack" for "cocaine." Crack was suddenly all over the place. Gangs were selling it. People were killing neighbors for a $10 vial.

"Sometimes we'd go to crime scenes and people would be shooting out of their windows," Kolatch recalled. "I was a 5-foot Jewish white girl. If I went to the projects, everybody knew who I was." Same went for the two accompanying homicide detectives. They'd all sprint from their cars into crime-scene buildings out of fear of getting shot.

Small children were caught in the cross fire. "These projects were just horrendous," Kolatch said. "In that Coney Island neighborhood, the odds of kids getting out then weren't good. . . . Every kid in Coney Island knew someone who was murdered."

In fact, Sebastian Telfair would often say he knew of more friends, acquaintances, and neighbors who were murdered than he could count. "And Coney Island is a better place now," Kolatch said. "I still wouldn't want to live in those projects, but they're not as dangerous as they used to be."

Otis would attest to that. "In the late 1980s," he said, "you'd come home and all you heard was gunfire. It was Dodge City around here." Coney Island was a place where problems were often solved on the street, just like they were on August 7, 1988, when Otis was jumped by three men. He had been fishing on the pier with a few of his kids. Otis said he left them to get bait, and that he stopped at a friend's home on the way back. When he left his friend's home, Otis's life changed for keeps.

"They beat the shit out of me," Otis said. "They kicked my teeth in, and then they took the money that I had in my shirt pocket. I went home, thought about it for 5 minutes, and then I went back outside."

On the corner of Mermaid and West 19th, Telfair did what he'd been trained in Vietnam to do. He located the enemy and aimed his loaded gun.

o   o   o   o   o

Sylvester Telfair was out of school and out of work when he decided he wanted to become a Marine. He failed their test before passing the Army's exam. "I was 19," Telfair said, "and suddenly I was being trained how to kill."

Soon enough he was overseas with the Army, boxing on German military bases. He was 149 pounds and good with his hands. The Army's team trainer called him "Sweet O," for some unknown reason, a nickname that evolved into "Otis," the name Telfair would carry back to the States.

Telfair did one tour in Vietnam before returning home. Like many veterans, he didn't easily share tales from the crypt of that war. Telfair would say he never appreciated the way history kept score.

"We won all the battles but lost the war," he said. "Don't get it twisted: We could've won there. At times, I'm bitter about the whole experience. I feel it altered my life and gave me a lifestyle I didn't like."

Otis hadn't even smoked his first cigarette yet, and here were men being shredded and slaughtered right before his eyes. "It's not like in the movies and on TV, where it's clean and glorified," Otis said. "I've seen what bullets really do to bodies, and it's the worst horror you can imagine.

"You had to be a violent person to survive. I got Agent Orange. I think I got it in Lai Khe, but I don't know. I got jaundice, too. When I came back, I was completely yellow, my eyes and everything."

His right eye was permanently damaged when struck by a branch released by an American soldier barreling through the bush. Otis would spend more than 2 months in a New York hospital, where he was treated for posttraumatic stress disorder. The government would award him $2,000 a month in disability. Another vet Otis knew, a vet who had lost his arms and legs, got more than double that amount.

"I saw worse things in the veterans hospital than I saw in the jungle," Otis said. He never took a bullet in Vietnam, but dodged his share of artillery fire in Lai Khe.

Survival didn't guarantee a happy ending. "We didn't get any kind of welcome when we got back," Otis said. "All we ended up getting were some names on a wall." Otis would recognize too many names on that memorial wall, and he would come to see the survivors reading those names as casualties all the same. The war, he said, "did fuck a lot of us up."

Back from Vietnam and out of the hospital, Telfair found work driving 18-wheelers, a job he grew to love. But long before he approached his assailants on August 7, 1988, Telfair's life had come undone. In 1983, he was convicted and jailed on charges of criminal possession of a weapon in the third degree, criminal sale of a controlled substance in the fifth degree, and criminal possession of a controlled substance in the fourth degree.

So he carried a felony record with his gun to the corner of Mermaid and West 19th on that fateful August night. Two of his three muggers had fled, but a 28-year-old man named Edwin Arroyo had not. Arroyo had just been discharged from prison and admitted into a work release program after serving time on an attempted robbery conviction.

At approximately 5:50 P.M., Otis Telfair fired his weapon and ended Arroyo's life. According to police and court records, a .25-caliber pistol, a magazine clip, and four spent shells were recovered at the scene.

The first officer on that scene, Donna Bianco, saw a man running south on 19th Street with a weapon in his hand. Bianco apprehended Telfair and placed him under arrest.

Two boys in the area told investigators they saw a man run, stop, and throw a gun into a junkyard lot. In separate viewings, the boys identified Telfair as the man who had disposed of the gun.

When first brought into the 60th Precinct, Telfair told a detective named Daniel Rizzo that he shot Arroyo only after the victim had pulled a gun on him, according to a police memo. Telfair told Rizzo that Arroyo's gun went off during their struggle. John O'Connor, assistant district attorney, videotaped Telfair's statement and decided "the case looked like it would be justifiable."

"Three days later," Telfair recalled, "they changed it. They said once I went back home and thought about it, I was no longer in danger. It wasn't self-defense anymore."

Telfair was indicted by a grand jury on the charges of murder in the second degree, criminal possession of a weapon in the second degree, and criminal possession of a weapon in the third degree. One year and one day after the killing, Telfair stood before the Honorable Ruth Moskowitz inside State Supreme Court in Brooklyn. Telfair was represented by Barry Krinsky; the people were represented by Sari Kolatch. The judge confirmed that the parties had negotiated a plea bargain and that Telfair was a repeat felon. Before he was sent back to prison, Telfair was asked if he had anything he wished to say.

"Yes," he said, according to court records. "To the Court, I would like to say there was no intentional, uh, murder. I'm charged with manslaughter. I'm guilty of manslaughter. But I didn't intentionally set out to kill no man."

"That's why I permitted the plea to manslaughter," Moskowitz said.

"And I'm sorry for a death to be involved," Telfair continued. "I'm sorry that this man wound up dying. I ask God and the court to forgive me for my sin, because a death was involved. I'm happy that the court took into consideration the circumstances of the case and reduced this to a manslaughter. And I feel that I'm going to serve my sentence and go home to my wife and kids."

"That's good," Moskowitz said. "The plea was agreed to because of the circumstances. It's uncontested that you were attacked by the persons, one of them being the person who was eventually killed, prior to the time that this incident took place. And that's why the people offered—and I agreed—to impose the sentence I am glad to impose, which is, you're sentenced to a minimum of 6 years and maximum of 12 to the New York State Department of Correctional Services. And the mandatory surcharge is waived."

Krinsky then asked the judge if she would consider recommending his client for the earliest possible parole release, given the fact that he was beaten, and beaten by men with criminal records. Moskowitz asked Krinsky if Telfair had a narcotics problem. "He had a narcotics problem many years ago," Krinsky said.

Moskowitz then pledged to write a letter to the parole board in the event Telfair used his jail time to participate in educational programs. Krinsky thanked the judge, who then advised Telfair that he had a right to appeal the sentence just imposed.

Finally, Moskowitz said, "Defendant remanded."

"Thank you," the defendant responded.

Some 15 years later, Telfair said this of his day of rage in the Brooklyn killing fields: "People think I'm some crazy killer, a murderer, and I'm not. I'm not crazy or sick. . . . I just left a fishing pier and didn't come home until 8 years later."

o   o   o   o   o

Sebastian Telfair was 3 years old when his father killed Edwin Arroyo. To hear Telfair tell it, his one-parent childhood was just another obstacle to clear, just another cone for a young Coney Island point guard to dribble around.

"When you come from the projects," Telfair said, "you can adapt to any environment. We visited my father in jail a lot. My mother made sure we knew who our father was. We'd go see him like once a month. He was in jail 8 straight years, came back, then went back for violating parole. But if (the killing) happened the way it looked like it happened, he would've been in jail a lot longer than 10 years. He would've done 25. He would've been in there forever."

It seemed like forever all the same.

Otis Telfair lifted weights in prison. Lifted weights and read the Bible, the Koran, and the Torah. "The scripture says we're made out of dust, dirt, and the mud of the earth," Otis said. "Go out on the beach and grab a handful of sand and put it under a magnifying glass. You're going to see a billion colors, right? If we're made from that, then that means there's every color in every one of us."

Over time, the Telfair home became its own kaleidoscope. Danny, Helen, and Terica were Erica's children by Dan Turner, who left the family when Danny, the oldest, was 5. "A coward," Danny said of his father, who died of a heart attack years after leaving the home. "My mother had to be my father, too."

Jamel and Deon Thomas were taken in after their mother was shot dead. Sylvester, Sylvia, Sebastian, Octavia, and Ethan were born to Otis and Erica, making 10 in all, not counting Jerry Ferguson, the cousin the Telfairs treated like a son. Rasheem "Bubba" Barker, Sebastian's closest friend, and the Marburys would come and go through the Telfair home like the Telfairs, Turners, and Thomases would come and go through the Marbury home.

"A lot more than 10 kids lived here," Erica said.

"And I don't take any credit for raising these kids the right way," Otis said. "I never willingly left my family; I was taken out of the home. But when I was away, my wife held everything together."

Erica raised six boys and four girls in the projects, which surely earned her a free pass to heaven. She was a large, warm, and gregarious woman who often shouted when she spoke, the natural yield of talking above the prattle of so many kids. Erica's children often marveled over the fact that she never used drugs, never so much as rolled a joint, even when practically everyone she knew was lost in a cloud of smoke.

"The perfect mom," Danny Turner said. "Basically, she taught us how to be a man."

Once when Jamel was about 12, he came upstairs crying after losing a fight with a bigger kid. Erica Telfair sent Jamel right downstairs to resume the battle. She stood there as Jamel took another beating, refusing to let any of his siblings jump in. When Jamel went down, she yelled, "Get up. Get up."

"She was teaching us to stand on our own," Turner said. "She was the spine of our book. Without her, the book would've fallen apart."

And the city-owned Surfside Gardens was an easy place for a family to fall apart. Surfside was a five-building, 597-unit complex bordered by West 31st and 33rd Streets and Surf and Neptune Avenues. The area was surrounded by vacant lots squared off by twisted chain fences and choked by wildly overgrown weeds and piles of sheetrock and plywood.

The ocean boardwalk across the street was home to abandoned shacks and run-down hamburger huts with shattered windows. The neighborhood high-rises had a mind-numbing sameness to them, block after block of cement-colored projects that were home to welfare families trying to negotiate their children through a maze of homeless men nodding on park benches, teenage truants huddling on street corners, and drug dealers doing business through car windows.

Outside Surfside Gardens, ballers were forever running full-court games on the legendary court known as the Garden. Inside the Telfairs' 15-story building on 2940-42 West 31st Street, dark and narrow stairwells were littered with garbage and defaced with profane scribblings. The drab yellowish hallways and reddish brown apartment doors were in dire need of paint jobs, and the relentless odor of urine told a resident he or she was home, bittersweet home.

Erica had lived in this building since it opened in 1969. She'd lived with Otis and the children on the 11th floor, in a three-bedroom unit, before petitioning the city for a bigger place, one flight below the Marburys. "We had to go to court," Otis said, "and the judge awarded it to us. We ended up with one of the largest apartments in the projects. Five bedrooms, two bathrooms, a kitchen, living room, and dining room.

"The only income we had was my government check, but it could've been a lot worse." The Telfairs had enough to pay the rent, buy food, cover the phone bill. They had each other, too. "When I wasn't (in prison) upstate," Otis said, "we were one of the few families with two parents around. Sebastian once told me that not one of his friends had his dad at home, and I didn't believe him until he started naming names."

Somehow, some way, Sebastian Telfair counted himself among the blessed in Coney Island. He had older brothers to act as his shepherds. He had a mother who was drug-free. And he had a father who was in the home, with the family, when he wasn't doing time upstate.

"I'm not going to put my father down," Sebastian said. "I love him so much. He'd die for us right now." He didn't prod his father about Vietnam; the kid harbored an unspoken respect for the soldier's sacrifice and valor. But Sebastian was very much Erica's son.

When Otis was in prison, Sebastian said, "my momma always made sure we had food. But we were poor. Poor poor. We didn't have shit. We'd go down to the Salvation Army right before Christmas to pick out a toy because we couldn't afford anything else. At some point, we needed a break as a family. We needed something to happen to turn everything around."

. . . . .

Jamel Thomas didn't happen, not the way the Telfairs had hoped. He would play in Europe, land an occasional 10-day contract in the NBA, and send back whatever money he could. It wasn't enough to get the Telfairs out of the projects.

The Marburys had already made it out through basketball, through the millions Stephon scored as the fourth overall pick in the NBA draft, and the Telfairs figured their best hope, their only hope, was to follow the same trail. Danny Turner had played high school basketball but was built like a noseguard; no scholarship offers came his way. Jamel's brother, Deon, earned a degree at St. John's like Jamel had earned one at Providence but didn't play college ball.

Sylvester Telfair was a role player at Lincoln, a kid who had enough trouble staying in school and out of jail. His hands weren't reliable enough to carry the family's future, a future so fragile it needed to be handled with the utmost care.

The Telfairs needed a quarterback, a point guard, their very own Stephon. Suddenly, they needed to believe what people had been trying to tell them all along: Their eighth child was the one.

So after Jamel Thomas "failed," in the words of Otis Telfair, the family drew up a new play. The time had come to give young Sebastian the ball.

2

Erica Telfair figured the only white men who knocked on the doors of Surfside Gardens were detectives looking for a perp or a victim's next of kin. So when Erica looked through her peephole and eyed Thomas Sicignano, she could say only three words.

Oh . . . my . . . God.

She opened the door anyway. "Hello," Sicignano said. "Your uncle, Don Marbury, sent me here. You're Sebastian's mom, right?" Sicignano explained that he was a basketball coach. "I saw your little boy out there playing, and I'd like to take an interest in him. Would you let him go with me?"

Erica asked Sicignano to have a seat. She was busy in the kitchen and needed her oldest son, Danny Turner, to come home and make this call.

Mother and guest talked about Sebastian, the player Sicignano had first seen on the court adjacent to the Surfside Gardens complex, the court known as the Garden. Erica had a story to tell, and she wasn't sure how the white man sitting in her living room would react to it.

Sebastian walked into the apartment one day and didn't say a word, Erica told him. Something about the way Sebastian came in, the way he marched into the kitchen and then right back out, had stirred a mother's instinct. Erica told the white man that she pulled up Sebastian's shirt and found a butcher's knife tucked inside. She pulled it away from him and told Sebastian to find another way to deal with the bigger kids who'd been bullying him outside.

"Wait a minute," Sicignano interrupted. "That's the killer instinct I want; we've just got to channel it."

Erica held firm. "If Danny comes home and says he can go with you," she said, "then he can go."

Turner came home and gave his blessing. At the ripe old age of 9, Sebastian was off to the manic world of New York summer circuit ball. He would be the crown jewel in the Brooklyn USA program run by Sicignano, universally known on the circuit as Ziggy.

Erica assigned Turner the task of bodyguard. Turner was one of the good guys in Coney Island, round and friendly in a teddy bear way. He was the one responsible for ensuring that the local drug dealers stayed clear of Sebastian, and he didn't have to flex too much muscle. The dealers operated under a singular code of honor. "If you're trying to do something with your life," Turner said, "they don't pressure you. They knew Sebastian was special. They all knew what we were trying to do with him, so they stayed away."

Turner helped establish a drug-free playground zone so Sebastian could work on his game. Ziggy was the coach, Turner the boss. Ziggy knew he couldn't afford to blow this one, not after coaching Sebastian's older cousin, Stephon Marbury, until the day Marbury decided he liked the bigger budget and higher profile of the Gauchos youth basketball program in the Bronx.

Born and raised in Flatbush, Ziggy had been a tough 5-foot-11 guard at William Grady High, a white kid with good enough hops to play above the rim. Ziggy got a few looks from Division I scouts, none that piqued his interest. Ziggy's mother, father, brothers, and sisters all went to college, he said. "But I was one of those guys who would rather walk through a wall than an open door."

Marbury was Ziggy's first prodigy. In their 3½ years together, Ziggy believed Marbury taught him how to coach a championship player.

"I wasn't mad at Stephon for leaving," Ziggy said. "I was mad at myself for not having the money to keep him." Don Marbury had assured Ziggy that his son never would have left had Brooklyn USA operated under a bigger budget. Don Marbury would tell his niece, Erica Telfair, "As long as Ziggy wants Sebastian, keep Sebastian with him."

It wasn't long before the decision to go with Ziggy began paying off. One Fourth of July day, Ziggy hurried over to Surfside Gardens, where the Telfairs were having a cookout. The coach had a magazine in his hands. Inside that edition of *The Hoop Scoop*, a self-styled recruiting analyst named Clark Francis had named Telfair the number one fourth-grade player in America.

Ziggy had called Francis to tell him he had a young playmaker who might be better than his cousin, Marbury. "You see," Ziggy shouted to the gathering Telfair masses. "I told you this would happen if he played with me."

Then the Brooklyn USA coach fixed his eyes on Sebastian. "You're going to be like a gunslinger walking into a bar now," Ziggy told him. "Everybody will want to take you on."

Over the years, Francis saw scores of references to his Telfair ranking, some claiming he'd made Telfair number one in fifth grade, others in fourth. Francis said he first ranked Telfair number one in fourth grade. Telfair had been left back in fourth grade, according to Turner, a development that likely created the confusion (and gave the player a significant advantage over the competition).

Either way, Ziggy was right. Everyone started aiming for the new gunslinger in town.

"I kept getting calls from coaches saying, 'I've got a kid who's better than Sebastian Telfair,'" Francis said. "And every time I went out to see those players, they weren't as good."

Ziggy shared with Telfair everything he'd learned from Marbury about coaching a pro on training wheels. Ziggy would run him through point guard drills, take him to tournaments all over the country, drive him up to Providence to visit Jamel Thomas, and offer a healthy dose of tough-love guidance.

Brooklyn USA was playing a tournament in Harlem once, and a 10-year-old Sebastian was acting like a jackass to the refs, his opponents, everyone. Ziggy cursed him out, and Sebastian returned the favor. The kid said he wanted to go home, and the coach handed him a subway token. Sebastian walked away, turned back, and sat at the end of the bench while Ziggy ignored him. The coach agreed to put his young star back in the game only after he apologized to all the wronged parties.

"That was part of making him a man," Ziggy said. So was the time when Sebastian, then in eighth grade, fumed that Ziggy had taken him out of that big tournament at Fordham, the Rumble in the Bronx. "Shut the fuck up and sit down," Ziggy had barked at him. Sebastian was playing against guys 3 and 4 years older than him, and Ziggy was just trying to get him a breather. "He was named MVP," the coach recalled, "and then he tells me, 'You were right. I was fresh in the fourth quarter. I needed that rest.'"

As it turned out, Telfair needed more than a rest. He needed a break from Ziggy Sicignano. The Rumble in the Bronx ended Sebastian's 5-year stay with Brooklyn USA, as the relationship was severed, predictably enough, along sneaker-war lines.

Ziggy had set up a meeting with Telfair, Turner, their mother, and Don Crenshaw of Nike. Three years earlier, Ziggy had told George Raveling, Nike's grassroots chief, that Telfair might surpass Marbury. Nike had come to suspect that Ziggy's word was prophecy.

"In my eighth-grade year," Telfair said, "it seemed like Nike was in Coney Island for the whole summer."

Ziggy was feuding with Adidas's Sonny Vaccaro over the failure of an Adidas store Ziggy ran in Brooklyn. So Ziggy needed Crenshaw and Nike. He told Turner he'd make sure Nike took care of him "if Sebastian goes to their camps. Sonny's good for giving you 100 sneakers, but he doesn't have the money Nike has."

Turner, Erica, and Ziggy met Crenshaw at a restaurant, and they waited and waited for the guest of honor. Sebastian had been driving around with the Lincoln High coach, Dwayne (Tiny) Morton. By the time Sebastian arrived, Crenshaw was about ready to leave.

No deal would be struck that night for Telfair to pledge his allegiance to the swoosh. Morton was trying to pry Telfair away from Ziggy, and he needed a place for the point guard to play. Morton didn't have his own summer team—not yet, anyway—and so he convinced Telfair to sign up with the Long Island Panthers, run by Gary Charles.

Charles didn't give Sebastian enough playing time to satisfy the point guard's camp, inspiring Morton and Turner to start their own summer league team through Adidas, a team they'd call the Juice All-Stars. Vaccaro bankrolled the Juice All-Stars and sponsored Telfair's Lincoln High team in the hope of keeping the playmaker in the Adidas pipeline until he was ready to turn pro and sign an endorsement deal. Vaccaro did this against the advice of his lieutenant, Charles.

"I just washed my hands of Tiny," Charles said. "He'd said, 'Wherever Sebastian goes, I've got to go, too,' and something about that I didn't like. . . . I told Tiny, 'You think this is going to be your free ride?'. . . On the Sebastian thing, I told Sonny, 'I'm not feeling this one.'"

Vaccaro often listened to Charles, but not this time. He gave Lincoln sneakers and gear and funded Morton's new Juice All-Stars to the tune of $22,500 a year. Vaccaro also told Turner that Ziggy could never have a role in their Adidas-backed relationship.

Sebastian tore it up at Vaccaro's prestigious ABCD camp—the ABCD stood for Academic Betterment and Career Development, but the camp was known as a basketball talent show where 200 of America's finest prospects auditioned for college coaches and pro scouts. Telfair tore it up as the first eighth-grader ever invited to compete.

In the weeks following the camp, Ziggy hoped against hope. Telfair didn't show at practice. Telfair wouldn't come to the phone. One day, Ziggy waited for him on the corner of Atlantic and Flatbush, waited in vain to take him to a Brooklyn USA tournament.

"I knew it was over then," Ziggy said. "He didn't even have enough respect for the 5 years I coached him to tell me to my face."

Turner and Erica simply felt Sebastian had outgrown Ziggy. This opinion enraged Ziggy, who felt Brooklyn USA belonged among the top summer programs in New York. Telfair had thrived under him, to the point where Ziggy thought his eighth-grade playmaker was more advanced than Marbury was at the same age.

"People took Sebastian," Ziggy said, "because they saw a pot of gold for themselves."

Ziggy's pot of gold.

Telfair never again spoke to the first coach who came knocking on his Surfside Gardens door. The one courtesy Sebastian extended to Ziggy was his refusal to play in a Juice All-Stars matchup with Brooklyn USA.

"Me and Ziggy were about to take over the city," Sebastian would say. "Yo, I didn't outgrow Ziggy. I like everyone on the AAU scene, but I love Ziggy the most." But shit happens.

"It happened over time," Sebastian said. "I still love Zig, but I started doing my own thing at Lincoln and with the Juice. And then he started having his problems in the paper."

Yes, his problems in the paper. Ziggy always thought he'd end up in big, bold New York *Daily News* headlines as a do-gooder coach who saved young basketball players from the despair of the ghetto. He never thought he'd be the lead story in his hometown paper because he was working in a strip club that was allegedly married to the mob.

∘   ∘   ∘   ∘   ∘

Ziggy Sicignano was selling popcorn and working a newspaper stand in Penn Station when his millionaire boss, Steve Kaplan, asked if he'd work for him in Atlanta. Ziggy couldn't function outside of Brooklyn. He always said he'd rather be a pauper in his home borough than a rich man somewhere else. "If I die and there's one ounce of me left," he said, "it's in my will that they have to bring it back to Brooklyn."

Kaplan told Ziggy he could make some real dough in Atlanta; the millionaire couldn't understand how Ziggy could be happy making peanuts selling popcorn. Kaplan couldn't understand how Ziggy could be happy pouring so much of his life into his Brooklyn USA basketball team—and having so little to show for it in his checking account.

Ziggy bought the pitch in 1994. He became a "pointer-outer" at Kaplan's Gold Club, pointing out this and that to customers. He made $700 to $1,000 a week in Atlanta while running Brooklyn USA from afar, delegating basketball duties to his assistant coaches. Ziggy mostly worked winters at the Gold Club, so it wouldn't intrude on his passion for New York's summer circuit ball. The weekend trips would open the most revealing window on his double life.

Ziggy would get the call from Kaplan and fly first-class to Atlanta. Two men would meet him at the airport, fetch his bags, and escort him to a waiting limousine. When Ziggy arrived at the club, he'd walk into a locker room full of beautiful, naked women. They'd flatter him with false praise about his looks and charm. Through Kaplan's connections, Ziggy and friends would get the best tables at the best restaurants. "We were the stars of what was becoming the biggest show in town," Ziggy said.

But when it was time to return to Brooklyn, Ziggy would fetch his own bags, take the train to the airport, and settle into his middle seat in coach. Nobody was there to greet him at JFK. Ziggy would claim his luggage, take a taxi to the train, and then the train to his home. First thing he'd do was find a mirror. "When I came back to Brooklyn to coach basketball," Ziggy said, "I knew how ugly I was."

In fact, Ziggy was never uglier than he was the days and nights he surrounded himself with those beautiful, naked women. Only he didn't see it that way. He saw a business he said "treated women like garbage. . . . The majority of the women had been abused by the age of 10 by their father, stepfather, uncle, next-door neighbor, somebody." Ziggy said he changed all that by applying the principles of basketball to adult entertainment.

"The girls were our players," he said. "You wanted them to come to work happy."

Ziggy also saw himself as a beacon of progressive thought. The club had little interest in hiring black women. "I literally had to go to Steve and say, 'They have a Ku Klux Klan mentality down here, and . . . we're in a city that's 67 percent black,'" Ziggy said. Word spread about the new open-door policy at the Gold Club, and Ziggy would hire beautiful black women right out of their cars. "Some of them would cry and say, 'We've been trying to get a job here for 8 years,'" Ziggy said.

Before this wave of diverse hiring, Ziggy would survey the club a little past midnight, see only 20 dancers available for 400 male customers, and tell Kaplan, "We can't have 380 guys jerking off."

So Ziggy flooded the floor with dozens of fresh hires. Kaplan, a devout Knicks fan, took Ziggy's basketball principles to a new Gold Club level: He wanted famous ballplayers as regular customers. He figured that was the surest ticket to making the Gold Club the number one strip joint in America.

Six years later, some of those ballplayers took the stand in a most salacious racketeering case, a federal case that put Ziggy in big, bold *Daily News* type. The feds had hit Kaplan and six associates with charges of promoting prostitution, credit card fraud, and making payments to the Gambino crime family.

The government's star witness? None other than Sebastian Telfair's coach, Ziggy Sicignano, the man who came up with the nickname "Griffey" (as in Junior Griffey) for Kaplan's friend, John Gotti Jr., for fear of referring to "Junior" Gotti by name.

Ziggy testified that the club ripped off customers by overbilling their credit cards, and that Kaplan arranged for dancers to have sex with star athletes. Patrick Ewing of the New York Knicks and Andruw Jones of the Atlanta Braves were among the stars to testify that they engaged in sex with Gold Club dancers. In response, Kaplan claimed Ziggy was the one running a one-man prostitution ring within the club.

Antonio Davis sued Ziggy for $50 million for naming him—falsely, Davis said—as one of the NBA players who had sex with a dancer; Ziggy claimed he was never served with the lawsuit papers.

In the end, Kaplan cut his own deal. He agreed to a guilty plea that earned him a sentence of 16 months in federal prison and a $5 million fine.

The Gold Club was converted into a church, and Ziggy returned to Brooklyn with a brand of notoriety he'd never fathomed. He estimated that Kaplan had contributed between $50,000 and $75,000 to his Brooklyn USA basketball program, a deal that made summer circuit observers uncomfortable.

"Who else was going to give me that money?" Ziggy said. "I was going to charge 14-year-old kids to play for me? I helped their grandmas pay the rent, electricity, phone bills. I bought the kids school clothes. I didn't have a job or money, and Kaplan offered me both."

The arrangement only complicated the mystery that was Ziggy, who was never arrested or charged in the Gold Club case. People didn't know what to make of the summer basketball coach who had become such a prominent figure in such a sensational tale. On his return, half of Brooklyn thought Ziggy was in the mob, and the other half thought he was being hunted by the mob.

Bald on top, with black hair slicked across the sides, Ziggy had a roundish face and enough of a 40-something paunch to pass for James Gandolfini's brother. But no matter how easily Ziggy could have fit inside the back room of the Bada Bing, the Brooklyn USA coach was never linked to organized crime.

"I testified that there was no mob activity," Ziggy said, "and that Steve wasn't sending money to the mob. My testimony didn't hurt the Gambino crime family, that's the way I thought. But to the whole world, you're going up against the Gambino family and they're going to whack you.

"People were kind of shocked I was still walking around. But I never feared any mob retaliation. The truth of the matter is, if they wanted me dead, they'd send a hit squad in 20 minutes and I'm dead. They'd send two shooters and two backups. What am I going to do, carry a gun and have a shoot-out? I just stood tall and tried to remain confident and a little cocky."

The feds offered Ziggy witness protection, but he turned it down.

"Mr. Sicignano testified at a substantial risk to himself, and he never flinched," said Art Leach, the assistant U.S. attorney who prosecuted the case. "I thought he'd leave Brooklyn, but he absolutely refused to do that. Naturally, anybody in a situation like that would be fearful, but he wasn't. It's not at all a general practice to offer protection . . . and most witnesses have nothing to fear, but he did."

It didn't matter. Ziggy was returning to Brooklyn as the hunter, not the hunted. He had one target in mind, and it wasn't anyone remotely connected to the Gambino crime family.

Ziggy had lost more than a piece of his good name, after all; he'd lost Sebastian Telfair, too. Someone had to pay for that, and Ziggy figured it should be the head basketball coach at Abraham Lincoln High.

o   o   o   o   o

Tiny Morton was anything but an easy mark. He was a Coney Island survivor, a 33-year-old basketball coach and junior high math teacher with a working wife, two kids, and a penchant for the great escape.

He barely survived Ziggy Sicignano's first attack, but survive he did. It went down in 2002, when the Department of Education launched an investigation of Morton based on information provided by the government's star witness in the Gold Club case, a man whom Assistant U.S. Attorney Art Leach would call "a witness who was credible in any way I know."

Ziggy told an investigator that Morton was illegally recruiting players and encouraging players from other schools to falsify police reports in order to secure safety transfers to Lincoln. In the irony of ironies, the former "pointer-outer" at the Gold Club also accused Morton of taking his players to a strip club.

Morton raged when informed that Ziggy was his chief accuser. He denied the accusations and told reporters at the time that Ziggy was someone "with a questionable character."

Morton was reportedly cleared of the charge of taking players to a strip club, but enough of the allegations stuck for Dennis Boyles, the Department of Education investigator, to recommend that Morton be fired. "And Boyles told me they do as he recommends 99 percent of the time," Ziggy said. Morton was suspended for the first round of the play-offs and wasn't expected to return to the Railsplitters' bench ever again.

But before Lincoln's second-round game, the Department of Education reinstated Morton and said it would continue to investigate the charges against him at season's end. Education officials reasoned that since the alleged recruiting violations involved players who weren't on Lincoln's roster, the team shouldn't be deprived of its head coach in the play-offs.

Morton might have been spared because at least one influential man had stepped in on his behalf: Assemblyman Roger Green, father of Morton's assistant, Khalid Green, and mentor to Lincoln star Karron

Clarke. Green's political career would later unravel when he pleaded guilty to stealing from the state by submitting fraudulent expense reports.

"My father was helping Tiny out for a lot of reasons," Khalid Green said. "He felt those kids didn't deserve to go down like that. . . . My father wasn't saving Tiny so much, but Karron. Some people say he made a mistake, but we don't live with regret."

Khalid Green said there was no doubt the Department of Education was influenced by his father's wishes in the Morton matter. "My father is a very influential politician," he said. "I'm not bullshitting you. There's no way the Board of Ed would not listen to his advice and wisdom."

Renan Ebeid, the Lincoln athletic director, said she was never given a specific reason why Morton was suspended or reinstated. "But I heard Khalid Green's father played a big role in him coming back," Ebeid said. "A lot of people stepped up to the plate and . . . now they all regret it."

Disgusted with the Department of Education's failure to punish Morton beyond a one-game suspension, Ziggy was fixing to take the edge off everyone's regret. While Morton was winning his first city title in 2002, and then repeating in 2003, Ziggy was mapping out a plan to put away the Lincoln coach for keeps, sending more allegations of illegal recruiting Dennis Boyles's way. Ziggy kept after Morton not only because Tiny had taken away Sebastian Telfair; Morton had also convinced Xaverian High star Chris Taft to leave Brooklyn USA for the Juice All-Stars.

"After Chris Taft," Ziggy recalled, "I said, 'Fuck it. Enough is enough.'" Ziggy was furious that Morton was trying to convince Taft to transfer from Xaverian, "which was a great place for Chris," he said. Ziggy confronted Tiny in the one and only conversation the two men had.

"You do this again with another kid, make him false promises of money and gifts, I'll get you fired and locked up," Ziggy said.

"How are you going to get me arrested?" Tiny responded.

"You ever hear of a safety transfer?" Ziggy said. "If you instruct a kid to file a false police report, that's a felony."

Tiny didn't respond.

"I'd told him, 'Stay away from Brooklyn USA,'" Ziggy said, "and he didn't listen to my warning."

So Ziggy moved to destroy the career of the man who took his dream point guard, Sebastian Telfair. There was no forgive and forget in this Machiavellian world. Ziggy fancied himself a community servant, but he was also a slave to his own ambitions. Sebastian represented a chance for him to climb the basketball ladder. Losing the point guard meant losing any restraint when it came to Morton.

Ziggy would often remind people of his network of powerful Brooklyn connections—he once coached the children of Charles Hynes, the district attorney—as if to suggest that he was holding an anvil over Morton's career. But Tiny would deny all of Ziggy's charges and ridicule his attempt to nail him on an allegation of taking players to a strip joint. "I don't know Ziggy," Morton said. "The only thing I know is what I've heard. . . . I found out about him when I read in the paper that he was involved in that strip club and then turning on those NBA guys. I didn't have to do any more research. That was it. His character was out there.

"He was just trying to put his thing on me, and it didn't work. But I'm not dealing with Ziggy. I don't trust him. . . . I might try to get (the police) on him and get an order of protection."

The line was drawn in the Coney Island sand. Ziggy had a wife, a daughter, an adopted son, and letters of thanks and support from the likes of Dean Smith and Jerry Tarkanian. He also had an NBA success story to call his own—Jamaal Tinsley was his personal project. Ziggy had taken a serial truant and guided him to junior college, to Iowa State, and then to the starting backcourt of the Indiana Pacers.

But the coach couldn't escape that Gold Club stigma. Ziggy was fond of saying that all of Coney Island watched *The Sopranos* and figured that anyone having anything to do with the Gold Club case was a candidate for a late-night hit outside a midtown steakhouse.

"If I was in the mob," Ziggy countered, "Tiny would be dead. Sebastian was the prize, and then he went after Taft. How many chances do you think the mob would give Tiny?"

The way Ziggy saw it, Tiny would have already been fired if the Department of Education knew what it was doing. This time around, Ziggy said he had evidence Tiny was taking money from agents. The Brooklyn USA coach was confident he would ultimately win this street fight.

"Personally," Ziggy said, "I think it's going to be a one-punch knockout."

George Karl was on the verge of being shit-canned by the Milwaukee Bucks, and yet he had the undivided attention of 200 of America's finest high school basketball players. Never mind that Karl had coached a team of NBA stars with home-court advantage in the Indiana heartland to a glorious sixth-place finish at the World Championships, then blamed "the greed of the NBA" for his team's pathetic showing—this while he was banking a $7 million wage.

Karl had an Adidas logo stitched to his shirt at the Adidas Athletes Betterment and Career Development camp, so Sebastian Telfair and 199 other young men sitting in a loose circle on the floor of the Fairleigh Dickinson University gym would hang on his every word. Truth was, Telfair and friends wouldn't have cared if George Karl were George Carlin.

Everything was immaterial to the pursuit of a summertime reputation that could mean full scholarships from the best college programs or draft lottery millions from the worst NBA teams.

Vaccaro founded the camp while working for Nike and named it the Academic Betterment and Career Development camp. Though ABCD officials still shepherded players into college and SAT prep classes wedged between workouts and games, Vaccaro would ultimately substitute "Athletes" for "Academic" as a concession to the obvious: ABCD was all about basketball. Nothing more, nothing less.

Vaccaro was the camp's judge, jury, and commissioner. He decided which high school prospects were worthy of his 200 invitations. He decided which players competed for which teams. He decided which prospects could someday sell a sneaker in exchange for millions in endorsement wages.

So the young black players listened to Vaccaro's guy, George Karl. They listened to yet another jowly white coach lecture them on the "right way" to play a game black players had been dominating ever since the barriers blocking their participation came tumbling down.

"One thing you have to understand about the NBA is we worry about attitude as much as we do talent," Karl barked as he worked the circle in Phil Donahue form. "I saw a lot of you guys work out yesterday, and I think you guys are acting a little too cool. Think about playing the game the right way."

The ballplayers eventually clapped and broke for their assigned stations on the Rothman Center's four side-by-side courts. They resumed fundamental passing and shooting drills, just instituted at the camp to answer claims that Americans were being passed and shot into oblivion by their European peers.

Coaches everywhere were demanding that young players quit perfecting their rim-rocking, self-celebrating moves and start practicing their basic team-first skills. Even Adidas bought in. While Nike ran its closed-door exercises in footwork in its sterile lab, the anything-goes Adidas camp was forever known as a wild, woolly, everyone's-welcome-to-watch celebration of fast breaks and alley-oop dunks.

"A four-day orgy of transition basketball," said Tom Konchalski, the New York–based recruiting analyst.

In other words, the camp was a reflection of its 63-year-old head counselor, Sonny Vaccaro, a crapped-out Vegas gambler who had become one of the most colorful and controversial power brokers in all of basketball.

Nike's by-the-book camp in Indianapolis was better suited for big men who wanted to plant themselves in the post; guards were expected to make enough passes to get them the ball. Now Vaccaro had come to see the fundamental light. It was time for his ABCD campers to relearn the alphabet.

"That's okay," said Sebastian Telfair, the biggest name in high school basketball in the Year 1 A.L. (After LeBron). "My goal is to lead the camp in assists."

Well, that was his third goal.

"I want to prove I'm the best player in the country," Telfair said.

Well, that was his second goal. Above all, Telfair wanted to prove this: "That I can play in the NBA next year if I decide to go. . . . I'd love to be the first 6-footer to make that jump."

You'd laugh if you didn't know any better. With his grade-school face and Everyman body, Telfair looked more like the sports editor of the Abraham Lincoln High School weekly than he did the baddest ballplayer in the land. But Telfair didn't see anything funny about what would transpire across these four days and nights of nonstop games.

He had overwhelmed the college coaches and pro scouts as a 5-foot-8, 130-pound eighth-grade graduate, as the youngest player ever invited to ABCD, firing behind-the-back passes and fearlessly attacking the rim. As a rising sophomore, Telfair had conquered a fleet of older playmakers and shared MVP honors with LeBron James in the underclassman all-star game.

But the summer of 2002 changed everything. The coaches and scouts started whispering that Telfair was overrated, that he was taking too many jump shots, and that he couldn't hang with the new kid on the ABCD block, Darius Washington of Edgewater High in Orlando, who traveled with a stage dad bearing a slight facial resemblance and full verbal resemblance to Warren Sapp.

Telfair and Washington were named co-MVPs of the 2002 ABCD underclassman all-star game, but everyone knew who had won the week. Sebastian slipped in the national rankings, and he wanted his good name back.

He wanted to leave this fourth and final camp with Washington in his hip pocket.

The showdown was set for 4:30 P.M. on Wednesday: Telfair's Jazz against Washington's Nets on Court 2. Two years earlier, on the same court, LeBron and Lenny Cooke had squared off in the most anticipated matchup in ABCD history.

James dropped 24 points and a 40-foot game winner at the buzzer on

Cooke, whose between-the-legs dribbling left him with 9 points, out of the money in every possible way.

"The myth of Lenny Cooke was debunked here in camp," Vaccaro said.

The legend of LeBron was not. He signed for more than $100 million in salary and endorsements, while Cooke attended his fifth high school, went undrafted, got cut by the Columbus Riverdragons of the NBA's Developmental League (NBDL), and ended up making $400 a week for the Brooklyn Kings of the United States Basketball League before heading to the Philippines.

So nobody could convince Telfair or Washington this was just another mano a mano to get through a summer day in Hackensack. They would square off before rows of NBA reps and big-name college coaches.

The camp's roster of guests included Mike Krzyzewski, Jim Boeheim, Tubby Smith, Jim Calhoun, Lute Olson, Billy Donovan, and on and on. Not only were Roy Williams, the new North Carolina coach, and Matt Doherty, the fired North Carolina coach, among the customers eyeing the goods from the bleachers, but they actually sat together and chatted as if they were arranging a tee time.

It was one big dysfunctional family that had gathered for this basketball feast.

And there was no doubting what was on the menu. The ABCD camp was an annual summertime ritual in the never-ending search for the next Michael Jordan or LeBron James. The camp allowed young ballplayers to market themselves to the scouts whose evaluations could mean a pot of gold for one kid, a pot to piss in for another.

The thin line representing the riches from the rags was on display inside the lobby of the camp's home base, the Hilton Hasbrouck Heights, decorated with banners listing previous camp MVPs. Stephon Marbury and LeBron were among the posted names. But riding shotgun with those multimillionaires were Cooke and Leon Smith, the poor soul who was drafted out of a Chicago high school, traded from the San Antonio Spurs to the Dallas Mavericks, and then released by the Mavericks after allegedly threatening his ex-girlfriend with a gun, attempting to commit suicide by swallowing 250 aspirin, and landing in a psychiatric ward.

And then there was Kobe Bryant. He was the Adidas 1995 senior MVP long before he skipped college, won three titles with the Lakers, and then found himself facing sexual assault charges in Colorado.

The fresh Kobe allegations didn't hang over the camp like a toxic cloud, not with the high school players seeing sunshine and blue skies. "Better him than me" seemed to be the prevailing attitude, as the kids turned their attention to something really important, like the duel between Telfair and Washington.

On Tuesday, Washington would tear into Shaun Livingston, a 6-foot-7 guard from Peoria, Illinois, and Duke recruit hailed as a better prospect than Telfair and Washington. Livingston finished with 2 points and 4 assists, Washington with 16 points and 10 assists. Krzyzewski's prize playmaker left the court shaking his head and appearing on the verge of tears.

Though the setback did little to temper Livingston's belief that he could take a flying leap over Coach K and into the NBA fire, Telfair was more vocal about his own potential flight. "I'm leaning more toward (the NBA) now than ever before," he said.

For that reason, the entire ABCD crowd—including a few grown men in Telfair jerseys—leaned away from the other 4:30 games as Wednesday's main event arrived. On one side of the gym, players, family members, friends, and fans shifted to their left to get a better view of Court 2. On the other side, the coaches shifted to their right in defiance of the major-college prospects filling up Courts 3 and 4.

But there was one college coach observing the Telfair-Washington duel, and then there was everybody else. Rick Pitino wasn't about to sit with the competition. No, he stood against that waist-high railing under the basket, getting as close to Telfair as the rules allowed him to get.

Pitino was wearing a maroon Louisville Cardinals golf shirt, and it wasn't meant to attract Washington's attention. The Orlando star had already committed to Memphis and John Calipari, whom Pitino couldn't stand (the feeling was mutual).

Only the Louisville coach wasn't worried about Calipari. Pitino was desperate to match the national championship success he had at Kentucky, and to ease the sting of his $50 million Boston Celtics flop. For the sake of his stripped aura and diminished legacy, Pitino needed to return to the Final Four.

He needed to sign Sebastian Telfair in the worst way.

And so Pitino stood guard over Court 2 as Telfair and Washington warmed up; the Louisville coach gazed at the Lincoln High playmaker as if he were falling madly in love.

"You'd have to love to play for a guy like that," Telfair said.

So play for Pitino Telfair did. With the 6-foot-11 star from Atlanta, Dwight Howard, roaring up and down the adjacent Court 3, looking like the cross between Kevin Garnett and Tim Duncan his high school coach had claimed him to be, Pitino and the rest of the basketball world ignored him while two ordinary-size kids raced each other to an extraordinary place.

At 6-foot-1, Washington stood taller than his counterpart. Telfair had slightly better muscle definition. Washington had a better vertical leap. Telfair had a better handle. Washington was dressed in the navy blue colors of his Nets, Telfair in the orange colors of the Jazz, complete with orange headband and wristband.

They were the smallest players on the court, and yet the other eight prospects were invisible to the naked eye. Telfair had by his side 6-foot-9, 330-pound Glen Davis of Baton Rouge, a center who looked all of 360 pounds, and 6-foot-9 Michael Williams of Alabama and 6-foot-8 Bryant Dunston of New York. Washington had by his side a frail 6-foot-11 kid from New Hampshire, Luke Bonner, and a pair of sturdy 6-foot-7 forwards in Maryland's Michael Beasley and Arkansas's Mark Winston.

Right away, Vaccaro's stated goal of spreading the talent evenly across the 10 teams named, appropriately enough, for NBA franchises had come under attack from a predictable source.

"Sometimes adults set kids up to fail," Darius Washington Sr. said. "Sebastian has the better team, and Darius is at a disadvantage."

Washington took his concerns straight to the top of the ABCD alphabet.

"This is the Sebastian Telfair Show," he told Vaccaro.

"We're in New York," Vaccaro responded. "What show did you think it was going to be?"

Darius Sr. had another beef. ABCD rules stated that all 10 players on a team must play two quarters in every game. The best players usually started the game on the bench and played the second and fourth quarters.

But Telfair's team was missing a player. The Jazz suited up only nine. That meant the Jazz were free to give Telfair extra time, free to play him in the final minutes of the first quarter while Washington sat cold on the Nets' bench.

"With all due respect," Darius Sr. told Vaccaro, "this is bullshit."

Vaccaro was positively loving every minute of this. His was a star-search business, and the hopefuls on his stage went head to head, pump fake to pump fake, in an attempt to win Vaccaro's affection. That affection comes in the vague promise of cold, hard cash.

Vaccaro had started this basketball gold rush a quarter century earlier, when he convinced Nike to give him the money needed to cut deals with college coaches willing to outfit their teams in the swoosh. "Joe Dean was running Converse at the time," Vaccaro said, "and he said, 'What a stupid thing. We'll never pay schools. We'll never pay coaches.'" In the retelling of this tale, Vaccaro grew giddy over his own punch line. "Nike just bought Converse," he said through a laugh. "No more Chuck Taylors. Now Nike will get the Chucks, make them retro, and make $100 million off it."

Five years later, the big money started finding its way to the players: Vaccaro signed a North Carolina guard named Michael Jordan for a half million bucks and a percentage of sales. Nike came out with its Air Jordan signature shoe, made a killing, and the rest was sneaker-war history.

Not every consumer wore football spikes, baseball cleats, or hockey skates; every consumer did wear sneakers. This truth made basketball the most fertile ground for athletes looking to score endorsement contracts, and for shoe companies looking to use athletes to reach average everyday families.

Basketball allowed for more creative individuality than other major team sports, another reason why superstars in that sport were best positioned to land sneaker deals. The basketball star could come across as bigger than the team, and Sonny Vaccaro fancied himself the master recruiter of those stars.

The man who signed Jordan for Nike long before he lost LeBron to the same company would remain the very face of the power sneaker companies held over players, coaches, and schools. Every dreamy kid at ABCD understood that Vaccaro's relentless recruitment of LeBron on behalf of Adidas forced Nike to pay $103 million for the phenom's signature; the Cleveland Cavaliers, LeBron's NBA employer, "only" handed him a $12.96 million guarantee.

This time around, Vaccaro was hell-bent on beating his former employer, Nike, at its own game. He wanted the next star to package and sell to the masses, and he believed Telfair might have been the young man for the job. Telfair was a sound and respectful student, a clean-cut kid with a killer smile and a handle to die for. In other words, he was a guidance counselor's dream, a regular Jack Armstrong or Chip Hilton smack in the middle of the 'hood.

"He's not going to be a $100 million sneaker guy; we won't see another one of those for a while," Vaccaro said. "But he could be the next darling. Unlike his cousin, Stephon, he's going to smile for the world."

This was why Vaccaro always paid more attention to Telfair than to Howard, the Atlanta high school center projected to be the first player taken in the 2004 draft. Joe Six Pack could better relate to an average-size star such as Telfair than he could a giant such as Howard. The average fan could watch the 5-foot-11 Telfair use his speed and ball-handling abilities to make fools of opponents who were a foot taller, and imagine himself doing the same. The average fan couldn't picture himself executing a reverse dunk.

This was the appeal of Telfair and players like him. His size might have been a curse in the eyes of scouts, but it was a blessing in the eyes of marketeers.

"If Dwight Howard elects to go to college," Vaccaro said, "he'll have more chance to lead his team to the Final Four than Sebastian simply because of his position. But no one will even think of that. Sebastian will be the one to sell tickets and get on TV. The (college) coach . . . who gets him will be expected to win the national championship, and Sebastian will be the darling.

"First of all, he's cute, he's good looking, and he speaks well. . . . Sebastian has the mystique of being Stephon's cousin, and he's from New York. You can sell that easier than Dwight Howard."

Everything had come easy to Sebastian at this camp, at least in his younger days. He was a comet streaking across the sky then, a flash of stardust that left dozens of grizzled coaches and scouts in awe.

Over time, the scouts started paying more attention to his flaws. "He's our first 4-year prodigy," Vaccaro said. "In a sense, he's been around here too long."

Telfair was fiercely determined to go out with a bang. Washington was his vehicle of retribution. Just as Darius Jr. and Darius Sr. feared, Telfair entered the game late in the first quarter and buried a mid-range jumper and a three-pointer.

When the second quarter came, all of America's basketball elders moved to the edges of their seats. The night before in Orlando, LeBron made his rookie-league debut with the Cleveland Cavaliers, attracted 15,123 fans and 175 media members and allowed scalpers to charge $80 for $5 seats. LeBron finished with 14 points, 7 assists, 6 rebounds, and 1 superhuman reverse layup in 23 minutes, inspiring teammate Darius Miles to call him "an athletic Magic Johnson."

Neither Telfair nor Washington was that kind of specimen. But both had special talents all their own, and the tension between them matched the tension that existed between LeBron and Lenny Cooke before one exploded into megastardom and the other crashed and burned.

Telfair, wearing number 31, took the first possession straight at number 15, Washington, beating him on the dribble but failing to convert. Telfair missed on a short jumper before drawing a charge on Washington to foil a Nets fast break.

This one-on-one game was overwhelming the five-on-five, and not a single player or coach was moved to complain. Telfair blew past Washington on his signature crossover dribble and missed an open finger roll to a chorus of ooohs and aaahs.

Each point guard was trying too hard to humiliate the other. Telfair missed a layup on the break, then dribbled between his legs and threw a left-handed pass that found a teammate and bought the Jazz two free throws. Washington would soon rise high to grab a rebound with one hand and attempt to dunk it in the same motion, but he bounced the ball off the back of the rim. Telfair answered with a beautiful left-handed reverse layup on the dead run, a basket that compelled Washington to drive recklessly into the lane and loft a shot that was easily rejected.

Halftime found Pitino grinning like a Cheshire cat and refusing to budge from his position behind the railing. Telfair was taking it to Washington in a big way, and Pitino imagined him doing the same next year at the expense of the great Coach Cal.

The third quarter came and went without fanfare. Telfair and Washington were on the bench, and the Nets' big comeback was the only relevant event: It allowed Telfair and Washington to play the final quarter with the game at stake.

The Jazz held a 53–51 lead when Telfair made a clean strip and fed Glen Davis, known as Baby Shaq, for an uncontested dunk. Telfair then rose for an open jumper, drew the defense, and fired a perfect pass to Michael Williams for a 59–51 advantage.

Sure enough, Washington's Nets roared back to make it 61–61 with 4 minutes to play, setting the stage for the defining possessions in this rivalry. The other games had ended, so the crowd thickened with the plot.

Near the top of the key, Telfair dribbled between his legs from front to back, and again from back to front, and then blew past Washington and hung in midair for a layup that rolled in for a 65–61 lead. A minute later, Telfair made the move of the day, using the kind of double crossover that had turned the Rucker crowd in Harlem upside down, scoring for a 69–66 lead. Telfair matched that move with less than 2 minutes to play, using a left-to-right crossover on the right wing to beat Washington and send the crowd into a fresh tizzy.

"Sebastian has the best crossover since Columbus left Spain," said Konchalski, the recruiting analyst.

Raging mad, Washington charged into the lane and attempted a dunk in vain. He grabbed the rebound in a fit of desperation, drew a foul, and sank both free throws to cut the Jazz lead to 73–70. Pitino was standing statue-still now, his eyes fixed on Telfair as Louisville's most coveted recruit missed the front end of a one-and-one and handed the Nets a chance to tie.

But Washington sought a day's worth of payback in one misguided drive. He was whistled for charging, again, and the next time Telfair went to the line, with 34 seconds to play, he made both foul shots and extended the Jazz lead to 5. There would be one more punctuation mark, an alley-oop pass from Telfair to Williams for a dunk that shook the building's foundation and sent the redeemed playmaker running out of the gym, handing a young boy his orange headband along the way.

"I tried to come out and destroy (Washington)," Telfair said. "Last year he caught me sleeping. I know it's not over, but I think I showed I'm the best."

Telfair finished with 15 points, 9 assists, and 2 steals, and shot 6 for 13 from the field.

Washington finished with 5 points, 1 assist, and 0 steals, and shot 1 for 11 from the field.

The box score said it was a slam dunk, but one father-and-son tag team figured the numbers told a big, fat lie.

"Sebastian's the golden boy," Darius Jr. said. "Every time he throws a bounce pass, everybody goes oooh and aaah. But all that dribbling he does? That's not basketball. That's for the Harlem Globetrotters. I play fundamental basketball and he doesn't. Sebastian knows deep down who's the best point guard in the country, and it isn't him.

"Sebastian's got no heart. Every time I go at him, he fouls. He doesn't play any defense. He doesn't get down low in the stance. He bails himself out. If we were in a real game today, he'd probably have fouled out."

As Darius Jr. delivered his unique analysis, his father stood by his side, nodding on every syllable. Darius Sr. found this the appropriate time to question the reported stories of Sebastian's predawn workout routine.

"There's no way you can tell me Sebastian wakes up at 6:00 every morning and runs stairs in his building," Darius Sr. said in his rapid-fire delivery. "That's just a nice story. . . . That's just New York hype. We're from Florida. Nobody came out of Florida but Tracy McGrady and Vince Carter, and New York's the media capital of the world. You know, we have a relative in the league, too. Chucky Atkins of Detroit is our cousin. But we don't run around talking about it like Sebastian does with Stephon Marbury.

"Darius has more heart than Sebastian does, more athleticism, his shot is better, and he trains harder."

But Washington wasn't ready for the NBA, at least in the biased opinion of college coaches. Though Washington said he'd consider passing on Memphis and turning pro "if I have the opportunity to be the first point guard to go instead of Sebastian," Pitino and Boeheim were busy pouring ice water on the thought.

Boeheim had Carmelo Anthony as his ultimate recruiting tool. Anthony might have gone anywhere from 12 to 15 in the first round had he entered the draft straight out of high school; he was taken third by the Denver Nuggets after winning a national title for Syracuse.

"NBA teams always want big guys early, anyway," Boeheim said.

What else was Boeheim supposed to say? What else was Pitino supposed to say?

The Louisville coach left Fairleigh Dickinson's Rothman Center with a message for Telfair, in the event the kid's dusting of Washington had swelled his head to NBA proportions.

"I haven't seen any point guards this year who are ready to make the jump (to the NBA)," Pitino said. "There's nobody close to being ready. . . . When you draft a big man like Kwame Brown, he doesn't have to be fundamentally sound in all areas. But a point guard can't have any blemishes, and I just don't see any high school point guard without any blemishes."

In other words, Rick Pitino just didn't see Sebastian Telfair rejecting the Louisville coach's offer to fix all of his flaws.

°   °   °   °   °

Two weeks after the close of the ABCD camp, Sebastian Telfair was wearing a black Adidas jersey, black Adidas shorts, and the look of an 18-year-old kid without a care in the world. He was in his element on a steamy Sunday. He was playing pickup ball at Surf Playground, off Surf Avenue, with the Coney Island projects on one side and the Atlantic Ocean on the other.

A half-mile away, the amusement park and boardwalk were packed with an eclectic mix of locals, tourists, and suburbanites who had driven in for the day, the sons and daughters of former Coney Islanders who had taken off in the white flight. The seagulls had established air superiority in the cloudless sky. The smells of salt water and Nathan's franks hung low over the court where Telfair had defeated Stephon Marbury in a pickup game for the ages the year before.

It was one of many such neighborhood parks for Telfair and friends to choose from. "Basketball courts," said Tiny Morton, head coach at Lincoln High. "That's all we got around here."

Morton had just parked his new Cadillac Escalade next to a cement-colored building with box after box of exposed and tangled wiring racing up its rear wall. He corrected himself and reminded me that Coney Island had something other than basketball courts.

"Water," he said. "We've got Surf, Mermaid, Neptune, Sea Park. Everything in Coney Island is named after water."

After all, it was known as a sink-or-swim place.

"I'm definitely carrying other people's hopes and the community's hopes," Telfair said after he was through with 90 minutes of stress-free balling. "It's pressure, but that's the situation you put yourself in. So if you can't handle it, you're in the wrong place."

Telfair was in the right place on this day. He was among the people who treated him as a natural resource to be protected at all costs. While he played ball with 15 or so lesser talents, making sure to embarrass no one, homeless men picked through the park's garbage bins. Three players, waiting for next, relieved themselves behind various benches and trees.

Telfair acted as the deputy mayor of these people and this park.

"They're not on the same level as you," he said, "but those people make you who you are. They're going to go buy the magazine you're in, and they're going to go buy your sneakers and go to your games. You should always be nice to them."

Telfair said he was looking forward to some late summer nights on the boardwalk, in the amusement park, on the beach. The next morning, Morton and his Adidas-sponsored summer team, the Juice All-Stars, would take a 7:00 A.M. flight to Vegas for the Adidas Big Time Tournament. Telfair had stunned everyone by announcing that he wouldn't go, that he needed a break, that he simply had nothing left to prove. He didn't care that his absence would drop him in the recruiting analysts' rankings.

"I'm just tired of it all," Telfair said.

He didn't even finish off the ABCD camp with any dramatic stand. Shaun Livingston, who'd been destroyed by Washington, took it to Telfair in the camp's final days and denied the Lincoln legend at least a share of a third straight MVP award.

But with his fourth and final ABCD camp in his rearview mirror, Telfair was too spent to care. Summer after summer of trips and tournaments and magazine shoots had finally caught up to him. He was ready for his senior season and a chance to move on.

"It's like a dream trying to come true," he said.

Coney Island's dream.

"See those guys over there?" Telfair asked me on the perimeter of Surf Playground, pointing to two men lighting marijuana cigarettes while a nearby infant napped in a stroller. "They won't smoke around me. They're only starting now because I'm leaving, and that's the ultimate respect."

With that, the genius playmaker dribbled for home. The projects were on one wing, the deep blue sea on the other.

Sebastian Telfair had no clear lane to greatness. His was a Cyclone ride all the way, and the twists and turns of a senior season would put his high-speed ambitions to the ultimate test.

4

What a day for a news conference. The adults making a larger-than-life figure out of a 5-foot-11 kid had been on a home-run roll, but they struck out here. Sebastian Telfair was about to deliver his big Brooklyn announcement 4 hours before the Yankees and Red Sox would meet in the Bronx in Game 7 of a play-off series colored in apocalyptic shades.

Sure to be reduced to a footnote in the morning tabs, Telfair wasn't about to call the whole thing off. He'd been waiting for this moment since the first time a summer basketball coach handed him a free pair of sneakers. He'd been waiting for this moment since the day his junior high principal walked into his classroom and barked out his name.

Telfair thought he was in big trouble, at least until the principal handed him a letter.

His very first recruiting letter, from the good people at Michigan State.

The kid was too busy staring wide-eyed at the envelope to open it. He brought the letter to his home inside the Coney Island projects and handed it over to his mother, Erica, who would sit near Sebastian inside the Lincoln High gym on the afternoon of October 16, 2003, and listen to him announce a decision that could secure or squander a multimillion-dollar score.

Telfair would pick among all the Division I schools that had offered space in their backcourts, or simply state his intentions to enter the 2004 NBA draft. There was no margin for error here. No fouls to give. After collecting between 300 and 400 pairs of free sneakers and thousands of recruiting letters and postcards, Telfair finally had to declare himself.

He would do so in an old gym with faded brick walls, a railed-off running track high above the court, and the silhouette of the 16th President of the United States marking the middle of the floor. If the gym looked like it belonged in the Indiana heartland, the black Adidas banner signifying the team's sponsor and framing Telfair's announcement reminded everyone that this wasn't *Hoosiers*.

A large *L* marked the midcourt podium, below the cluster of microphones. About a dozen photographers and cameramen jostled for position with the New York sportswriters who weren't assigned to track George Steinbrenner's volcanic mood swings. Jonathan Hock, the filmmaker who did ESPN's *Streetball* series, had his documentary team in place.

To the left of the podium sat officials from New York's Public Schools Athletic League (PSAL)—a 100-year-old confederacy made up of the public high school sports teams across the city's five boroughs—and Bobby Hartstein, Lincoln's special ed dean and the man who had coached Stephon Marbury and Jamel Thomas to the city title. To the right sat the family of the hour. Telfair had gone GQ all the way—navy pin-striped suit, powder blue shirt, and a light gray tie. His father, Otis, went for a less formal look. He wore a black shirt and several silver chains around his neck, one of them dangling a large crucifix. Otis also wore a USA cap graced by the image of an eagle, a button supporting national child welfare, and another button carrying the word "Airborne."

"First Infantry Division, Vietnam," he explained to a reporter before hobbling toward his seat with the help of his cane.

Across the court and behind the assembled media stood various this-is-your-life figures in Telfair's world. Security guards who walked the Lincoln hallways. Father Robert Lacombe, the former Providence College teacher who had baptized Thomas. And Lincoln High faculty members. Telfair was a solid B student who had asked his favorite teachers to share in his big day.

But Telfair kept everyone waiting a bit, and not for any false dramatic effect. The coolest hand in Brooklyn was on the verge of an emotional breakdown. Renan Ebeid, Lincoln's athletic director, saw it in Telfair's face in the manic minutes before the announcement, and she pulled him into her office outside the gym and slammed the door shut.

With the cameras and notebooks finally locked out of his *Truman Show* life, Sebastian did what any 18-year-old might in the same situation. He began crying hysterically. The AD knew Sebastian felt like a frayed rope pulled in opposite directions by Morton and Hartstein, the protégé and mentor who were forever at odds and who were whispering conflicting words of wisdom in the point guard's ear.

But this problem ran deeper than the divide between past and present Lincoln coaches.

"What's wrong?" Ebeid asked Telfair.

"Everyone's telling me I'm doing the wrong thing," Telfair answered.

"What do you feel?"

"I feel like I'm doing the right thing. But Miss Ebeid, you have to understand. It's my family. My family's always telling me one thing, and I know I'm doing the right thing."

People began banging on Ebeid's door, shouting that the press conference had to begin. The AD threw water on Telfair's face to help him camouflage his tears.

"You keep crying up there and you're going to make me cry and ruin my makeup," Ebeid said in an attempt to make Telfair laugh.

"Miss Ebeid, I want to do this for you. I want to make sure that you're less stressful this year. So if I tell people my decision, they won't be calling you all year and asking what I'm going to do."

"Make the decision for yourself. If you feel this is the right decision, then go with it. Just know who was there for you before. People who are popping into your life now don't really want anything but your money."

Telfair finally told Ebeid he was ready to roll. She threw open her door and explained to inquiring minds that she was only giving her point guard a pep talk.

"His father was against the decision," Ebeid would say later, "but you have to understand that his father hasn't really been a part of his life. Sebastian's more concerned about his mother and little brother. His mother is very nervous. She's seen a lot of failures in her family. Jamel didn't get drafted, and she doesn't want to get her hopes up too high."

But this was a day of high hopes, a day when all of Coney Island would discover where Telfair planned on representing the neighborhood next. "NBA or College?" read the T-shirts handed out to the members of the girls and boys teams who were sitting in the wooden bleachers behind the podium, waiting for their cue.

The Lincoln principal, Corinne Heslin, who could have passed for an old-school nun, was first to the mike. "Sebastian is a wonderful young man," Heslin said. "He's respectful and he works hard. . . . But the good thing is we have him for all of this year. You're ours for one more year."

Heslin gave way to Ebeid, who quickly called a dry-eyed Telfair to the podium. The point guard had arrived at a decision. What a long, strange trip it had been.

°   °   °   °   °

Rick Pitino had never intended to leave his Camelot at the University of Kentucky for the Boston Celtics. He instructed his business manager, Rick Avare, to ask Boston officials for a record salary of $6 million only on the premise that those officials would make Pitino's decision easy by telling him to get lost. "In that case," Avare told Pitino, "why don't we ask for $7 million?"

So they made their ridiculous request for a long-term contract at $7 million a year.

"You're never going to believe this," Avare told Pitino in their next phone conversation, "but the Celtics went for it." Six coaching years at $7 million a pop, plus 4 general managing years at $2 million a pop for a grand total of $50 million.

Pitino got rich beyond his wildest dreams, but he paid a heavy price with his aura. He drafted the wrong players and made too many moves in a vain rush to glory. The Celtics disaster left him a basketball emperor with no clothes until the University of Louisville pulled him in from the cold, in part to shoot a dagger at the Cardinals' hated rivals in Lexington. To fully recover his good name, Pitino needed to find that one special prospect who could return him to the college basketball mount.

"Sebastian Telfair," Pitino would say, "is the one who can get me back to the Final Four."

More than any high school player, Telfair understood what it meant to be recruited. As far back as elementary school, he'd been courted by every sneaker-sponsored summer team in New York. Out of eighth grade he'd been coveted by all the powers inside the city's Catholic High Schools Athletic Association (CHAA), considered the most competitive league in America.

But in Pitino, Telfair had met his match. As a young Syracuse assistant hired on his wedding night, Pitino left his honeymoon to recruit a prospect named Louis Orr. Age never altered Pitino's approach: He stopped at nothing to get his man.

In the summer between his freshman and sophomore years at Lincoln High, the 5-foot-9 Telfair instantly became the playmaker Pitino would have left a second honeymoon for.

"Tiny Archibald is the fastest New York point guard I ever saw, but Sebastian is faster than all the rest," Pitino said. "And this young man has something Pearl Washington, Kenny Anderson, and Stephon Marbury did not have. He has unbelievable charisma. He's lit up every room he's ever entered."

This mass appeal made Telfair the eye of every college coach who would dream of landing that one career-making talent. Every college coach except the one next door, Mike Jarvis of St. John's.

Jarvis was on his way out, anyway, before his program became engulfed in a sex scandal. But a Telfair signing might have guaranteed the coach a new contract at St. John's, a fact that didn't influence Jarvis's thinking.

"Even though he's the biggest high school name in the country, we're not really recruiting Sebastian," Jarvis said. "He really seems to want to go to the NBA, and we've already been down that road with Omar Cook, who played 1 year for us before making a disastrous decision to turn pro.

"Sebastian should definitely go to college. It's a potential tragedy if he doesn't go to school, but we hear he's leaning toward the NBA."

By passing on the Telfair sweepstakes, St. John's opened the door for other suitors. Duke showed early interest. Georgia Tech was the 1-year home to Stephon Marbury, only Telfair wasn't about to follow every step of his cousin's career.

Syracuse appeared an ideal fit. Jim Boeheim had just won the national title, his first after an endless wait. But he had to keep feeding the beast. He had to keep filling up the Carrier Dome, meaning he had to find a successor to Carmelo Anthony.

The Syracuse coach twice visited Telfair. "A terrific kid," Boeheim said. But as big as Boeheim scored with another Brooklyn sensation, Pearl Washington, something was telling him to leave Telfair for someone else.

"I don't want to get involved in a long, drawn-out process where Sebastian ends up in the NBA anyway," Boeheim said.

Boeheim's experience recruiting Telfair's cousin also played a role in that decision. On a muggy September night in 1998, Boeheim and his assistant, Wayne Morgan, met up with Lincoln assistant Gerard Bell. Bell played chaperone for their home visit at the Marbury residence, as Bobby Hartstein was in the hospital with stomach problems.

"I remember it was hot as hell in the house," Bell said. He also remembered that Stephon's father and two of Stephon's brothers, Donnie and Eric, sat in on the visit. "Donnie and Eric took Wayne back to the bathroom and left me in the living room with Mr. Marbury and Steph and Boeheim," Bell said, "and we continued talking academics. When Wayne came back, he was definitely frustrated. He was angry. You could see it on his face. You knew something came down. He was looking to get out of there."

Now the head coach at Iowa State, Morgan did confirm Bell's claim that Stephon's older brothers took him into the bathroom for a talk. But Morgan would not reveal the nature of that alleged bathroom conversation.

Marbury signed with Georgia Tech.

On the same night that Providence nearly ended its recruitment of

Jamel Thomas because of Marbury interference, Bell didn't hear any of the Marburys ask the Syracuse coaches for an improper inducement. "But one time Mr. Marbury asked me to take a ride with him, and I knew shit was going to happen," Bell recalled. "I'm not an idiot."

When asked to comment on Syracuse's recruiting visit, Don Sr., said, "We didn't do anything wrong. We didn't ask for anything. I basically listened to what the boys said. You can't argue with experience, and they had far more experience as far as the recruiting process was concerned."

Donnie confirmed that he and his brother Eric, "were very involved in (Stephon's) recruiting" but denied that there was any bathroom meeting with Morgan. "The rumors that surfaced about us are just from people who don't know us. That's part of recruiting; people always make up things."

Hartstein later claimed the Marbury brothers made up an allegation that the Lincoln coach had cashed in on Stephon's college choice. "They said the word on the street is that I got paid from Georgia Tech," Hartstein said. "I heard $50,000, and I heard $100,000. Never in my life was I more offended by anything. I actually started to cry. . . . They couldn't believe I didn't get paid, even though I didn't get a nickel.

"I'll tell you what I could've gotten if I'd packaged Stephon and Jamel together, or even Stephon by himself. There are plenty of schools that I could've cashed in on, and I would've wanted a lot more than ($50,000). . . . There's so many ways I could've gotten paid for Stephon."

Hartstein said two small gestures represented the grand sum of his Georgia Tech take.

"I even told Stephon that the only thing (Bobby) Cremins did for me was for (Stephon's) first game there," Hartstein said. "I was there with five guys from Bay Ridge, and Cremins picked up my hotel bill. Not for the other guys, just me. That's the only thing Cremins ever did for me. That and I went to a game in the Garden to watch (Stephon) play Allen Iverson, and Cremins got me tickets. That's it."

College recruiters didn't chase after Telfair like they had after Marbury, in part because Telfair was weighing the NBA option more seriously than his older cousin had. But there was more to it than that.

"Some people were scared off by what happened with Stephon," said Louisville assistant Kevin Willard. "That was a wild circus, and that was not the case with Sebastian. Once you got to know Sebastian, he's a great kid and fun to talk to on the phone. . . . It wasn't a wild circus."

But enough major Division I coaches either figured it would be, or figured they'd be wasting their time recruiting a kid who would never step foot on a college campus.

"Listen," Boeheim said, "Sebastian's one of the best point guards I've ever seen at that level. But Sebastian's problem, as far as the NBA is concerned, is that he stopped growing.

"How's a skinny 6-foot teenager going to play Jason Kidd at 6-foot-4, 220 one night and then Gary Payton at 6-foot-4, 190 the next? We're not talking about LeBron James here. LeBron is the most ready player I've ever seen coming out of high school. LeBron's a 6-foot-8 chiseled freak of nature, as physical as anyone playing the wing in the NBA. He gets up and down the floor better than anybody in the league. So Sebastian should go to college. It didn't hurt Magic, Bird, Jordan, or Isiah to go to college."

Boeheim's former assistant couldn't have agreed more, but Rick Pitino knew the trick would be convincing the precocious playmaker to at least tap the brakes on his high-speed career. The Louisville coach was burdened by the same thoughts that drove so many recruiters out of this arms race. While shadowing Telfair's every move for more than 2 years, Pitino wondered if he was wasting his time.

But Pitino kept pushing, prodding, and selling against hope. He was the leader in the clubhouse for Tracy McGrady and Jermaine O'Neal before they decided to skip college, and yet Pitino decided Telfair was worth the risk of an unwanted three-peat.

If nothing else, the Louisville coach had Telfair's academic standing working in his favor. Unlike many recruits straddling the college/NBA fence, Telfair had no standardized test concerns. He'd scored a 1070 on his first SAT attempt—184 points higher than the most recent recorded average for a Lincoln student.

Telfair did fine in the classroom, but his high SAT score raised some eyebrows across the city's high school basketball scene. "Every person who knows Sebastian knows he didn't take it," claimed one PSAL head coach whose team played Lincoln. "But he did it on the first try, so nobody can challenge it."

Nobody produced evidence that Telfair used what is known on the recruiting trail as a "pinch hitter," but a culture of suspicion was created by a tidal wave of fraudulent scores, according to Rob Johnson, the most recognizable middleman in the street scouting market. "I'd say 70 percent of big-time New York players use pinch hitters," Johnson said. "The kid goes to a person he knows, a coach or whatever, and an arrangement is made to pay a guy to take the test. In most schools in New York the proctors don't check IDs. It's the easiest thing that ever happened, and the NCAA hasn't done anything about it. The key is to cheat on the first try, because then nobody can compare your high score to a low one you took earlier when you didn't cheat."

Telfair was universally liked and respected by his teachers, and he was never one to cut corners. Sebastian was many things, but a liar wasn't among them. It was hard to believe he'd cheat on anything, never mind his college entrance exam. Telfair called the test "long and hard" but said his high score simply reflected his hard work and his attendance in a preparatory course, nothing more. "I took a class that helped me because they gave us last year's test," Telfair said. "That really helped me get an understanding of what it was about. When I got the results, I was so happy. I didn't think I'd score that high."

So Telfair was in the academic clear long before Pitino spent a September night inside the Surfside Gardens housing project, the same Coney Island building that had become the center of the major-college universe 9 years earlier, when Cremins won the fight for Stephon Marbury's services.

Pitino arrived at the Telfairs' door accompanied by his assistant, Kevin

Willard, the son of Holy Cross coach Ralph Willard, himself a former Pitino aide. Kevin Willard had been promoted into the place of Mick Cronin, who had taken the head job at Murray State. Telfair was Willard's first official recruit. Telfair's father would say that Willard "sends me something every day. Every single day. A card, a letter. I guess he's just trying to make a contact."

He was trying to make the score of a young coach's life.

But Telfair wasn't about to go to Louisville for the sake of Kevin Willard. This was Pitino's game to win or lose. And on the official recruiting visit to the Coney Island projects, the game started over the hors d'oeuvres Telfair's mother, Erica, had cooked up for her guests.

"It was more a social visit between long-lost friends than it was a recruitment," Pitino said. "It was the longest visit I ever made."

Telfair's father, Otis, said the meeting went a good 5½ hours. Pitino brought along oversize photos of the Louisville campus, but no matter how grim and gray life on the Coney Island peninsula could be, Telfair wouldn't choose a school for its green grass and fresh country air.

The kid only wanted to know if a season with Pitino would improve his NBA stock, or if the Louisville coach was just another unnecessary middleman to be dismissed from the process.

"You'll win a national championship at Louisville," Pitino told Sebastian that night, "and that will put you as the number one pick in the first round."

Pitino went on about the veteran nucleus that would return, and about the recruiting class he was assembling. Of course, the sales pitch to Telfair would have been moot had the Lincoln star been ruled ineligible to play at Louisville or any Division I school.

LeBron James would have never gained NCAA eligibility after accepting that Hummer and those free throwback jerseys, and after engaging in a season-long food fight with Ohio athletic officials who yearned for the days when their teams weren't cutting pay-per-view deals and riding inside white limousines on some promoter's expense account.

Pitino understood that Telfair would succeed LeBron as the most watched player in America. He understood this even before a report in the *Courier-Journal* of Louisville questioned whether Telfair had compromised his amateur eligibility before his senior season at Lincoln by appearing in a *Slam* magazine ad for the Pass the Roc clothing line, an ad that showed Telfair wearing the company's clothes above a caption that read, "It's no secret. Just ask Mr. Sebastian Telfair. The number one and hottest point guard in the country!"

Telfair explained he received no payment for the photo and never authorized it to be used in an ad, claims that apparently satisfied the NCAA. "But I don't think Sebastian realizes that the NCAA is going to follow him everywhere his senior season," Pitino said. "I spent a half-hour of our recruiting visit conversation reminding him of that." Pitino told Sebastian, "You're not in Montana or South Dakota. You're in New York City. There are more eyes here than anywhere in the world."

Pitino hoped Telfair had learned from his friend, LeBron, and his cousin, Stephon, who faced NCAA scrutiny at Lincoln after he was given use of a car by Lou d'Almeida, head of the famed Bronx Gauchos summer program (Marbury was cleared when investigators found that his family's relationship with d'Almeida predated his rise as a basketball phenom).

Pitino pleaded with Sebastian to reject the advances of agents and hoped the point guard would see him not as a recruiter with a self-serving agenda, but as a partner with the kid's best interests at heart. "Being from New York," Pitino said, "(Sebastian) needed someone he could believe in. All point guards who are 5-foot-11 or 6 feet and trying to go to the NBA need someone they can trust."

Pitino told Sebastian about his business partnerships with former Kentucky players such as Jamal Mashburn, Walter McCarty, Ron Mercer, and Derek Anderson. "We have Lexus and Toyota car dealerships, Outback steakhouses, a glass company, you name it," the coach said.

Before Pitino finally left the Telfair apartment, he needed Sebastian to believe that he wouldn't deceive him. The Louisville coach told the point guard he'd advise him to turn pro when he was ready. Pitino told Telfair to listen to the right people, namely his would-be college coach. "There's so many voices in New York," Pitino said, "and Lenny Cooke and Omar Cook listened to the wrong ones."

°   °   °   °   °

At 4:39 P.M., October 16, 2003, Sebastian Telfair slapped down his cards faceup. "Now I came to tell you," he said, "that I will be attending the school of the University of Louisville, Rick Pitino."

On those words, the Lincoln boys and girls players sitting behind Telfair and wearing those "NBA or College?" T-shirts rose to face the assembled media and did a jump spin in place. "Telfair Says Louisville," read the announcement on their backs. The words "For Now" weren't visible to the naked eye.

Family members, teachers, and school and PSAL officials cheered this seminal moment in a prodigy's life.

"When you're a kid," Telfair said, "you dream of playing in the NBA. You want to go to somebody who can help you live your dreams. . . . Coach Pitino is the person who can do that for me."

Heslin and Ebeid hugged and kissed their boy king. Bobby Hartstein beamed about Marbury's more telegenic cousin. "Sebastian's a media machine," Hartstein shrieked. "A public relations dream."

The next day, the ESPN crawler kept delivering this bulletin: "High school PG Sebastian Telfair announces he will attend Louisville instead of entering NBA Draft." Only Telfair never quite said that. In fact, not a single one of the high school megastars who preceded him had declared for the draft before his senior season; even LeBron James waited until his St. Vincent-St. Mary career was complete.

"As of right now," Telfair said, "I'm definitely going to be playing college basketball."

Pitino fully understood the implication of those first four words. But weeks later, after Telfair sent in a signed letter of intent that did not prohibit him from declaring for the draft, Pitino held a press conference to bask in the reflected glory of his coup.

"(Telfair) is everything the marquee says about him," he said.

A half-hour after Telfair's big Brooklyn announcement and 3 hours before the Yankees and Red Sox began an epic Game 7 that would drive that announcement deep into New York's sports sections, I asked Telfair if Pitino really had him locked up.

"Nah, I just needed to get people off my back," he said through his million-dollar smile.

"If I'm in the top 15 of the draft, I'm gone."

The Lincoln team did not pull up to 2630 Benson Avenue in Brooklyn in the yellow school bus that was the picture of high school sports for most of Americana. The players came by train, by cab, by Danny Turner's Trailblazer, by Tiny Morton's Escalade, and by Sebastian Telfair's shiny new Nissan 350Z.

The Railsplitters had come to Lafayette High for their season opener, and by all appearances, Telfair hadn't heeded Rick Pitino's warning. He said his car was a gift from Jamel Thomas, who was making about $150,000 a season in Greece. The Z had a James Bondish look to it, and for a high school star from the projects, the car couldn't have demanded more attention.

Actually, Bassy originally wanted a Benz. "We had to talk him down from that," Turner said. "But it's in Jamel's name. He leased it and pays about $430 a month."

Thomas said the gift was "just something I wanted to do for Sebastian. . . . I help my friends with cars, too. I don't pay for them but help them out if they need a couple of dollars."

Already uneasy over the fact that Morton was driving a new Escalade, Lincoln athletic director Renan Ebeid had summoned Telfair into her office. "Sebastian, you can't be driving around in a fancy car and you know it," Ebeid told him. "You're going to bring attention to yourself."

Sebastian replied that the car was legally registered through Jamel. "They put it under the name of Jamel's aunt, an Aunt Nella," Ebeid would say.

That would be Nella Davis, a 47-year-old woman who lived in Providence. The Nissan's registration papers showed the mailing address as a post office box in Sacramento. The papers also showed the color of the vehicle as red; Telfair's car was silver. A law enforcement official who viewed the document said the discrepancy could have suggested an honest mistake, or the possibility that the tags were taken from another car.

All of which begged the question: Why would a New York man use his aunt in Rhode Island to register a car for a teenager in Coney Island and then have the bills sent to Sacramento? When I called the number listed at Davis's Providence residence, the woman who answered the phone identified herself as Nella Davis. She said she was Thomas's aunt and then declined to be interviewed. Thomas didn't respond to numerous interview requests. Telfair said he knew only that Thomas handled the transaction and "did everything the right way."

"You have a good reputation," Ebeid told Telfair in their meeting about his car. "Don't mess it up."

Telfair drove the Z with the Rhode Island plates all year, even though tags were required to be changed within 30 days of arrival in a new state. The local cops knew the Z was Telfair's, according to Turner, who said he was stopped and arrested one day simply because he was driving it. "I have a different last name, so they didn't believe I was Sebastian's brother," Turner said. "They thought I stole the car, and they took me to the precinct."

Turner said the subject of Telfair's car came up in a preseason meeting with an NCAA official, but that the official was satisfied with their explanation. Dan Matheson, an assistant director of enforcement, met with Telfair and Turner after the point guard appeared in the *Slam* magazine ad for a clothing line. Matheson told Telfair that he needed to be careful, that he could jeopardize his amateur status if he accepted any money or gifts based on his athletic talent. The NCAA rep handed Telfair his card and a sheet of paper titled "Principles of Ethical Conduct."

Pitino was a prophet. The NCAA was already monitoring Telfair's senior season, maybe the most anticipated season in the storied history of New York City ball.

The Lincoln players wouldn't show up as one for the opener of that season; the school couldn't fit a bus or driver into its budget. So they arrived in small, staggered clusters, marching up the Lafayette steps, through the doors, and into a school notorious for its high rate of disturbances. Not a single Railsplitter had a clue that Lafayette was the home to the most celebrated Brooklyn baller of them all: Sandy Koufax.

The borough's legend of the moment was Sebastian Telfair, Lincoln's number 31, the point guard who wore a number in honor of his home—31st Street. Telfair prepped for the first game of his final season by shooting alone on one basket while his teammates dressed in a Lafayette classroom. The home fans heckled Telfair while he shot jumpers in Lafayette's dark bandbox gym, a gym with the feel of a small bingo hall.

Three rows of wooden bleachers lined both sides of the court, enough seating for a few hundred people. Lafayette provided no public address announcer, and all of one pro scout—Jay Cyriac of the Philadelphia 76ers—had bothered to show up. It was a hell of a setting for a 5-foot-11 teenager fixing to go straight into the 2004 NBA draft lottery, but Telfair always knew how to dribble his way out of a jam.

He would need help to make this happen, help from a team that was suffering a crisis of depth after losing eight seniors from the year before. Sebastian would need guidance from his Coney Island–bred coach. He would need support from his four fellow Lincoln starters—one from Ghana, one from Russia, one from Queens, and one from Brownsville—to make this crazy Coney Island fantasy come to be.

o   o   o   o   o

Tiny Morton counted some 30 friends and acquaintances who had been arrested or killed. "Man, you've dodged a lot of bullets," one of his jailed friends had told him.

Morton grew up in what he called a two-parent home. Yeah, two parents. "My mom and my grandmother," he said. With no father in his life, Morton made his own way on the basketball court, where he topped out at 5-foot-8 and yet became a big Coney Island name with his clever ball-handling and reliable left-handed stroke.

He starred for Bobby Hartstein at Lincoln, then played prep ball at

Virginia's Flint Hill School. Boston College was among the interested schools, before Morton was removed from the Flint Hill lineup. His friend's aunt had been murdered. She took a bullet in the head during a robbery, and Morton wanted to go home for the funeral. Flint Hill had a big game on ESPN, Morton said, "and my coach told me I had to make it back in time to play." Morton didn't make it back in time. His days as a Flint Hill point guard were done.

He returned to Coney Island to finish high school. Boston College would sign another guard, and Morton would find refuge at Westchester Community College, and then at Central Connecticut State, and then at Long Island University (LIU). He sank a couple of buzzer beaters along the way and made progress toward a master's degree. But Morton couldn't make it through his senior year at LIU without a near-death experience in the school cafeteria.

A woman had struck him during a disagreement, and he struck her back. "The only time I've ever done that," Morton said. The woman responded by fetching her boyfriend. When they approached Morton, the boyfriend pulled out a gun. He squeezed the trigger, but the gun didn't go off. Tiny fled the scene. He said LIU officials would order him to leave school because he was a detriment to his fellow students. "But I went back and got my master's," he said. "I should've filed charges and sued the school. I could've sued her for hitting me first, and I could've sued the school for letting her stay in the dorms and keeping me out."

Morton started his post-grad life as a construction worker and substitute teacher before Hartstein put him on the bench, where Tiny grew close to Stephon Marbury, the star who would lead the Railsplitters to the 1995 city crown. When Hartstein decided to take a sabbatical, Morton was given the promotion. He waited five seasons for his very own Marbury. Sebastian Telfair didn't just represent a shot at a city title or three; he represented a crack at a brand-new life.

Morton would often field the charge that he was trying to cash in on Telfair. "I used to get upset when I heard that," he said. "That was until I sat back and said to Sebastian, 'What if I do get a job because of you?

What's wrong with that? Isn't that part of life?' Every coach gets ahead on talent."

Morton had a list of enemies that ran longer than the shoreline. But he was a father who was affectionate in public with his 9-year-old son, Trevonn, and 7-year-old daughter, Malaysia, holding their hands and kissing their foreheads—doing things many fathers in Coney Island weren't around to do. While his wife worked, Morton would pick up his children after school and take them to practices and games.

"He really is a loving, caring man," said Morton's wife, Indira, a welfare investigator for the city. "When you need something, he's always there. The kids he teaches love him. Sometimes we get notes from them saying, 'You're my favorite teacher.'"

But Morton had a way of opening himself to scrutiny. He was forever being investigated by the Department of Education for alleged recruiting violations—high school coaches were prohibited from offering inducements (gifts, promises of more playing time, promises of better college opportunities) to players at other schools in an attempt to convince them to transfer.

The Lincoln coach refused to lie low. Before Telfair's senior season, Morton began driving an ultra-conspicuous brand-new Escalade, and one with Virginia plates. Morton conceded that some students saw his wheels "and thought I got the car from an agent or sneaker company." In fact, the Lincoln coach said, his household income was about $100,000. "If I'm making fifty and my wife's making fifty," he said, "hey, I'm a math teacher. It's not too difficult to live on that."

Tiny's registration papers showed his Escalade in his name, at a Stafford, Virginia, address. Asked to explain why a lifelong New York resident would have Virginia tags, Morton would say only that "I've got a lot of family in Virginia. My sister lives there."

Despite the plates, Morton was all Brooklyn. Weather permitting, he often walked the streets wearing tank-top shirts that highlighted his muscular arms. Under his favorite Yankees cap, Tiny resembled a younger, smaller Willie Randolph. He knew his way around the bases, that much was sure. Morton was never an easy guy to pick off.

That's why he'd won two straight city titles. That's why he was assuring friends a three-peat was in the bag.

°   °   °   °   °

Eugene Lawrence was something with a violin, even if his coach and teammates didn't know it. Having a talent for the violin wasn't something you bragged about in Mike Tyson's Brownsville.

Lawrence was good enough in grade school to earn a Saturday school scholarship at the Brooklyn Academy of Music. He stopped playing when basketball assumed a bigger role in his life, yet came out of retirement one day during his junior year at Canarsie High, where nobody believed that the rugged 6-foot-1 star of the school's basketball team could actually make beautiful music with a violin.

"I shocked everyone that day," Lawrence said.

He kept an A average and hit the books hard enough to meet his SAT requirements for freshman eligibility in college. Only that made his transfer to Lincoln for his senior year all the more surprising. For 3 years, Lawrence had been a model student-athlete at Canarsie. Suddenly, he left it all behind for a place next to Sebastian Telfair in the Lincoln backcourt.

"I practically begged him not to come," said Tiny Morton, who coached Lawrence on his Adidas-sponsored Juice All-Stars summer team. Morton said he didn't want the scrutiny sure to hit in the wake of a controversial transfer. When Canarsie coach Tommie Allen was informed of Morton's claims, he laughed.

"Me and Tiny were friends," Allen said. "Tiny said, 'Tommie, don't believe any of this stuff you're hearing about Eugene ending up at Lincoln.'. . . With this No Child Left Behind rule, Eugene won't be the last high-profile player to do this."

The No Child Left Behind law allowed students in low-performing schools to transfer to better-performing schools within their districts (athletes wouldn't lose eligibility in such moves). Only Lawrence arrived at Lincoln as a safety transfer, as a kid who claimed he needed a new classroom setting because he felt threatened in his existing one. And Lawrence wasn't one to cower in anyone's presence.

"They got a safety transfer at the end of August and, what, he didn't feel imperiled in June and July?" said Tom Konchalski, the New York–based recruiting analyst. "Look at him. He's the strongest guy on the team. That's an absolute joke. . . . In the end, Eugene lives in Brownsville and Lincoln isn't in his district. He shouldn't be in that school."

Renan Ebeid had questioned Morton, Lawrence, and Lawrence's parents before the transfer was approved. Ebeid's instincts told her this wasn't a move she should support. "I'm the softball coach," she said, "and if a girl I'd coached for 3 years left me as a senior, I would've hated that."

Canarsie found itself on Mayor Michael Bloomberg's dirty dozen list—his list of the 12 most dangerous schools in the city. But at a fat-free 185 pounds, and with a business-only expression forever glued to his face, Lawrence himself conceded that he didn't feel threatened at Canarsie, and that he wanted to attend Lincoln in the hope of drawing interest from the major Big East and Atlantic Coast Conference (ACC) schools that had ignored him.

"You can't turn a kid away on a safety transfer," Ebeid said. "You have to go to the precinct to sign off on it, and (Canarsie) did. Tommie Allen's pissed off, but Tommie Allen's part of the school, and they signed off on it."

Lawrence had heard from Harvard, Bucknell, and Cornell, and there weren't too many ballplayers in Brooklyn who drew interest from schools like those. "But none of the big horses have contacted us," said his father, Gerard, a postal worker. So his son traded in the local school for a two-subway-line, 40-minute commute to Lincoln. Allen couldn't even understand the move on a basketball level. Major college scouts figured Lawrence was too small to play shooting guard on their level; they wanted to see him exhibit point guard skills. Why, then, go to a team that already had the best playmaker in America?

Morton said he'd use Lawrence and Telfair the way the old Pistons used Isiah Thomas and Joe Dumars. Tommie Allen? He would be left to talk up some 6-foot-3 freshman, a prospect who reminded the coach of a young Tracy McGrady.

"He could be special for us," Allen said. "That's if somebody doesn't try to steal him."

∘   ∘   ∘   ∘   ∘

Antonio Pena nearly pulled a Eugene Lawrence in reverse. The 6-foot-8, 225-pound center nearly walked away from Lincoln after his sophomore season to enroll at St. Benedict's Prep in Newark, New Jersey.

St. Benedict's appeared to be a good fit. Pena could have lived on the Newark campus and liberated himself from the nearly 4-hour round-trip commute from Queens he faced every day, giving him more time to focus on the core courses he desperately needed to become eligible to play Division I ball. Only Tiny Morton wasn't about to sit back and let perhaps the best big man in the city walk out on him the way Lawrence had walked out on Canarsie.

Pena grew up in Coney Island but lived with his mother out near Queens College. He'd rise between 5:00 and 5:30 A.M. every morning to prepare for a bus and train odyssey that landed him at Lincoln in time for his first class.

Pena maintained that his commute was worth the payoff. Ebeid wasn't so sure. "My first thing was, 'Why do you have a Queens address and why are you here?'" she said. "He said, 'I wanted to come to Lincoln because they have a good reputation in basketball.' I'm unhappy with the travel time because Antonio needs a lot of (academic) help."

John Pena, Antonio's uncle, was among the more visible parental figures at Lincoln games. He had respect for Morton as his nephew's coach, but had little use for the pressure Morton applied in an attempt to convince Antonio to leave Gary Charles's summer powerhouse, the Panthers, for a home with Morton's Juice All-Stars.

The issue was a constant source of tension between Morton and his center, though not one that destroyed the relationship. John Pena hadn't forgotten Morton's act of kindness during the worst week of his life. A technician at Verizon, John was working the graveyard shift one night when he was told to get to the hospital. By the time John arrived, his 2-year-old son, Kheri, was gone.

"He had asthma," John said, "and we gave him the nebulizer that night and he never woke up." The Lincoln team attended the funeral. Tiny removed a championship ring from his finger and gave it to John so he could place it in his son's casket.

Antonio felt his own obligation to Telfair, this after an entirely different act of kindness. The scene was the Glens Falls Civic Center, the event was the 2003 state championship game against Christ the King, and the development was the awarding of the MVP trophy to Telfair after he'd fouled out with 5:12 left in regulation.

Pena had made two foul shots with 5 seconds left to send the game into overtime and then scored 8 of his 18 points in the extra session to give Lincoln the victory. With fans jeering the MVP announcement, Telfair handed the plaque to Pena. "He deserved it," the point guard said, "a lot more than I did."

Telfair's philanthropy would have its limits. During the first preseason practice, the point guard dribbled between his legs and threw a no-look left-handed pass that bounced off Pena's forehead and into the hands of a younger, lesser intrasquad opponent. "You can't let these little skinny freshman asses beat us," Telfair screamed at Pena. "Elbow someone in the face."

After another lost intrasquad scrimmage 3 weeks later, Telfair found Pena emerging from the water fountain in the corner of the Lincoln gym. "Where's Tone?" he shouted. "Tone. Tone. I've got to say this. You're a bitch." Four days later, Pena ripped down a rim while dunking in Lincoln's auxiliary gym. Morton screamed at his center for causing such damage but privately celebrated the center's rare show of force.

"Tony needs to be more powerful down low," Morton said. "If he doesn't start balling, we ain't winning shit."

o   o   o   o   o

Yuriy Matsakov saw the vile smoke billowing above the smoldering towers, saw it the way everyone around Coney Island saw it. He wondered how the terror he thought he'd left behind in Russia had followed him across the world.

Six years earlier, he said, Chechen rebels blew a hole through a train station not far from his Pyatigorsk home. Three people died, and at least three people fled.

Yuriy, his sister, and their mother came to Brooklyn for those old Ellis Island reasons. Opportunity, freedom, a better and safer life. Then out of a clear blue September sky, terrorists made war against America's symbols of economic and military might. The Matsakovs were on a train bound for a Manhattan immigration office when their new world screeched to a grinding halt.

"I couldn't believe that 9/11 could happen in this powerful country," Svetlana said through her son's translation. "We thought we were safer here. That's why we came."

In the wake of the 9/11 attacks, Yuriy's grandfather thought Yuriy would be wise to return to their home in the southwest corner of Russia. The family overruled him. When Yuriy visited his homeland in August of 2003, his grandfather used the blackout that hit New York and other eastern U.S. cities to remind the boy that "things look worse in America than they do in Russia."

Only Yuriy wasn't about to turn back. At a lean 6-foot-5, he was developing into a promising ballplayer at Lincoln. Matsakov wasn't ever going to be Sebastian Telfair or even Antonio Pena, but he was the walking definition of upside. He only started playing basketball when he arrived from Russia in the middle of his freshman year; soccer had been his game of choice.

With his Siberian pallor, blond buzz cut, and angular frame and features, Matsakov could have passed for Andrei Kirilenko of the Utah Jazz. The Lincoln players called him Dirk, in honor of Dirk Nowitzki, the German star of the Dallas Mavericks. Matsakov wore Nowitzki's number, 41, yet showed nothing remotely approaching a young Nowitzki's talent when he first showed up in the Lincoln gym.

But the Lincoln players didn't make fun of him. "They encouraged me because I was tall," Matsakov said. Telfair was among the most supportive, a truth that inspired confidence in Yuriy.

Matsakov was subjected to occasional teasing as the Railsplitters' lone white player, "but only in a good way," he said. "Sometimes that made me feel special."

He didn't speak a word of English on arrival, like hundreds of Russian students from the Brighton Beach area. To walk the Lincoln perimeter during lunch hour was to sometimes imagine yourself visiting a school in Moscow. Russian kids gathered in noisy circles outside the Lincoln doors to smoke cigarettes and speak in their native tongue.

Like Pena, Matsakov was a young man who didn't waste a syllable. For instance, Yuriy never bothered to correct Morton and other Lincoln officials who kept spelling his name "Iouri," a spelling lifted from an old passport. But his slow, heavily accented English was good enough to meet the team's rapid-fire Brooklynese halfway.

"I like Tiny," Matsakov said. "He's made me a better player."

Matsakov's father was a mechanic back in Russia, his mother a home attendant in Brooklyn. They were children of the Cold War who agreed Yuriy needed a red, white, and blue upbringing.

On the basketball court, the future was now for Yuriy. He had impressed Russian coaches on his summer visit home—"I was killing the junior national team players in practice," he said—and if Yuriy wanted any shot at a college scholarship, he needed to impress the U.S. recruiters who attended Lincoln's games.

His family had sent him from Russia, with love, to chase an American dream, a dream that was less elusive to those who could put the ball in the hole.

o   o   o   o   o

Like Yuriy Matsakov, Nyan Boateng came to America for an education his mother didn't see available back home. Life was different in

Ghana. "Teachers beat you with canes if you didn't do your work," Boateng said. So kids had to take their studies seriously.

"But still," Boateng said, "my mother thought the educational opportunities would be better over here."

Theresa Adupoku first arrived in America in 1979. She found work caring for an elderly woman, returned to Ghana each summer, then decided her children should live permanently in the States. In 1994, she sent for her two young sons, Nyan and Dominic Osei, who would join her two daughters in New York.

The boys were glad to learn that no misstep in a Brooklyn classroom was met with the sensation of a cane raging against exposed human flesh. "Oh Mommy," Boateng would say, "school here is so easy." Adupoku reminded her children that life in Coney Island wasn't always so forgiving. Sometimes a sketch of a man under a "Wanted for Rape" posting near their building elevators did the reminding for her.

"In Africa," Adupoku said, "you can leave your door open and you don't have to be afraid somebody will rob you or point a gun at you."

By all accounts, Boateng and Osei were polite, respectful kids. But they were teased and bullied over their accents, leading to schoolyard fights. Soon enough, they forged a lasting peace the hard way. The brothers who found an occasional NBA game on the tube in Ghana earned the respect of the locals with their ballplaying skill.

They lived two blocks from the Telfair home and a parking lot away from Tiny Morton's apartment. Boateng and Osei grew up with Telfair on the Coney Island playgrounds. "Tiny eventually said, 'Come work with me,' and that's what we did," Nyan said.

Over time, the relationship between Morton and Boateng would deteriorate and become a constant source of conversation in the cramped 16th-floor apartment Adupoku shared with her boys and their stepfather, an apartment cluttered with her sons' trophies. The discord began with Osei, a senior on the 2003 team that won the city and state titles. Osei was a borderline Division I player who felt Morton couldn't have done less to help him earn a scholarship.

"It was all Sebastian doing this and doing that," Osei said. "We had a lot of seniors who didn't have scholarships, and guys were stressing out. That's the main reason we won the state; everybody knew they had to play well to get into college.

"Sebastian's a real nice person, so it was nothing against him. It was how Tiny was treating the seniors. He just used us to win championships."

In the heat of summer, with time running out and his options dwindling, Osei did land a last-second scholarship to Fordham. He credited a family friend and 1954 Lincoln High captain, Norm Ostrin, for arranging an unofficial tryout before new Fordham coach Dereck Whittenburg.

Morton refuted Osei's claim that he didn't attempt to help him find a Division I taker—"I definitely made calls for him," the coach said—and dismissed Osei's assessment that he was a Telfair-obsessed coach who ignored his seniors.

Either way, Boateng knew before his junior season at Lincoln that he wouldn't have to sweat out a full ride, and his relationship with Morton, the way his older brother had. Boateng, a 6-foot-3 wide receiver, was already being heralded as one of the best young football prospects ever to come out of New York City, never known as a football hotbed.

Boateng, not Telfair, was Lincoln's best athlete. His 185-pound body appeared to be one long and lean fast-twitch muscle. He had a ballerina's waist, a wide upper back, and rippling shoulders and arms. His vertical leap was measured at 40 inches, and he could run the 40-yard dash in less than 4½ seconds.

But Boateng nearly transferred to a private school, Poly Prep, to get away from Morton. Boateng said he decided to stay out of loyalty to his football coach, Shawn O'Connor, whose relationship with Boateng was in stark contrast to Morton's.

"If (O'Connor) wasn't there," Boateng said, "I was gone. . . . I think (Morton) hates the fact I'm playing football and getting a lot of media attention. But Tiny knows I'm not afraid of him, and Dominic wasn't afraid of him. (Pena) and the rest of them are afraid of Tiny, and Eugene hasn't been around long enough to know better. We're foreigners, so our parents aren't going to go in and sit there, and Tiny tries to use that to his advantage."

On the surface, it would seem absurd that an African-American coach would resent the success of an African-born player. But this is what Boateng and his mother came to believe, and not simply because Morton would often reference Nyan's heritage in misguided attempts at humor.

"I tried to set up meetings with him and he avoided me," Adupoku said. "I think he had something personal against Nyan and Dominic, the idea they were from Africa. If Nyan or Dominic were black Americans, that would've never happened. . . . Maybe he knows that if he treats some (American) kid badly, the father or mother would come with a gun or something bad. He knows in Africa we don't use guns."

Morton dismissed these claims as "ridiculous." He said that he never had any personal issues with Boateng or Osei, and that their differences amounted to garden-variety coach-player differences. In fact, Morton wasn't alone in believing that Boateng had trouble dealing with the fact that he wasn't "the man" in basketball the way he was in football.

"I'm just trying to teach them and motivate them," Morton said. "I don't single out anyone. I don't get on Nyan. . . . We're trying to get guys to play their roles, and sometimes there's conflict. That's normal. Every team on every level has that."

Morton was right: Every team on every level did have that. Some teams thrived on internal conflict, and others came unglued because of it. Which path would Lincoln High take?

o   o   o   o   o

The first game of the 2003–04 season was in the books, and Tiny Morton was acting some kind of pissed off in the Lafayette classroom that served as the Lincoln dressing room.

"I want everybody to remember what that girl said," Morton said of a Lafayette student who heckled the Railsplitters on her way out of the gym. "She said, 'We won. We won.' Most of you guys don't understand what she's talking about. They did win. They beat us."

The scoreboard said Lincoln had won, 100–70, over a dreadful PSAL opponent. But after being down 44 points, Lafayette closed with a 16-to-2 "run" against the Lincoln reserves that actually had the home crowd dancing to a March Madness beat.

It was a tough day all around. The refs wanted to begin the game at 4:00 P.M., a half-hour before Lincoln thought its season was scheduled to start and 10 minutes after Antonio Pena was supposed to be liberated from his last class. The Railsplitters were so notoriously late for everything that their clocks were said to be set to LST—Lincoln Standard Time.

Somehow, Morton got five players on the court for the 4:29 opening jump. Other than John Pena and his omnipresent videocam, there was no Lincoln presence in the stands. Lafayette was a notoriously rough place; later in the school year its principal would be knocked unconscious by a student fleeing police. Attending any PSAL game was an exhausting exercise in declaring your identity and purpose. It wasn't enough to pay a few bucks for a ticket, not after past brawls had spilled from the stands onto the floor. Gyms were often turned into police states. School security agents, cops, and out-of-season coaches were forever ringing the perimeter of the court, stopping fans from going this way and that.

Sometimes the hassle of attending a PSAL game just wasn't worth it. And besides, Lincoln fans had come to know Lafayette as a pushover unworthy of the commute. That sentiment clearly trickled down to the players.

So Sebastian Telfair would miss some layups, force some wild passes, and deliver a sloppy 26-point debut that made his NBA ambition seem like a wild fantasy. Only Telfair was the least of Morton's problems. His bench appeared even weaker than expected.

"It's unbelievable how unready you are," the coach told his team.

Kenny Pretlow, Morton's second assistant, would remain quietly seated in this session. Pretlow was a first-year man at Lincoln, a tall, bespectacled coach who made his name working with the Riverside Hawks of summertime fame. He was true to his professorial, voice-of-reason look.

In contrast, Danny Turner launched into a minirage. Turner was the kind of assistant who didn't say much but made an impact when he did. He ripped Pena for scoring 12 lousy points. "You play like bums," he shouted. "Sebastian, too." Turner promised to rip into Telfair when the two made it home.

"Ain't nobody knocked (Sebastian) down in practice yet," Turner said. "Last year he'd be knocked down."

Morton wondered aloud if he'd cut the wrong players from the team. "It's going to be a long season," he said. "A loooooooong season."

"Better buckle up," Telfair responded from the back of the room. "Let's go for the ride."

Ride? Turner wasn't about to give anyone a ride in his Trailblazer. "I ain't driving nobody home," he said. "They're walking."

With that, the Railsplitters headed out into the night, left to find their own way back to Coney Island. Telfair was wearing an Adidas cap as he stopped on the Lafayette steps, while LeBron James's best friend and Nike coworker, Maverick Carter, waited for him in an idling car.

"This gave us a reality check," Telfair said. "I'm glad we played like this. But fuck that. I'm not getting down. It's time to play ball. I'm tired of everything, of people saying how great we are, how great I am. I'm just relieved it started. It's time to play."

Lincoln's second scheduled game was its first "national" game, a date in a Fresno, California, tournament sponsored by Adidas. It seemed like an awfully long way to travel for one game, especially when that one game wasn't being staged in Shangri-la. But I figured this was just another manifestation of the new age of big-time high school ball.

"I'll see you at the airport," I said to Morton as he walked away from a bittersweet night inside Lafayette High.

"No, you won't," he said in reply.

The Adidas Showdown represented the shoe company's attempt to beat its former carnival barker, Sonny Vaccaro, to the West Coast punch. Vaccaro had left for Reebok in a huff over his failure to sign LeBron James, and Adidas wanted to establish a major high school tournament in California before its former employee could.

Adidas guessed that Sebastian Telfair would be a fish worth hauling in from 3,000 miles away.

The Showdown, also sponsored by EA Sports, would feature seven games at Fresno State's Selland Arena, with most participating teams coming from the Fresno area. The event would be run by an Adidas man, Darren Matsubara, coach of the Elite Basketball Organization summer program that produced Carlos Boozer and DeShawn Stevenson, the latter making the NBA jump straight from 12th grade.

The tournament was supposed to stay local in its first year, go statewide in its second, and then go national in its third. "But then Tiny Morton called," Matsubara recalled, "and I said, 'What the heck?' You don't turn down Sebastian Telfair."

It didn't matter that Fresno wouldn't have made any Lincoln player's top 20 list of places to see. And it didn't matter that most national high school tournaments, shoot-outs, showdowns, whatever, were played around the Christmas and New Year's holidays, when students had their weeklong break.

The Railsplitters were going to cross the country twice within 3 days to play one game the Saturday after Thanksgiving, and they were going to do it with smiles on their faces.

Morton knew Matsubara from their days on the summer camp circuit. "I want to keep a connection with EA Sports," Morton said. "Having Sebastian communicate with those guys will help him out with endorsements down the road. Sebastian did a lot for me, so I'm trying to do things to benefit him."

Stephon Marbury had an endorsement deal with EA Sports, so why not Telfair? Lincoln would face off against Stevenson's former high school, Washington Union of Fresno, and its star guard, Dwight O'Neil.

Matsubara guessed that Telfair's appearance would ensure a crowd of 5,000 for his all-day card, with Lincoln as the 8:00 P.M. headliner. Matsubara also guessed that this business proposition was a two-way street.

"The Sebastian camp is making a good case to get a shoe deal," Matsubara said. "He goes to an Adidas high school. He plays in the Adidas camp. He plays for an Adidas AAU team. It all puts him in a nice position. Adidas might give him a deal on loyalty, and if outside companies like Nike and Reebok try to get him, they'll say, 'God, he's locked into Adidas. We're going to have to come in with a real big offer to get him.'"

Fresno was supposed to be the first stop on Telfair's road show, the first stop on the journey the Lincoln point guard wanted in the wake of the Scholastic Fantastic LeBron James Tour. The Railsplitters would also play in Philadelphia, Los Angeles, and Louisville. They would play an ESPN2 game at Fordham. They would play in Trenton on George Steinbrenner's YES Network.

Telfair certainly wasn't the equal of LeBron, easily the most hyped American high school player of all time. But Telfair was LeBron's friend, Marbury's cousin, and a kid with enough Coney Island street cred and suburban crossover appeal to serve as an invaluable commodity for a school that could use the positive marketing images and whatever financial reward could be reaped from those images.

So Lincoln administrators weren't eager to park their national basketball schedule before it got out of the garage. But at the 11th hour, the Railsplitters canceled on Fresno, setting in motion a series of events that landed the aborted trip in the middle of the New York Department of Education's investigation of Tiny Morton.

Lincoln hadn't even taken to the road, and already there were charges of an improper side deal and a violated contract that would be heard by school lawyers and Department of Education investigators. The most ambitious high school tour of the 2003–04 season had started right where the most ambitious high school tour of the 2002–03 season left off: in trouble.

St. Vincent-St. Mary High of Akron, Ohio, had been where Lincoln High of Brooklyn was trying to go. One year later, nobody in Ohio was quite sure if the gain was worth the pain.

o o o o o

Frank Jessie left his job as athletic director of St. Vincent-St. Mary because of those dreaded "philosophical differences." Jessie wanted high school basketball to be high school basketball. Before LeBron James's senior season, that sentiment made the AD a member of a small parish.

Jessie didn't want to criticize his alma mater from his new office at Purcell Marian High School in Cincinnati. He said he didn't think it was right to run down a place he'd grown to love. Jessie was president of the St. Vincent-St. Mary alumni association, after all, and he thought LeBron James was a damn good kid to boot.

But Jessie wanted no part of the packaging and selling of a high school kid. He was a basketball lifer, a former assistant under Bob Huggins. Everyone knew you didn't coach and recruit at Cincinnati without developing a taste for high stakes ball.

Only that was college and this was not. When St. Vincent-St. Mary trustees started drumming up the idea of asking for five-figure appearance fees, Jessie knew he needed a new job.

"I had a problem with guarantees," he said. "A lot of the schedule was predicated on who was paying you the most, and I don't know if that was the role of high school sports. When you get big money involved, some issues start to surface that I don't think are the best for anyone. Then you start to get the official Vegas line, or you see things in the paper and on the Internet about gambling lines and how many points somebody's going to get, and those are the things that caused a lot of the problems in college."

Jessie had a problem with schools negotiating with promoters, especially since one such promoter offered him $5,000 for his pocket if he signed on the dotted line. "Now, I'm not a saint," Jessie said. "But if I'm going down, it's not going to be for $5,000. Make it $5 million and I'll think about it. So if people are offering me that much, how much is being offered to people close to some of these programs?"

St. Vincent-St. Mary faced a relentless wave of criticism for allegedly turning James into its very own ATM. A trip to the school's Web site made a visitor feel like he or she had stumbled upon a promotional agent of the ultimate college sports money machine, Notre Dame. To one and all, the site announced, "There is nothing like an Irish road trip to see your number one nationally ranked Irish basketball team."

Not that Notre Dame ever had a player like LeBron James.

St. Vincent-St. Mary moved home games to the University of Akron to draw bigger crowds at higher ticket prices, put some games on pay-per-view, and requested and received $15,000 a pop for allowing its basketball genius to play in a promoter's friendly neighborhood gym.

After agreeing to let ESPN televise two earlier games, the school rejected the network's request to televise James's final regular season game. St. Vincent-St. Mary was worn from taking a coast-to-coast pounding from commentators and columnists. It needed a time-out after LeBron James was suspended for accepting free throwback jerseys from a sporting goods store, and after LeBron received a new Hummer, with three televisions, as a birthday gift from his mother, Gloria, who was said to have made the purchase through a bank loan.

"But St. Vincent-St. Mary took all that criticism over money and didn't get near the money it should've gotten," Jessie said. "If you're going to make the decision to do (a tour), don't go halfway. If you have a 15,000-seat arena and the average ticket price is $20, and that's conservative, that's $300,000. Now you're telling me you've decided to do this and you're going to take the criticism and you're only going to get 15 grand? What happens to the rest of the money?

"After expenses, some promoters could make $100,000 on a single game. Hey, if you're going to make money, *make money*. Don't put $100,000 in some bozo's pocket."

If St. Vincent-St. Mary didn't make enough money, it did make enough enemies. Some of its traditional local rivals decided against scheduling the Irish as payback for the school's choice to go national and leave them in the proverbial dust.

"There was some jealousy," said Grant Innocenzi, Jessie's replacement at St. Vincent-St. Mary. But Innocenzi claimed there was no regret, at least not on his school's end.

"Most of our kids won't end up in the NBA," the AD said. "For some it will be the only chance to get to California, or to play in front of 15,000 fans. We didn't miss any school. We looked at these as field trips. It wasn't like we were prostituting anybody, not when they could see different cities and cultures.

"We could've played a couple more away games and charged $25,000, and we didn't do that. We didn't sell LeBron shirts or bobbleheads. Look at the sales of LeBron's Cleveland Cavaliers jerseys, and then figure how much we could've made if we sold his number 23 Irish jersey. But we didn't do that because that would've been exploitation."

St. Vincent-St. Mary wasn't always so conservative in its approach, according to Bobby Jacobs, executive director of Delaware's Slam Dunk to the Beach tournament, the biggest Christmastime event in the land. Jacobs thought he had an agreement with the Akron school to make a return appearance in his 2002 field.

"Then the school called me," he recalled, "and said they wanted $15,000 a game as an appearance fee, 20 motel rooms that had to be on the oceanfront, and five first-class plane tickets among the 20 we'd give them. They would play two games, so that would be $30,000 in appearance fees. I've had requests before, like teams asking to stay near the outlets or some asking to stay near the water because they don't live near water. But this was way beyond that. The school was saying, 'We want this, and this is how many we want, and this is how much money we want, and if we don't get it, we're not coming.'"

Jacobs said he wasn't left with a difficult choice. Even LeBron wasn't bigger than his one-size-fits-all basketball show.

"They were like, 'You're turning us down?'" Jacobs recalled. "And I said, 'Well, that's pretty much what I just did.' . . . I think I set a precedent when I said, 'No.' There's also a rule that nobody follows, but I do, and it says that whatever you do for one school in your tournament, you must do for every school."

St. Vincent-St. Mary nearly boycotted a game during Jacobs's 2001 tournament, though no school official deserved the blame. LeBron's surrogate father, Eddie Jackson, was irate when he phoned Jacobs and demanded that the promoter send away the vans parked outside the team hotel and waiting to take the St. Vincent-St. Mary team to the gym.

"We ain't showing up," Jackson shouted. "You better get Greyhound or something, because LeBron don't ride any yellow fucking school bus."

Jacobs got a coach bus to the hotel in time, and the band played on.

Back in Ohio, St. Vincent-St. Mary did raise some 2002–03 ticket prices from $5 and $6 to $12 and $13, though it kept student prices at $3. Innocenzi claimed the school broke even, or lost money, on its pay-per-view arrangement with local outlets. "Our total revenue was $400,000 for the athletic department," he said. "With that, we were barely in the black. Maybe $500 or $1,000 in the black."

Yet there remained enough outcry over alleged St. Vincent-St. Mary greed that state athletic officials limited the amount of road trips a high school team could make. The LeBron Rule would allow teams to play as many road games as they wanted in contiguous states, but limit them to one long-distance trip (without any missed class time).

During James's rookie season in Cleveland, his alma mater never traveled beyond Columbus. What a difference a year makes. Jessie would have never left St. Vincent-St. Mary if it had played the schedule in the 2002–03 season that it played in 2003–04.

"I hate to go back to the *Hoosiers* type of situation and be cornball about it," Jessie said, "but there's something to be said about growing up in your neighborhood and playing with the same group of people. There's a lot to be said for the local fan support and the loyalty of the neighborhood high school. Some of the reasons we played high school sports in the past are not even in the picture today.

"We used to have camp with fundamentals stations, and now . . . they're only putting kids against someone else so the college and pro scouts can evaluate them at a very young age. And in AAU ball, basically the people with the best teams are those who give their players the most. So at a very young age people are learning that you have to have your hand out, and I just don't think seventh and eighth graders need to be going to the highest bidder."

Jessie's successor, Innocenzi, shared some of his concerns. He said he worried about too many kids putting too many eggs in too many athletic baskets after watching the local teen wonder, James, become one of the more recognizable sports figures in America.

But the AD was a realist. He knew that kids would strive to be the next LeBron, and schools would strive to be the next St. Vincent-St. Mary. He knew that Sebastian Telfair and Lincoln fit both bills.

So one year after watching his Fighting Irish basketball team get more publicity—good and bad—than Notre Dame's Fighting Irish basketball team, Innocenzi was willing to offer some unsolicited advice to the bigger high school with the smaller star.

"I would tell Lincoln to develop a positive relationship with the parents," Innocenzi said. "Be honest with each other, and make sure you deliver on what you say you're going to do. I would tell them to keep school time as normal as possible. School is school. It's not a time for media or autograph seekers. And once you get things set, you're probably going to have to hire a couple of extra people to help you with ticket and media requests."

No public school budget in Brooklyn was allowing for a ticket and publicity manager. Still, Telfair's senior season would offer a critical public relations opportunity for Lincoln, an overcrowded school tethered to the neglect and despair weighing down its home community, Coney Island, where the locals had one thing, if only one thing, on their better-off neighbors:

The best damn team in New York.

Lincoln High delivered to the world two Nobel Laureates in chemistry (Dr. Paul Berg and Dr. Jerome Karle), one Pulitzer Prize–winning playwright (Arthur Miller), the entertainers Neil Diamond and Neil Sedaka, the actors John Forsythe and Louis Gossett Jr., the sportscaster Marv Albert, and the Baltimore Orioles' manager Lee Mazzilli. Yet no two students ever brought more attention to the school than its Nobel Laureates of the hardwood, Stephon Marbury and Sebastian Telfair.

By winning city titles and wearing the Lincoln label on TV and in big-city newspaper photos, Marbury and Telfair were speed-dribbling messengers of a not-so-subliminal thought: Lincoln was a place where hoop dreams came true.

Marbury was an NBA point guard good enough to score more than $100 million in wages. His little cousin, Telfair, would run enough successful fast breaks to seriously consider skipping the one year of college ball Marbury played at Georgia Tech.

"We're thrilled with our basketball success," said Corinne Heslin, the Lincoln principal. "But I worry about one thing: Lincoln is an educational institution. Our job is to get athletes a diploma, not to make them pro athletes. . . . Sometimes I think that students who are interested in basketball say, 'Lincoln equals basketball. If we go there, we're going to be Sebastian Telfair or Stephon Marbury.'"

Heslin had seen plenty of young students who burned to be the next Marbury or Telfair, only to fall short of those baseline-to-baseline standards. On a wall outside Heslin's office hung "Lincoln's Failures," a framed recounting of the disappointments in the life of the 16th president. Badly beaten in a legislature race. Badly beaten in a Congressional race. Badly beaten in a Senate race. And on and on and on.

"If anything," Heslin said, "I want the basketball team to know that if you persevere, you can become more than you really think."

No, this principal wasn't about to let her young ballplayers cheat her or themselves. She wasn't about to let the Railsplitters believe that basketball was their only hope, or that Lincoln High was merely an appendage of its most prominent athletic team.

Heslin spent 20 years as Lincoln's assistant principal in charge of guidance before she got the big promotion. She was a stout, white-haired woman who would say only that she was "over 55." If Heslin wasn't Joe Clark of Paterson (New Jersey) Eastside High, carrying a baseball bat and a bullhorn on daily patrols, she remained a hallway presence to be reckoned with.

The school was in dire need of her firm leadership. Lincoln's student body of 3,000 was five times larger than that of St. Vincent-St. Mary, and 33 percent bigger than it was meant to be. The closings of failed schools conspired with the No Child Left Behind legislation to create a barely tenable situation. Though it wasn't among the city's more dangerous schools, Lincoln did experience a sharp rise in incidents largely because of its swelled ranks.

To see the Lincoln hallways between classes was to see Penn Station and Port Authority merge inside the school's grand old building off the Belt and tree-lined Ocean Parkway. Lincoln was a fading yellow brick structure surrounded by just enough grass, small businesses, and well-maintained co-op and rental complexes to suggest a tranquility that didn't exist between the classrooms, never mind inside the nearby projects.

Kids screeching. Security guards shouting. Students bumping. Fights erupting.

"About 10 to 15 years ago, we had a lot of Coney Island versus crosstown incidents," Heslin said. Crosstown included Flatbush, Bushwick, Bedford-Stuyvesant, and Brownsville. "Maybe some of the crosstown kids felt they were more middle class than the Coney Island kids, and the Coney Island kids resented that and there were clashes.

"We haven't had that as much, but there have been a couple of recent incidents between those groups. Whenever a school is so overcrowded, you have kids constantly rubbing or bumping in the hall by accident. If you're in a bad mood, things happen."

Lincoln had only one security guard for every 300 students. The school was supposed to have an armed police officer on the premises every day, but when the officer had vacation time or was sick or stuck in court, Lincoln did without. In an attempt to ease the burdens, the school decided to go from two staggered class sessions to three. That didn't work, either.

"So early in the year was horrendous," said Renan Ebeid. "We got a new group of freshmen, and a lot of them couldn't read. We had to target some of the trouble kids, put handcuffs on them, and show them we were serious.

"Some of our kids have it a lot worse at home. Single-parent families, low income, uneducated parents, drugs, you name it. They can't get involved in activities because they have to babysit their sister, their son, their niece or nephew. These kids don't need that negativity. You hang around the projects and you see kids smoking marijuana all the time."

Given the alternatives, Lincoln was generally a desired location. "It's been known as one of the safer schools," Ebeid said. "We have a very nurturing staff, and kids respond to that."

By most accounts, racial tensions were not particularly high at Lincoln despite the presence of enough sons and daughters of Russian immigrants to make up 20 percent of the student body. This relatively peaceful coexistence manifested itself on a basketball team comprised of black and Hispanic players who treated their lone white teammate, Yuriy Matsakov, as an equal partner in their quest for PSAL history.

But that quest drove a wedge between the school's academic mission and its basketball team's extra-large ambitions. Morton had nearly been fired after the first Department of Education investigation into his alleged recruiting. Two years later, with the Department of Education back on the hunt, some school officials believed the time had come to rein in the coach.

Ebeid was among those officials. "I'm disgusted with the whole basketball thing," she said. "I just think kids should come to high school and you teach them sportsmanship and leadership skills so they can learn stuff for the future and play ball. Everyone here is about winning, and to me that's not what coaching high school kids is about."

A teacher, assistant principal, and head softball coach who got her athletic start as a trainer at Howard Garfinkel's Five-Star Basketball Camp, Ebeid had just established herself inside the male haven of high school sports. She was only 3 years on the job as athletic director and, at 28, she was striking enough for coaches to call her the J-Lo of the PSAL.

Ebeid had to overcome her good looks. "I think I've earned everyone's respect," she said, "because I've put a lot of coaches in their place. I've heard comments like, 'You're young and beautiful,' but coaches now know they need to stop before crossing that line."

Ebeid served as the football team's trainer during her first year at Lincoln. She grew so uncomfortable taping up teenage athletes who were constantly hitting on her that she'd wear ponytails and baseball caps just to calm them down. As it was, the promotion to the athletic director's chair didn't make her life any easier. "My first year was a year from hell," Ebeid said. She was a young woman suddenly lording over a male-dominated world, and coaches tested her at every turn. "Everything was, 'This is how we do it at Lincoln,'" Ebeid recalled. "And I'd say, 'That's nice. Thanks for letting me know. This is how I want you to do it now.'"

Ebeid mandated equal access to the main gym for the girls basketball team. That wasn't Morton's problem with his boss. He felt Ebeid didn't appreciate his team's success relative to that of the football team run by Shawn O'Connor, who enjoyed a strong working relationship with the AD and a healthy coach-star relationship with Nyan Boateng.

"Football gets treated like kings by Miss Ebeid," Morton said, "and look at everything we've done for this school. We've never gotten the respect we deserve. Miss Ebeid hasn't done right by us."

Ebeid didn't see it that way, but did concede she had a problem with Morton's involvement in the summer basketball circuit. The AD didn't believe a high school coach should also run a sneaker-sponsored enterprise such as the Juice All-Stars, who traveled across the country from one major tournament to the next.

Ebeid thought of Morton as "a very good basketball coach. . . . But all the negativity (Morton) has with the outside AAU team tends to come into Lincoln, and that's the one thing I don't like. . . . In the end, he needs to do right by the kids, by me, and by the principal."

o   o   o   o   o

Tiny Morton signed a contract with a Fresno-based promoter he wasn't authorized to sign. Morton promised to deliver Lincoln to the first inaugural Adidas Showdown, and his own principal would come to believe he took an improper inducement in exchange for that pledge.

Lincoln never made the cross-country flight because Morton didn't submit the required paperwork for the trip until days before the team was scheduled to leave. "Ever since 9/11," Ebeid said, "New York City wants the hotel insurance information and the fire inspection certificate." Ebeid asked for that paperwork to be turned in 2 weeks before the event. When Morton failed to meet that deadline, the trip was canceled.

"That's not fair," Morton told Ebeid. "What will I tell the kids?"

"Tell the kids you screwed up," Ebeid replied.

Heslin had problems with Lincoln's scheduled appearance that went beyond Morton's failure to hand in the paperwork on time.

"He can't sign for Abraham Lincoln," Heslin said. "I can or Miss Ebeid can because she's my designee in that area. . . . I didn't sign the contract, and so I didn't feel I had any obligation to honor the contract."

Morton and Danny Turner lobbied Heslin to change her mind. Morton set up several meetings with the principal. Turner went over Heslin's head, straight to the superintendent. "It was like a house of cards that started to tumble," Heslin said. Turner's decision to contact the superintendent backfired. "If Danny hadn't gone there, it would've been within the school," Heslin said. "But then the lawyers for the Board got involved because now it's a contract and the people in California are saying you're reneging on the contract. So it became a little bit messy, and the best thing was not to go."

Heslin had one other reason for keeping the Railsplitters in Brooklyn: She knew that half the players wouldn't attend Monday classes after a 6,000-mile, Friday-to-Sunday odyssey, and that the other half would be fast asleep at their desks. For two games in San Francisco, maybe she could have accepted that. For one game in Fresno, fat chance.

The drama hardly ended there. Darren Matsubara wasn't about to let his main attraction bail on his tournament without a fight.

Matsubara was a most familiar presence on the summer circuit scene, where the coach and promoter known to friend and foe as "Mats" had a noisy past. When his former player, DeShawn Stevenson, decided to skip college and enter the 2000 draft, Stevenson's mother and stepfather ripped Matsubara and Adidas in the *Fresno Bee* for pushing DeShawn toward the NBA.

Stevenson was the second high school guard—after Kobe Bryant—to successfully make the jump into the first round (Utah picked him at number 23), and, like Bryant, he would stand accused of sexual misconduct. In his second season, Stevenson was sentenced to 2 years probation and 100 hours of community service after pleading no contest to a charge of having sex with a 14-year-old girl. The NBA suspended Stevenson for three games without pay, slapping an exclamation point on the notion that he'd entered a man's world much too soon.

Away from the Stevenson case, Matsubara was involved in a lawsuit brought against the agent, Dan Fegan. A former Fegan employee, Brian Dyke, said in a sworn deposition first reported by the *SportsBusiness Journal* that his former employer had made cash payments to Matsubara and other Adidas-backed summer coaches; Fegan strongly denied the charge, and the suit was settled out of court.

"Someone was throwing me under the truck," Matsubara said, "and I want to set the record straight. It wasn't true."

Either way, Mats was hell-bent on surviving. He was a viable candidate for a seat on the grassroots board of directors that would replace the not-so-dearly departed Vaccaro. So it was clear why Matsubara wanted his first Adidas Showdown to be a smash hit, and why he wanted to avoid the embarrassment of a Lincoln-Telfair no-show.

Matsubara had already spent thousands of dollars on the Railsplitters' airfare, and he also figured to lose more cash on the extra Selland Arena seats Telfair would have filled. According to Lincoln officials, Matsubara was prepared to spend money to save money.

"Now the phone calls start coming in," Ebeid said. "At first, (Matsubara) wasn't calling me. 'So you're calling me up now and asking me how come I'm not sending the team? You ask the coach. Now you want to deal with me?'. . . . They decided to do everything through Dwayne, and he didn't abide by the rules. So (Matsubara) said, 'Is there anything we can do to have them come?' I said, 'Like what?' He said, 'Can we offer you anything?'"

Ebeid said Matsubara called Heslin and said, "We're not giving anyone else money, but we'll give you guys money." Matsubara denied ever offering Ebeid or Heslin an appearance fee in exchange for making the paperwork problem go away. He said there was language in the contract "that was a little bit unclear," and that he could understand how Lincoln officials might interpret the language as indicating an appearance fee. But Matsubara insisted the only compensation offered involved travel expenses. He said at no time did he tell Ebeid or Heslin he would give the school money.

The Lincoln principal disputed Matsubara's account and confirmed Ebeid's version of events, saying the tournament organizer did offer an appearance fee without stating a specific amount. But Heslin took the matter to an entirely different level by saying, "I think (Matsubara) had already given, in my heart of hearts, Dwayne something."

With Ebeid sitting in her office, Heslin had asked her coach if he'd taken an improper inducement. Morton said he hadn't, but the Department of Education wouldn't take Morton's word for it. During an investigation of Morton that would drag through the season and into summer, investigator Dennis Boyles asked about the aborted Fresno trip and claims of a Matsubara-Morton side deal.

Boyles didn't return messages seeking comment on his investigation, but a source close to the inquiry said Boyles had come up with no hard evidence that Morton received an improper inducement.

Sonny Vaccaro, the Reebok executive who had regarded Matsubara as a protégé when they both worked under the Adidas banner, suspected something else. "You have Lincoln High from Brooklyn going to Fresno, and how ridiculous is that?" Vaccaro said. "People in Fresno had no idea who the hell Lincoln was. They probably didn't even hear of Sebastian. They were going out there for what? For the experience of it? They weren't even going to be on TV or anything. One game in Fresno, what a joke."

Before being told of Vaccaro's comments, Matsubara had said, "I'm very close to Sonny." Apparently not as close as he thought.

"(Boyles) asked me if there was an appearance fee and I told him, 'No,'" Matsubara said. "I haven't heard back from them. . . . There was no appearance fee, no compensation fee."

Morton scoffed at Vaccaro's remarks and the idea that the Department of Education was asking questions about the canceled Fresno trip. "What? That's crazy," he said. "Sonny and (Matsubara) do business, so Sonny assumes it's dirty. It's ridiculous. . . . If that's the only thing they're looking into, then I'm fine."

In the end, the Adidas Showdown went off as scheduled. Some 3,500 fans paid to see two dozen Division I players compete in seven games. "We were able to recover the fumble," Matsubara said.

Meanwhile, Morton was back on his own 10-yard line. He had botched the first leg of the Sebastian Telfair Victory Tour, and his quarterback and team couldn't afford any more turnovers.

The Reebok sneakers emerged from a box listing China as its return address. The shoes were white and red, with Sebastian Telfair's initials gracing the sides, and their presence on the Fordham University scorer's table announced that the battle was joined and that Telfair needed to pick his weapon of choice.

Reebok, Nike, and Adidas. They all wanted the Lincoln High star to wear their brand on national TV. ESPN2 was in the house, and Telfair and Lincoln would face Orlando's Edgewater High and Telfair's old friend, Darius Washington, back from the ABCD crypt.

Telfair had seen enough of Washington, but this was the game ESPN2 wanted. This was the game a few matchmakers from the Paragon Marketing Group decided could best pique the interest of a nation that had tuned in to watch LeBron's St. Vincent-St. Mary High beat Oak Hill Academy the year before, a game that was among ESPN2's highest-rated programs.

More than anything, this was the game that would best capture the culture of the high school basketball celebrity, a phenomenon inspired by sneaker reps, rappers, writers, and scouts.

"Kids are expected to be cultural icons now," said Tom Konchalski, the recruiting analyst. "So LeBron and Sebastian don't have to be Michael Jordan, but Michael Jackson, too." Konchalski had recently seen a picture in the paper of Jay-Z gazing adoringly at LeBron. "If Lew Alcindor or Wilt Chamberlain were in a picture with Elvis Presley," he said, "it would've been the other way around."

On this day, December 11, 2003, Sebastian Telfair's color picture appeared on the front page of the *New York Times*. When I tried to explain to him what some foreign dignitaries would do to get even a below-the-fold piece of Pinch Sulzberger's A-1 pie, Telfair wasn't impressed. It didn't mean any more to him than a spread in *Slam* magazine.

But at least Telfair could measure the mark he was making at the multibillion-dollar intersection of hip-hop and sports when Jay-Z and Derek Jeter arrived at this game side by side, making Fordham's Rose Hill Gym, of all places, the sexiest spot in town.

John Carideo of the Denver Nuggets and Evan Pickman of the Los Angeles Clippers were among the scouts present to see if Telfair was worthy of guaranteed first-round cash. Personnel men around the NBA watched on TV. Rick Pitino sat on press row, a few chairs up from Jeter and Jay-Z and a hovering, hulking bodyguard big enough to fit Shaquille O'Neal in the palm of his hand.

Len Elmore, the stately NBA veteran, would call the game for ESPN2 with Mark Jones and Fran Fraschilla, former coach at New Mexico and St. John's. For every five fans in the Fordham gym there appeared one sneaker guy or summer coach or street agent who was busy shaking hands, patting backs, and whispering sweet somethings in somebody's ear.

This was Sonny Vaccaro's ABCD camp on steroids. Coaches and scouts waited in the stands, all of them eager to watch reputations made and broken on the floor. Nobody seemed to care that Shaun Livingston, the 6-foot-7 playmaker from Peoria, was recognized by most sanctioning bodies as America's reigning point guard champ.

"The focus on Sebastian Telfair and Darius Washington won't be as great as it is tonight until they're playing in the NCAA Tournament or Final Four," said Rashid Ghazi, vice president of Paragon Marketing Group. "At 18, being on the cover of the *New York Times* in a color photo is incredible for Sebastian. Now he can build the Telfair brand. If Sebastian wants to make the jump from the basketball world to the general marketing world, reaching cereal and fast-food companies and other potential endorsement sources, this is huge."

So huge that Pitino flew in for the occasion, showing up in his best pin-striped suit. He was there to let his star recruit know how much he appreciated that signature on his letter of intent. When the Louisville coach spotted Pickman, the Clippers' scout, they had the following exchange:

Pitino: "What are you doing here?"

Pickman: "Same thing you're doing here."

Pitino: "Then I guess I better get a new fucking point guard."

According to Pitino, Pickman told him the Clippers were already prepared to draft Telfair in June. "And I said, 'Would you really? But you'll be drafting so high,'" Pitino recalled. "Evan said, 'We're picking him because we think he's the best point guard in the country.'"

Telfair didn't do anything to allay Pitino's worst fears by making a fashion statement on the Fordham court: He was wearing white socks bearing the NBA logo.

Of course, the 6-foot-1 Washington had to wear black socks bearing the NBA logo. These were opposite talents and personalities attracting in the bright camera lights, staging their own *American Idol* face-off.

Paragon, the company responsible for first putting LeBron on national TV, pored over a list of 50 high school stars while determining which matchup would create the most curiosity. Livingston was a candidate. So were Dwight Howard, Al Jefferson, and Josh Smith. All four were taller than Telfair, and some would argue that all four were better than Telfair, but neither consideration ruled the day.

"This year, there wasn't any more publicized athlete than Sebastian Telfair," Ghazi said. "He's Stephon Marbury's cousin. He's won championships in the biggest city in the country, the city with the best tradition for point guards. He's also the athlete most associated with LeBron; they were on the cover of *Slam* together. . . . So putting on Sebastian against his main rival made the most sense. He'd answered the challenge of having that bull's-eye on his back for a lot of years."

Of course, there was that little matter of the bull's-eye on his feet. Telfair chose to remain loyal. That choice was made easier by Adidas's foresight in coming up with its own special sneaker for Telfair's big night. The white sneakers with blue stripes were small, mobile billboards showing Telfair's initials flanked by his number. Adidas's 3ST1 won out over Reebok's offering from Yao Ming's corner of the world.

Vaccaro had actually bet me a dime to a doughnut (his words) that Telfair would play the Edgewater game in Nikes. "I could've worn Nike because I could've worn anything I wanted," Telfair said. "Players aren't under contract, the school is. I chose to wear Adidas because they sponsor us and do a lot of nice things for the kids. It's the whole team, not me, and that's why I made that choice."

Telfair took the Fordham court in Adidas shoes, and Washington did the same. In the hour before tip-off, Washington was wearing Edgewater's red Adidas sweats and carrying a black Adidas bag. His father was wearing a blue Adidas sweatshirt and black Adidas cap. If there was no debate over which company won the marketing battle, the game the sneaker wars had reduced to a sidebar was finally ready to unfold.

"The world will finally find out what kind of player I am," Washington had told his father before they boarded their flight from Orlando. "Now is the time." In young Darius's mind, it was time to expose a New York myth once and for all.

°   °   °   °   °

"ESPN2?" Darius Washington said. "I thought this game was on ESPN. Nobody gets ESPN2."

"Everyone gets ESPN2," countered his father, Darius Sr. "It's the sister station. Don't worry, people will watch."

The kid frowned as he sunk into his chair. He was wearing gym shorts and a blue USA basketball jersey as he sat in his living room corner, next to a stack of gray tubs carrying every letter, postcard, and FedEx package from the institutions of higher learning soliciting his high hops.

"The game's going to be at St. John's, ain't it?" Darius Jr. asked.

"Fordham," said Darius Sr., the Warren Sapp lookalike and talkalike who was wearing an earpiece running from his omnipresent cell phone.

"Fordham?" the kid said. "Where's that at? I thought we were going to be at the Garden. Man, they're not going to have Spike Lee sitting front row at Fordham."

"They couldn't put enough people in the Garden," Darius Sr. explained. "The fans will be close to the court. . . . And Fordham's where they play the Rumble in the Bronx. Remember? That's the first time you ever saw Sebastian."

Yes, Sebastian. The entrée of this postdinner conversation on a warm November night in Orlando, where the Washington family lived in a comfortable four-bedroom, two-bath ranch. Telfair had Coney Island and the amusement parks that time forgot in his backyard; the Washingtons grew up at Disney and lived a three-pointer away from Universal Studios. Their environments were as different as their opinions on the hottest mano a mano on the summer circuit since LeBron James traded trash talk and jump shots with Lenny Cooke.

"I killed him at ABCD as juniors," said Darius Jr., the Memphis signee, "and everyone said Sebastian wasn't motivated because I'm a nobody. . . . I played with a bad ankle and tendinitis in my knee all summer, but if I have a bad game it's, 'Aw, he sucks.'"

"Yeah," Darius Sr. added, "New York backs its players. Here in the South, everybody's out for themselves."

"That's what's different," Darius Jr. said, "the hype all those New York guys get. I mean, I'd won a national championship at age 10 and had never heard of Sebastian. Suddenly he came out of nowhere and everyone's talking about how great he was." Darius Jr. and Sr. went on the Internet in search of the great Sebastian. At first, they had no luck. "Then one time," Darius Jr. recalled, "I'll never forget, it was late at night and we finally found a picture of him. It was a side view, and Coney Island was behind him while he was holding the ball. It was like, 'Oh, that's finally him.'"

Him. Father and son loved nothing more than talking about him. Theirs was a stand-up routine, and if the Washingtons were forever on cue, one immediately picking up where the other left off, it was because they didn't have to negotiate a wide generation gap.

Father and son were more like big brother and little brother. "We had Darius when I was in the 11th grade at Edgewater," Darius Sr. said as he nodded toward his wife, Tarchelle, who was holding fast to her cheerleader looks. The three of them grew up together.

Darius Sr. was an Edgewater star with NBA ambitions before fatherhood knocked him off course. "I went to 13 colleges," he claimed, and just as many minor league camps. He understood that his kid brother for a son wasn't destined to play for the Florida Beachdogs of the CBA. Darius Sr. hired a publicist for Darius Jr., put up a Web site devoted to his skills, and became Darius Jr.'s manager, promoter, and psychologist. Darius Sr. didn't care that some in the amateur basketball community saw him as the classic overbearing dad.

Darius Sr. cared only that his son was in demand. A 35-year-old assistant recreation chief at a local community center, Darius Sr. burned to channel that demand into everything he couldn't achieve or attain in his own fractured youth.

Darius Jr. was young, gifted, and good-looking; people told the Washingtons their boy should model clothes if he didn't make it in the NBA. But Darius Jr. wasn't thinking about anything but a career in ball. Out of those overflowing gray tubs came the one scholarship offer Darius Jr. accepted. He would play for John Calipari, perhaps for a year or two before making that Dajuan Wagner leap into the pros, and he would make his hard drives to the basket in the official shoe of the Memphis Tigers, Reebok.

"We're known as the Adidas family," Darius Sr. said, "so I sensed Sonny (Vaccaro) was pissed off that we didn't choose an Adidas school."

This, of course, was before Vaccaro's own big-money jump to Reebok.

"I don't think the shoes really make the person play," Darius Jr. said. "You don't think Michael Jordan could dunk unless he had Jordans on? These companies try to spoil kids at a young age, and hopefully those kids remember that. It's a business."

Darius Jr. was all set to play a season or two in Memphis, and inquiring neighborhood minds wanted to know why. Darius Sr. loosed a belly laugh when he brought up rumors that his son wasn't waiting on the NBA to play for pay.

"We hear that now," Darius Sr. said, "'Why would he pick Memphis? You had Duke and North Carolina? Oh, Calipari must've dropped you off.' So you know what I tell them? 'Shit, come to my house and let me show you these bills. Come on, baby, you want to see if I got dropped off?'"

From across the living room, his wife intercepted the thought.

"We supposedly got money from Adidas," Tarchelle said. "We got $90,000."

"Yeah, $90,000 from Adidas," Darius Sr. said, laughing.

"That one was going around for a good time," their son added. "That one was around for 3 or 4 months. The recent one was that they bought us a car."

"Yeah, we've turned down a lot of money from agents and people like that," Darius Sr. said. "I won't let those guys get to him. He's not going to get bought."

The Washingtons wouldn't take any sneaker company advice, but they would take the sneakers. Dozens and dozens of sneakers. Enough to inspire Darius Sr. to offer me a tour of his personal Adidas, Nike, and Reebok outlet, starting in his son's bedroom, where a life-size cardboard image of Vince Carter stood guard in the corner and a poster of Michael Jordan, Scottie Pippen, and Dennis Rodman hung above a shelf stacked with Darius Jr.'s trophies.

Darius Sr. opened his kid's closet to show off an overflow supply of Air Jordans and the like. Then it was on to the garage and more shelves of brand-new sneakers lined up Foot Locker–style above the family pool table.

The conversation eventually worked its way back to Telfair and big, bad New York City hype.

"When you see all these New York kids who don't make it," Darius Sr. said, "kids like Lenny Cooke and Omar Cook, you ask, 'Why put them out there so quickly?' At an early age those New York kids get confused. They run with a posse. The first time I ever saw Sebastian in person, he had all these people with him. We were getting on an elevator at ABCD. We're going to the all-star game and the elevator opened, and it was like Sebastian and his whole posse on there.

"When you've got all these people around you, you know somebody in that group is not telling you the right thing."

Nobody credible was telling Darius Jr. to apply immediately for the NBA draft, a fact encouraging the dissection of Telfair's game and celebrity. So when they were done singing those tired ABCD camp blues, the Washingtons brought up Edgewater's regular-season victory over Lincoln at the University of Central Florida during the 2002–03 season to support their fresh charge that Telfair wasn't a clean player.

Darius Jr. said Telfair had twice sucker-punched him when the refs weren't looking. "Let him hit me on (ESPN2)," Darius Jr. said. "On TV they'll be like, 'Let's run that back. Whoa, he's dirty.'"

"Sebastian is a great showman," Darius Sr. said. "But when he punched Darius, it was like when Tyson bit Holyfield's ear. The champ wasn't invincible anymore. Darius gave everyone belief, because that was the first time someone ever stood up to Sebastian."

o   o   o   o   o

Darius Washington Jr. was on a search-and-destroy mission, killing Lincoln with three-pointers, muscular drives to the basket, and high-risers in the lane. Edgewater was up five in the second quarter, and Sebastian Telfair was desperate to stem the tide. Jay-Z and Derek Jeter were in the house; their fashionably late arrival had caused a stir in the crowd.

This was Telfair's city, his night, his prime-time special, and it was all being pilfered by an adversary he thought he'd vanquished for good in July.

Then it happened. The gym stopped dead the way the city had stopped dead earlier in the day when word hit that Jeter's teammate, Andy Pettitte, had signed a contract with his hometown Houston Astros.

Telfair was down, screaming, grabbing at his right leg. It was a scene reminiscent of the 2000 college national championship game between Florida and Michigan State, a game that saw the Spartans' Mateen Cleaves crash to the floor and shout, "It's broke." Cleaves made a dramatic return from the locker room to secure the biggest victory of his career. The odds weren't good that Telfair was about to do the same.

His right ankle gave way when Edgewater guard Jeremie McClendon landed on it during a scramble for the ball. There were 27.1 seconds left in the first half, and the worst endgame thoughts were racing through so many minds.

This wasn't just an injured ballplayer. These were multimillion-dollar ambitions in that heap. Coney Island dreams, shoe company hopes, and Final Four aims.

Telfair screamed and bared his teeth. Pitino turned a ghostly shade of pale on press row, the blood rushing from his face to his toes. Renan Ebeid stood behind the ESPN crew and watched the replays on their monitor with her mouth open, her palms pressed against her cheeks, her eyes frozen wide with dread.

Danny Turner and Tiny Morton made a slow journey across the court, as if they didn't want to receive the news. Bubba Barker ended up out there, too. Telfair was down for 8 minutes before he sat up, wincing as a fan kept yelling "Brooklyn . . . Brooklyn." Telfair was lifted to his feet, and Washington and his Edgewater teammates came over to pay their respects, to ask their sworn enemy if he was able to continue the fight.

Telfair limped off with the aid of Turner and Bubba. The cheering crowd got louder as each Telfair step grew steadier. Before he reached the bench, Telfair turned back in an attempt to take the free throws already assigned to the reserve guard, Nich Leon. Telfair was led back to the bench, and he would watch Leon make both foul shots and then drain three more with one-tenth of a second left in the half, cutting the Lincoln deficit to 35–33 and sending the Railsplitters out of the gym feeling slightly less doomed.

At the bottom of the stairwell, the team turned right into its locker room and its star headed straight into the trainer's room. "You came out flat as hell," Morton shouted as he stood before a chalkboard. "I don't know if you're nervous or what."

Across the hall, Telfair was getting taped up tight. Diagnosis: severe ankle sprain. Prognosis: There was no time for a prognosis, not with the ESPN2 cameras waiting to capture its junior Willis Reed moment.

Telfair slid off the trainer's table and hobbled through the door and led his father, girlfriend, and athletic director toward a meeting with the Lincoln team at the foot of the stairs.

"Iverson plays when he's half dead," the father, Otis, told his son. "He plays with a broken leg. Suck it up, play in pain, and then you can go home and cry."

Telfair began to hobble up the steps. "Don't limp," Morton said. "Don't be limping on me." The orders didn't end there.

"You're letting the team lead you," Otis said. "You have to lead them. You've got to take over in the second half."

The crowd roared when Telfair appeared for warm-ups. At press row, Pitino asked me for an update, and I gave him what I thought was good news: The kid was about to give it a go. Pitino would have preferred otherwise. He didn't need his own master plan compromised by a high school injury made worse for some made-for-TV cause.

But start the second half Telfair did. Washington immediately hit a pair of three-pointers, threatening to run away with the game, before Telfair made a stand that defied the pain shooting up his leg. He drained a jump shot and then rejected a Washington drive with a wild sweep of his right hand, drawing ooohs and aaahs from the crowd.

Washington answered by making four free throws; he wasn't letting the momentum turn without a fight. Edgewater maintained a 62–57 lead at the end of the third quarter, and the score within the score looked less favorable to Lincoln: Washington had 32 points, Telfair 18.

Darius Sr. sat upright in his front-row seat and looked all cat-who-ate-the-canary proud. But if the NBA scouts were wondering if the wrong guard was weighing a jump into the draft, Telfair was about to set them straight.

His spinning layup a half-minute into the final quarter preceded a slap-steal on a Washington drive and a left-handed bank shot. Out of a time-out, Telfair flapped both arms toward the Rose Hill roof in request of more noise from a crowd already chanting, "Let's go Brooklyn." The tension was mounting. "It's louder in here than it will be for any Fordham game all year," said Dick "Hoops" Weiss of the New York *Daily News*, sitting courtside.

Attendance was a disappointment: Even the generous estimate of 2,500 left some 1,000 seats vacant. Neither Paragon nor ESPN accomplished much in the way of game-day buildup in the city tabs.

Still, there was a buzz in the gym all the same. Jay-Z and Jeter made up for those empty seats. Pitino's presence didn't hurt, and neither did the roster of heavyweight media types on press row. Elmore, Fraschilla, and Jones for ESPN2. Chris Lawlor of *USA Today*. Harvey Araton and Chris Broussard of the *Times*. Weiss of the *News*. Writers who regularly covered Lincoln and high school ball for the *News*, *Post*, and *Newsday*—Julian Garcia, Dan Martin, and Michael Weinreb—were pounding away on their laptops, chronicling Telfair's night in the white-hot LeBron lights.

He would give them all something to write about, the way stars always do. Telfair scored six straight points to start the fourth quarter. With 5:44 to play, he risked more bodily harm by sliding in front of the hard-charging Quintin Thornton, all 6-foot-8 of him, and drew an offensive foul. Forty seconds later, after scoring in the lane, Telfair drew another charge at midcourt, this time at the expense of Washington.

At the 5-minute mark, Telfair made a pretty kick-out to Eugene Lawrence, who drained the 3-pointer that gave Lincoln a 66–65 lead. Fans began chanting Telfair's name. When Washington took the free throws that tied the game with 2:10 left—his first points of the fourth quarter—hecklers mocked him for his disappearing act.

Telfair made a big steal and hit the two foul shots with 33.6 seconds left that gave Lincoln a 79–75 lead and the winning points, leaving Washington to berate a ref after attempting a wild, running 3-pointer.

With 8.3 seconds to go, Telfair faced his bench and banged his fist off his chest. The crowd was standing, stomping, and roaring its approval until it was distracted by the commotion behind the Edgewater bench. Darius Sr. had left his seat, grabbed a couple of large friends, and confronted some fans who had been riding his son. Darius Sr. had nearly brawled with a heckler in the stands of the ABCD all-star game, causing a delay in the action, and now he was claiming a fan had reached out and pushed Darius Jr. A few security guards in maroon blazers tempered the shouting and finger-pointing as the game ended and the teams lined up.

Telfair and Darius Jr. embraced.

"Good game," Washington said, "but this ain't the end."

"You're right," Telfair said.

Telfair finished with 27 points, 7 assists, and 4 turnovers. Washington finished with 36 points, 10 rebounds, and a triple-double-clinching 11 turnovers. On the way back to his Louisville season, Pitino confirmed his heart had stopped when his recruit went down in what looked like a season-ending pile. "But what a great performance," said Pitino, who maintained there was a "95 to 5 chance" that Telfair would play at least one season at Louisville.

Pitino said he wasn't allowed to meet with Telfair after the game; NCAA rules prohibited such in-season, face-to-face contact. "When you see him," Pitino asked me, "can you say hello for me?"

I found Telfair sitting in a chair in the back of his cramped locker room, where Lincoln players were picking through mounds of clothes in search of their baggy jeans and white Adidas winter coats. Telfair was wearing only shorts and the ankle tape his father was trying to yank off his leg. "You're killing me, Dad," Telfair said in full wince. "Just killing me."

"Man, in the NBA they play 100 games a year," Otis said. "You think Bassy's not going to get hurt sometimes? Well, he showed tonight he can play hurt and under pressure. I was just hoping his leg wasn't broken."

Above the din in a locker room filling up with the Coney Island regulars, Sebastian began shouting for someone to find his clothes. He slid on a Yankees cap. He said it was "a special feeling" to play before Jeter and Jay-Z.

"But the crowd kept me going," Sebastian said. "Anybody else would've sat down, especially when Darius was so hot. . . . It was surreal, man. This was one of the best times of my life."

His defeated opponent, Darius Jr., would say the same. He thought a few endgame calls could have gone Edgewater's way, but said he understood that home-court advantage was home-court advantage. Washington praised Morton for trapping him more in the second half and forcing lesser teammates to take shots. The Edgewater star reported no cheap shots thrown his way.

Of course, he wasn't about to award Telfair a free pass. "After the game I had 100 people call me to say Sebastian was limping on defense, but on offense he was going full speed," Washington said. "When I looked myself, I saw they were right."

Predictably enough, Washington's father advanced the theory that Telfair wasn't nearly as injured as he let on.

"I thought it was a cop-out," Darius Sr. said. "Darius was kicking his butt with 20 points in the first half. But I'll give Sebastian credit. I thought he should've fouled out, but he won the game."

Telfair won a game seen in 415,000 households. The 0.5 rating was fairly good news for ESPN2, which had shown major-college games at the same number. It wasn't LeBron's 2.0, but it wasn't far behind the ESPN2 rating for the second LeBron game it aired in 2003.

"LeBron had an aura and maturity about him, and Sebastian has a lot of those same characteristics," said Paragon's Ghazi. "He lived up to the hype."

When he was done telling reporters about the pain in his leg and the resolve in his heart, Telfair limped toward the exits in his stylish white parka, the one bearing his last name and the Adidas logo.

He gathered his girlfriend, Samantha Rodriguez, pushed through the gym doors, and headed for the Fordham parking lot. A few cars passed, a few students shouted from their windows, and then Sebastian and Samantha were all alone with their hopeful thoughts. They bumped at the shoulder and thigh as they walked, the chilled December night lit up by a near-full moon and the excitement a young couple feels when heading down a path to who knows where.

o   o   o   o   o

The Lincoln gym was packed, Spike Lee was sitting front row, and Sebastian Telfair was whipping no-look passes to teammates streaking to the hole. It was a wild and crazy Friday afternoon in Coney Island, only

20 hours after Telfair injured his ankle on national TV, and the visionary playmaker was taking it to Grady High from the top of the key.

Telfair couldn't drive. He couldn't change directions or chase loose balls or do much of anything except play traffic cop with the ball.

Telfair was the victim of a schedule that would have broken most pros: NBA stars don't play day games after night games. No way Telfair should have been out there, not after spending the morning in agony, in tears, and, finally, in Coney Island Hospital. "I was crying real bad," Telfair said. "I couldn't walk. We'd iced it at night, rubbed Epsom salt on it, but nothing helped."

By the time LeBron James called to offer congratulations, Telfair was already being examined by a doctor. "Good game," LeBron said. "You okay?" Telfair was a million miles from okay. He offered up his foot for X-rays, headed back to school before he could get the results, then laced up his sneakers before he could think about the payday he might be putting at risk.

Lincoln-Grady was Brooklyn's answer to Yankees-Red Sox, with a twist: Grady was right across the street from Lincoln. Given that Grady ballplayers grew up in the shadow of Lincoln legends, a victory over the mighty Railsplitters would have made their day, their week, their season.

"So I knew my team needed me," Telfair said. He gingerly tiptoed through the game, his ankle fitted inside a blue rubber wrap. Telfair was grimacing all the way, helping more in spirit than body. But he couldn't walk away from this 79–63 victory without putting his signature on it. Late in the third, as he dribbled near the hash and right in front of Lee, Telfair ripped off a stunning behind-the-back pass that made it all the way to the baseline and Antonio Pena, who scored the basket to advance his domination down low.

Lee rose out of his seat and appeared ready to faint. Everyone in the gym was taken by the show. Everyone but the Cardozo High coach, Ron Naclerio, who was fuming over the transfers in the starting lineup (Eugene Lawrence) and on the bench (Lawrence Alamilla).

"This is bullshit," he said. "That kid, Eugene, and that other muscle kid (Alamilla) from Sheepshead Bay, they shouldn't be here. Eugene was succeeding at Canarsie. If he was still there, Canarsie would probably make the play-offs.

"But I'll tell you right now, I'm right there with Lincoln. We might play them three times this year, including the city play-offs, and we've got three good guards and a big man. If Lincoln is human, I could beat them."

Telfair finished the Grady game with 12 points after obeying Tiny Morton's order to "be Jason Kidd and pass the ball." In a quiet corner of the Lincoln locker room, Telfair held a box of Nikes as he huddled with Daren Kalish of Adidas. Soon enough, Telfair pulled out the black Nikes labeled "Black Album." He laughed when I asked how the name of Jay-Z's album ended up on Nike heels when Jay-Z had his own Reebok shoe line.

"It's all politics, man," he said.

Politics. Telfair was an electoral college of one in his own sneaker race, but he needed his feet to win the popular vote. And while his performance against Grady was both earnest and inspiring, those 90 minutes of basketball would imperil his season and his chance to hit the lottery in every literal and figurative way.

The holiday shoppers did not look like ants from a window high above Fifth Avenue, at least not through the mind's eye of one rich and powerful man. They looked like ballplayers, high school ballplayers, swarming about the gates of the National Basketball Association and its commissioner, David Stern, who had a problem and no idea how to solve it.

He entered a conference room with the greatest of ease, extended a hand, and apologized not for his casual attire but for the construction that had shifted the commissioner and this meeting into temporary quarters. No harm, no foul. The large windows delivered a stunning view of St. Patrick's Cathedral, and a devilish sneak peek the commissioner was eager to share.

Stern navigated my eyes through the spires and toward an oval figure mostly cloaked by the sweeping grayness of the church. A satellite dish. I suggested that the cardinal might have caught Sebastian Telfair on ESPN2. Stern countered that he was probably too busy catching an NBA game with League Pass.

The gap between high school ball and the pros was narrowing at alarming speed, anyway, to the point where the telecast of one could have easily been mistaken for the telecast of another. But Stern said he didn't watch Telfair beat Darius Washington on ESPN2 because he was too busy watching the Cavaliers' teen wonder, LeBron James, take on the Pistons on TNT.

"Poor Darko," Stern sighed. Poor Darko Milicic of the Pistons. The second pick of the draft was already devolving into an embarrassment, a scrub who couldn't even finish off an uncontested dunk.

The commissioner didn't have to sweat it, not with the LeBron phenomenon in full swing. LeBron entered the league out of St. Vincent-St. Mary High School in Akron more hyped than any rookie before him, and Stern and his network partners weren't shy about seizing the opportunity that hype presented. The dog-ass Cavaliers became a fixture on TV. They were even part of the Christmas Day schedule, opposite another member of the prom-to-the-pros club, Tracy McGrady of the Orlando Magic.

But this was where Stern's problem came in. He wanted an age requirement to turn back the high school tide, and yet he found himself marketing high school players to his paying public. LeBron. T-Mac. Kobe. KG. In one breath, Stern celebrated their contributions to his game. In the next, he pledged his allegiance to the cause of stopping future LeBrons, T-Macs, Kobes, and KGs from showing up in his league before age 20.

"Have LeBron and Tracy and Kobe and Kevin and Al Harrington and Jermaine O'Neal been good additions to the NBA?" Stern asked. "Of course. Would they have been good additions had they come a year later? Of course. So it's really not about the players who make it. My continuing observation is that because we're a sport that's very popular and easily accessible, there's going to be tens of thousands and hundreds of thousands of 10-year-olds thinking they are the next Sebastian Telfair or LeBron James. And I just don't feel great about being associated with that."

Someone needed to be blamed for Stern feeling the way he did, and the commissioner wasn't looking in any mirror. He was looking only across his conference table, at me, credential-carrying member of a media that had made LeBron LeBron.

"Because of miscreants like you," Stern said through a half smile, "LeBron James is the best known first-round draft pick we've ever had. And we didn't raise a finger to do anything about it before he came into the NBA. He was who he was because of the media. . . . So the NBA promotes him. But he's a Rookie of the Year candidate. He's a great player and our network partners who happen to pay us $4 billion say we would like to put this team and this player on because we think our fans would like to see that. 'You got it.' . . . If they're members of the league, they're entitled to all the rights and privileges pertaining thereto."

Stern was right to assign blame to the media machine, and I offered to go straight from his office to a confessional booth next door. But Stern's claim that his league "didn't raise a finger" in the making of LeBron was absurd.

Every NBA team sent scouts and/or executives to watch LeBron play for St. Vincent-St. Mary. Their presence alone represented a courtship, an invitation for young King James to ascend to his play-for-pay throne. Throw in the anonymous Eastern Conference and Western Conference general managers who salivated over LeBron in print, and you have that lifted finger nudging him through the NBA door.

LeBron wasn't the exception to the rule. Sebastian Telfair told me he had compiled a list of 11 NBA teams that had contacted him or a family member in the preseason to check his schedule and gauge his interest in making the jump. But Stern maintained that team officials had no choice but to track high school players. A scout would lose his job, the commissioner argued, if he didn't beat the high school bushes. "If the body of work Sebastian Telfair is going to be judged upon is his senior season at Lincoln," Stern said, "then you'd better damn well make sure you're going to see his senior season."

Yes, scouts were just doing their jobs when they shadowed high school stars, and reporters were just doing theirs when they wrote about high school stars. So which came first, the scout or the scribe? It was a moot question. The genie was done living in that bottle.

Telfair's Class of 2004 was threatening to send more than 10 graduates straight to the NBA; the class was regarded as the best in 25 years. The value of the free marketing college basketball provided was coming into question. LeBron was more widely publicized before the draft, without attending college, than any predraft Jordan, Magic, or Bird who played college ball. "And now Sebastian," Stern said. "Front page of the *New York Times*. I'm sure *Access Hollywood* or *Inside Edition* will now be running a Sebastian piece at some point."

The commissioner was all over the place on the high school issue. He was in no-man's-land, a most unfamiliar place. Stern might have come across in public as an avuncular leader, but behind closed doors he was known to get loud until his positions became policy.

That style took an NBA that once broadcast its championship round on late night tape delay, an NBA that, in Stern's words, had been "written off as too black and too drug-infested," and shaped it into a wildly successful global enterprise. Whether he was right, wrong, or somewhere in between, Stern was forever sure of himself. That certainty was as much a symbol of the NBA as the dribbling silhouette of Jerry West.

And yet this one issue left him a hedging, contradicting mess. The high school ranks had produced some of the NBA's biggest attractions, and they had also produced some spectacular busts. The NBA had become more of a training league, and the quality of play suffered. Veterans who'd earned another two or three seasons of paychecks at the end of their careers were being forced off rosters to clear room for kids who hadn't yet started to shave. Major college basketball, Stern's former farm system, was being reduced to a temporary holding ground for players who feared they wouldn't go high enough in the draft.

Nobody was happy with the process, except the teenagers living large on their guaranteed seven-figure wages.

"The NBA guys know that 99.99 percent of the high school kids they're watching aren't anywhere near ready for the NBA," said Mike Jarvis, the former St. John's coach. "The sad part is kids see the NBA people watching them and it gives them a false sense about what they can do.

"If NBA scouts are in the gym, even if a kid is not that good, he'll say, 'Today must be my day. They're here to see me. It's my time to be discovered.' It's like the girl in Hollywood who goes to buy an ice cream soda in the same shop as Lana Turner in the hope she'll be discovered, too."

That doesn't mean the NBA guys have embraced their freedom to roam the high school gyms and sneaker camps that demand their presence. Almost to a man, NBA executives have said they would prefer an age requirement that would send them back to the NCAA Tournament to find their next first-round picks.

Jeff Nix was among those putting a voice to that sentiment. A widely respected executive in the Knicks front office, Nix railed against the youth basketball culture that was feeding the trend of college-skipping teenage stars.

"Most of the high school kids are getting bad advice," Nix said. "Kids are worrying about who's the next LeBron, and some of them aren't even ready for our development league, the NBDL. It's really sad. The Le-Brons, Kobes, McGradys, and Garnetts are so few and far between. LeBron was so far superior to other players; he was the varsity and everyone else was the jayvee.

"But so many people are in these kids' ears. It's so out of control now. And we're not allowed to give advice. I couldn't pull a kid aside in a gym and say, 'What are you thinking?' I felt embarrassed for some kids at the ABCD all-star game, the way they played the game. It was so selfish. These kids play 100 AAU games in a summer and don't get the proper instruction. There's a false sense of reality with all this traveling around the country to play tournaments, and it's hurting our product."

David Stern didn't disagree. But he was living in the world of 14-year-old prodigies such as Michelle Wie, the golfer, and Freddy Adu, America's Pelé-to-be. Teenage tennis players and figure skaters and gymnasts were all going for the gold, and Stern was hoping only that some high school junior wouldn't try to win a court case, skip his senior year, and enter the NBA draft in the near future.

O.J. Mayo, the Ohio freshman phenom, was already being mentioned in next-LeBron discussions. Stern figured that if Mayo were eligible for the 2004 draft, some GM would take him. "He would get put on the injured list for a couple of years," the commissioner said, "but you know he'd be drafted. When you put it in that context, it is really unseemly.

"But actually, and this is the part that you'd better fully understand, that's the European system. So maybe it's not so unseemly, because now our GMs are saying, 'Isn't it wonderful that you get a Tony Parker or Pau Gasol because they've been playing professionally since they're 15?'

So you figure it out and tell me what view I should have, because it's very confusing."

It was as confusing as the scoreboard separating the high school success stories from the disasters. LeBron, Kobe, T-Mac, KG, Jermaine O'Neal, and Amare Stoudemire were among the big winners, the all-stars, the multimillionaires. Lenny Cooke, Leon Smith, DeAngelo Collins, Korleone Young, and James Lang were among the big losers, the flameouts, the can't-miss prospects who missed.

"A troubling case to me is Lenny Cooke," Stern said. "He had the ability to grow, and there were interested hangers-on giving him bad information and flattering his ego. It was designed to cause him to go a particular way to get him money in the short run, and it caused him to make decisions at a time when he didn't have good advice."

o   o   o   o   o

Lenny Cooke was the name and face behind David Stern's push for a collectively bargained rule that would require entering players to be at least 20 years old. Lenny Cooke was LeBron before there was LeBron. He had the jump shot, the hops, the handle, that little bit of everything scouts look for when they're searching for a once-in-a-generation star.

Cooke didn't go to college. He did go to five high schools, though his education was never complete in the eyes of NBA scouts. Cooke didn't get drafted in 2002, not even in the second round.

"It's not Lenny's fault what happened to him," said Debbie Bortner, the New Jersey woman and summer coach who took Cooke into her home. "It is the fault of greedy adults who see the chance to ride on a child's coattails into the bank."

Bortner was the most unlikely summer coach in the history of the circuit. She was an upper-class white woman from the leafy Bergen County suburb of Old Tappan, and her mission was to go into Brooklyn and save Lenny Cooke from Bushwick, from himself, and from all those who wanted him to be ready for the NBA before the NBA was ready for him.

"They used the race card with him against me," Bortner said. "One black guy came in and said, 'What the fuck does that white bitch know?' People used anything they could use against me to get to Lenny."

All 6-foot-6 of him. The number one player in America, they all said. He was going to be rich enough someday to buy every five-bedroom spread in Old Tappan.

First Cooke had to make it out of Bushwick. Bortner was his ticket. Her son, Brian, had met and befriended Cooke while playing summer ball. One thing led to another, and soon enough, Bortner and her husband were offering Cooke more than a permanent place in their home.

They were flying him on their Lear jet to summer tournaments. They were letting him drive their Navigator and Mercedes convertible. They were sending him to school at Northern Valley Regional High, where Cooke toyed with Bergen County's vertically challenged 6-foot-1 centers. Cooke was a one-man band of Globetrotters, making his opponents look like wonderful candidates for the Washington Generals.

Bortner was living for this. She'd started getting involved in summer ball when Brian was in seventh grade. Brian never developed into a major Division I prospect, but Lenny Cooke most certainly did.

"You take a child who really has nothing," Bortner said, "the lifestyle he came from, the physical conditions, the dire circumstances, I mean, there's a whole fucking world of difference between where we were and where he came from. Lenny had less than nothing, and he moved into a situation where he had everything, and where I wanted him to have everything.

"He had friends in Brooklyn who were very bad influences on him. I allowed those friendships to continue in my home, and I shouldn't have. . . . Brian was a year ahead of Lenny in school, and once he left to go to college, it made a big difference. Lenny started gravitating back toward what I call the ghetto rats in Brooklyn."

Lenny was also pulled in the direction of another destructive force: LeBron James. LeBron tore him down at ABCD, and a deflated Cooke retreated to Old Tappan and a senior year that wouldn't offer him a chance to vent on those 6-foot-1 Bergen County centers. His wayward journey had caught up to him: Cooke was no longer eligible to play high school ball.

Without the game, Cooke couldn't possibly survive in some Rockwellian corner of Jersey. He left Bortner's home near winter's end in 2002. "I begged him, begged him, begged him to stay," Bortner said. "Just 3 more months. Just finish school, please."

Cooke hired an agent, Mike Harrison, and officially applied for the NBA draft at a Brooklyn restaurant news conference attended by the standard cross section of rappers and jocks. "The first week he moved out of my house," Bortner said, "he dropped in one mock draft from 3 to 19, and every week after he went lower and lower. The powers that be in the NBA said, 'If he's going to do that to her, what would he do to us?'"

On the first day of June's critical predraft camp in Chicago, Cooke suffered a hairline fracture of his big toe. The injury turned off scouts and executives already concerned that Cooke hadn't even played high school ball in more than a year.

Bortner blamed the agent for Cooke's disastrous choice to enter the draft. "Despicable," Bortner called Harrison's handling of Cooke. Harrison didn't return several messages left on his voice mail for comment on Bortner's assessment.

Cooke played the minor league circuit and ended up on a team in the Philippines. "These kids should only take advice from people that love them," Bortner said. "No newcomers allowed. AAU people don't love you. You look at Sebastian Telfair, he's got a long-term relationship with Tiny (Morton). Tiny's okay. He's hooked into the basketball pipeline, and I never was. I'm a mom. You want to characterize me? I'm a mom with a $60,000 car, a million-dollar property, and that's not my satisfaction. I get enormous satisfaction from the kids who e-mail me, kids I coached years ago.

"But in the end, these young black kids don't need some rich old white lady. They need young black men in their lives doing good things in the community . . . and there's just not enough out there."

o   o   o   o   o

As leader of a league with overwhelmingly black rosters and an over-whelmingly white management structure, David Stern was forever con-fronting America's third-rail issue: race. People kept asking why there was such a firestorm over the mass teenage exodus to the NBA when suburbanite tennis players were routinely skipping the junior prom to compete for big prize money.

Stern was a tennis fan who could rattle off the Hingises and Agassis with ease, and he was sensitive to the notion that whatever was okay for Buffy and Biff should be okay for T-Mac and LeBron.

But as he talked in his office about the holiday cheer LeBron was bring-ing to the NBA, Stern knew he couldn't win for winning. "In my opinion, they just want to draft niggers who are dumb and dumber—straight out of high school," Rasheed Wallace had just told the *Oregonian*. "That's why they're drafting all these high school cats, because they come into the league and they don't know better. . . . It's as if we're just going to shut up, sign for the money, and do what they tell us."

Stern would dismiss this as a misguided rant. "In light of the conver-sation we're having," Stern told me, "the fact that (Wallace) accuses us of wanting to draft young players who will stupidly drink the Kool-Aid, this is a very confused and enraged young man who doesn't understand what he's saying."

If the commissioner himself wasn't enraged, he was confused. Stern was caught between his desire to close the floodgates and his belief that young people shouldn't be denied the ability to exhibit their skills. His-tory wasn't helping him sort it all out.

The first three high school players who used the underclassman-lib-erating Spencer Haywood case to make the jump—Moses Malone, Darryl Dawkins, and Bill Willoughby—embodied the varying degrees of success and failure that met the teens who applied for the draft. Malone became a Hall of Famer, Dawkins an enigma who delivered fleeting flashes of greatness, and Willoughby a journeyman who claimed his agent ripped him off.

"I talked at ABCD to Sebastian Telfair, Dwight Howard, and Darius Washington," Willoughby said. "I had talked to Lenny Cooke before that, and he didn't listen and that made me mad. But I told these guys that people will try to take your money.

"Sebastian was in the back of the room and he was the only guy to come up and ask questions. I was like, 'Good, this is why I'm here.' I could tell he was going pro." Willoughby told Telfair that he needed to handle his own money, that he shouldn't even let immediate family members manage his cash.

"What about your girl?" Telfair asked him.

"Nobody," Willoughby replied. "Get a briefcase, take all your papers on the road, and write your own checks after shootarounds."

Some high school players who skipped college after Kevin Garnett became the fifth selection of the 1995 draft never had to worry about balancing an NBA checkbook. The casualty list: In 1996, the year Kobe Bryant went 13th and Jermaine O'Neal 17th, Taj McDavid wasn't drafted and never played in the league. In 1998, Korleone Young went in the second round, played a few games for the Pistons, and couldn't make it back; Ellis Richardson didn't get picked at all and ended up in jail on robbery charges.

In 2001, Ousmane Cisse was selected 47th and didn't stick; Tony Key went undrafted the same year. In 2002, Lenny Cooke, DeAngelo Collins, and Giedrius Rinkevicius never heard their names called. In 2003, the year of LeBron, James Lang went 48th to the Hornets, landed on the injured list, and was later released.

So when Stern reviewed the list of high school players who entered his league, he found horror stories, smash hits, and everything in between. No trend. No rhyme. No reason.

Stern could have blamed Garnett for this jumbled maze the commissioner had to negotiate. If only Garnett had achieved the standardized test scores necessary to play college ball as a freshman, he likely wouldn't have entered the 1995 draft and the seed for the high schoolers to follow him wouldn't have been planted.

Back then, the draft was forbidden teenage fruit. But when the 6-foot-

11 Garnett learned he'd be a sure top-10 pick if he came out, a seven-figure wage seemed more appealing than a full year of classes on a campus where he'd be ineligible to play as a freshman.

Garnett wouldn't just become a dominating player with the Timberwolves and, in 2004, the MVP of the entire league; he'd become the patron saint of every big kid looking to make a quick buck.

Like DeSagana Diop of Senegal, via Oak Hill Academy. Diop, a 6-foot-11, 300-pound center, was all set to pick between North Carolina and Virginia when Matt Doherty, then the coach of the Tar Heels, showed up one fateful spring day in 2001.

"Here comes Matt with his NBA salary scale for rookies," recalled Steve Smith, the Oak Hill coach. "As soon as I saw that scale, I knew Matt had made a mistake."

Doherty tried showing Diop that one year at Carolina would move him up in the draft and up that salary chart. "But as soon as DeSagana saw you could make $800,000 as the 29th pick, he was all fired up," Smith said. "He didn't have any money in Senegal."

Doherty called Smith to follow up and asked, "How did I do?"

"Not good, Matt," Smith told him. "Once he saw your pay scale, that was the end of that."

The Cleveland Cavaliers closed the deal. Diop was the eighth pick of the 2001 draft, earning him the money Doherty said he'd get if he played one year in Tar Heel blue.

"DeSagana got $2.69 million for his fourth year alone," Smith said. "He had them all fooled; they all thought he was the next Shaq. Two years before DeSagana was drafted, he couldn't make a left-handed layup. He had no upper-body strength and didn't run the floor well. He didn't even average 10 points a game for me as a senior. He beat the system.

"DeSagana gets paid for those 4 years he could've been in college, and those are years you don't get back. If he'd gone to college, he might never have been picked in the first round. . . . When Ndudi Ebi and Travis Outlaw came out (in 2003), I thought, 'Man, this high school stuff is going to stop. Those jokers aren't going in the first round.' But they sure went in the first round, and that's why you'll see about 10 kids come out of this next class."

The Class of 2004. The class of Dwight Howard, Josh Smith, Shaun Livingston, and Sebastian Telfair.

From his station above Fifth Avenue, from a view that made one feel top-of-the-world high, the NBA commissioner saw the rebellion taking form. The Class of 2004 was preparing to run an unprecedented fast break his way, and David Stern knew he was powerless to stop it.

LeBron James was stretching out his Greek God body on the locker-room floor, working those fast-twitch muscles that were about to take on the burdens of a 34-game road losing streak. The Cleveland Cavaliers were in Philadelphia on this December night, and LeBron was just starting to accept the terms of his nightly NBA engagement.

The Cavaliers were 6-19, and there wasn't a man, woman, or child in the Wachovia Center who thought the 6-foot-8, 240-pound rookie would leave Philly with a victory tucked inside his travel bag, even if he had Magic Johnson vision and Michael Jordan hops.

The locker room had cleared of all reporters and most of the players, and LeBron was tugging on his hamstrings when Darius Miles grabbed his attention from two stalls away. Miles himself had skipped college. He was the third pick of the 2000 draft out of East St. Louis High, and he'd already been dealt by the team that had selected him, the Los Angeles Clippers.

Nobody was confusing the 6-foot-9 Miles with some cross between Magic and Michael. He was a relative bust, out of coach Paul Silas's rotation for the moment, and wondering if the bulletin I'd just given him would have ever hit the wires had he played college ball.

Mike Jarvis of St. John's, the coach who signed Miles to a letter of intent, had just been fired. "You serious?" Miles said. "Yeah, I committed to St. John's. I think I fucked up the whole thing."

Miles maintained that he made the right decision to enter the draft— the right decision for him, if not for Jarvis. He hated the traveling, but said the NBA offered an easy life. I asked Miles if he expected more and more high school players to chase that easy life.

"Yes," he said. "I think at least three will come out every year." When I told Miles that some 10 members of the Class of 2004 were expected to enter the draft, he turned to his left and fixed his eyes on the burgeoning legend who appeared ready to take a nap on the locker-room floor.

"You heard any players coming out next year, coming out of high school?" Miles asked LeBron.

Miles checked out of the conversation before James had a chance to answer.

"Yeah, I heard who might," LeBron said, opening his eyes and looking in my direction. "Dwight Something."

"Dwight Howard," I said.

"I think Bassy's thinking about it," LeBron said. "Shaun Livingston."

"Josh Smith, too," I said.

"Yes, I think Sebastian might think about it," LeBron repeated.

"Al Jefferson," I threw at him.

"Oh shit," LeBron said. "He's been thinking about it since ninth grade."

"The big kid from California," I said. "Robert Swift."

"There's not going to be anyone left in high school," LeBron answered. "I was fortunate. The Cavs had the number one pick, and they just liked me because I live 30 minutes away in Akron. I don't know why they picked me. I can't play basketball."

LeBron smiled and closed his eyes. Even at 13 games under .500, he was waiting for someone to pinch him. He was still 11 days shy of his 19th birthday, December 30th, a birthday he shared with Tiger Woods, and already LeBron was cashing Nike checks that would have made Woods blush.

It was quite possible that no 18-year-old had ever been as good at anything as LeBron James was at playing basketball. Like his good friend and would-be protégé, Telfair, LeBron had emerged from tough times. His biological father was a nonperson in his life. His surrogate father went to jail for cocaine trafficking and fraud. His mother, Gloria, had LeBron when she was 16 and was fond of making herself as conspicuous as possible at her son's games.

"What's up, Mrs. James?" people would ask.

"LeBron James," she would often answer. "That's what's up."

LeBron became a *Sports Illustrated* cover boy as a St. Vincent-St. Mary junior, the cover proclaiming him "The Chosen One" and contributing to the bloodiest sneaker war to date.

Nike, Adidas, and Reebok pushed one another to the brink of the madness Nike finally stamped with its trademark swoosh. The shoe executives weren't dealing with any salary cap; they gave LeBron eight times the money guaranteed him by the Cavs, who hired Silas, the respected veteran coach, to tame the monster surely being spit out by a hype machine that knew no shame.

Despite making the play-offs, Silas had just been fired by the New Orleans Hornets. The Cavs originally offered Jeff Van Gundy the job and asked Van Gundy to keep that offer discreet before the former Knicks coach filled the Houston Rockets' vacancy instead. Cleveland officials wanted Silas to believe he was the first choice all along. They didn't want a new coach questioning his own position with management before his first confrontation with LeBron James.

There wouldn't be any confrontations with LeBron James. He arrived in Cleveland as the antidote to the Generation X star, as the answer to "The Answer," Allen Iverson, who looked forward to practice as much as one would look forward to hemorrhoid surgery.

LeBron was the first Cavalier on the pregame court for his professional debut in Philadelphia. If any Cav had an excuse to waste valuable preparation time in the locker room, it was LeBron. He was averaging 24.4 points for his previous five games, which included a 37-point outburst against the Celtics. LeBron's early season averages of 18 points and 6.1 rebounds blew away Kevin Garnett and all the high school lottery picks who followed him.

But LeBron was a solitary figure on Cleveland's end of the court, wearing Michael Jordan's number 23 and launching jump shot after jump shot. He stopped practicing only to fulfill his pregame commitment to the assembled media.

LeBron had come a long way since the last time he stepped on a

Philadelphia court one year earlier. His St. Vincent-St. Mary team had gone to the Palestra to play in the same event Sebastian Telfair would compete in the night after the Sixers-Cavs game, and so I asked him what advice he was giving Telfair about his options. "Basically, just work hard," LeBron said. "Don't let nobody make your decision. You've been playing basketball. Nobody has been playing basketball for you. You should make your own decision and do what's best for you and your family. You should go ahead and go for it."

LeBron said he told Telfair that NBA life was fun. "It's the best job in the world," he told Telfair. "You go out and compete every night against the best players in the world. You can't ask for nothing else."

Silas couldn't either, at least as it related to LeBron. Silas had his problems, no question about that. DeSagana Diop, the center out of Oak Hill, had all the makings of a disastrous high school pick even before he went on the injured list.

But LeBron had a way of easing his coach's mind. "He's one of the smartest players I've ever met," Silas said.

LeBron was smart enough that night to drop 36 points on the Sixers, to finish with the most points ever scored on the road by an NBA teenager, and to give the Cavs their first road victory since they won in Seattle 11 months earlier, smack in the middle of LeBron's senior season at St. Vincent-St. Mary.

He was 5-for-7 from 3-point range. He scored 8 straight points in a decisive fourth-quarter stretch. He dished out 5 assists, grabbed 4 rebounds, and stole the ball 4 times. Silas didn't want all this pressure on James to lead, but it was there and he had no choice but to let the kid deal with it. After all, LeBron was the only Cav who had his own sneaker debuting in stores later that night, at the stroke of midnight. Nike's Air Zoom Generation. It didn't have the ring of Air Jordan, but LeBron hardly cared.

"That's all you dream about," he said. "I used to wear Jordan. I wondered how he felt when he saw kids wear them, but I know I'll feel good."

LeBron would be in a merry postgame mood, his boyish smile reminding visitors that there was a child inside that grown-up body. So when the reporters on deadline rushed off to their laptops, leaving LeBron sitting in a corner all by himself, I asked him again about the one high school star who had his number on speed dial.

This is what Telfair told me about the advice LeBron was giving him: "He's telling me to leave. He's seen all these NBA point guards, and he told me I can play with these guys."

This is what LeBron told me about his discussions with Telfair: "I have no idea what he's going to do. There's no reason to tell a kid with that type of athletic ability and that type of game that he shouldn't make the jump. . . . A lot of people have athletic ability, especially coming out of New York, but he really works at it, and that's a big key for him."

They became friends, LeBron said, because that's what big-time high school players do on the summer circuit. "We kind of communicate with each other some way, somehow, and that's basically what me and Sebastian did," LeBron said. "I just love the way he plays and competes. He knows how to play basketball. His brother, Jamel, plays basketball, and his cousin, Stephon Marbury, has a good background, and that really helps him."

I asked LeBron if he thought Telfair would be a first-round pick in the next draft. "Definitely," he said. "Physically, he can make it. Gamewise, he could make it, too. It's all about working once you get here, and he works. I think he'll definitely be a star in this league."

o o o o o

At the moment, Sebastian Telfair just wanted to be a star in the Palestra. The kind of star who could fill college basketball's most historic gym with the buzz of greatness on training wheels.

Only one of those wheels was broken down, and threatening everything Telfair had worked for. He came up so big on ESPN2, but then his battered right ankle kept him benched for two easy PSAL victories before he tried a foolish comeback in the second half of a fiercely contested game at Sheepshead Bay High School.

Telfair sat out the first half; in addition to his ankle problems, he had tendinitis in his left knee and he'd missed school that day with the flu.

But with Sheepshead Bay playing way over its head, and with the crowd fired up by the return of Lawrence Alamilla, the Sheepshead transfer, Telfair left the court in street clothes and returned in full uniform with 4:12 left in the third quarter, his team down two.

He entered the game and violated PSAL rules—class attendance was required on game day. It was a lost cause, anyway. At the buzzer, with Lincoln's first defeat in the books, the home crowd flooded the court and celebrated as if its team had just secured a bid to the NCAA Tournament.

Telfair had been trying to protect the remote possibility of an undefeated season. Fair enough. But his decision to follow up LeBron James as the main attraction of Philly's Scholastic Play-by-Play Classic was rooted in his feeling that he couldn't let the Palestra promoter down.

Jeremy Treatman wasn't selling a New York-Philadelphia thing as much as he was selling a playmaking legend. This wasn't Lincoln versus Cardinal Dougherty. This was the one and only Sebastian Telfair versus Kyle Lowry, stud point guard and Villanova recruit. That's what the gray T-shirts said, anyway, the ones Danny Turner carried through the stands in a vain attempt to peddle them at 10 bucks a pop. "Telfair vs Lowry. Who's Number One?" It was a tough sell.

"These people don't know who Lowry is," Turner complained as he held a stack of shirts in each arm. "They know who Sebastian is, but that's it."

Treatman was banking on the notion that Sebastian's appeal would carry the night. He needed about 3,000 in the 8,700-seat Palestra to break even for his all-day Scholastic Play-by-Play Classic card, with Lincoln-Dougherty as the headliner. Treatman figured Telfair's national TV exposure guaranteed the promoter a profit. He was hoping for a crowd of 6,000.

"I'm a 5-foot-10 guy, and I can look eyeball to eyeball with (Telfair)," Treatman said. "Regular people can relate to him. . . . He's the closest thing to Isiah Thomas I've ever seen. I think he could be a 10-time NBA All-Star."

But how does a future 10-time NBA All-Star tell a breathless promoter that he can't play in his main event? Easy, he doesn't. Nobody at Lincoln bothered to warn Treatman that the attraction he was trying to push all over Philly was barely able to jog.

∘   ∘   ∘   ∘   ∘

Sebastian Telfair was flat on the locker-room floor, stretching the way LeBron James had stretched the night before, when he motioned for me to take the seat beside him.

"I don't think I should go," he said. But Telfair was going anyway. He was in his Lincoln warm-ups, and Danny Turner was reminding him of sports' least forgiving code: If you play, no excuses.

Sebastian's knee was acting up, and his ankle was throbbing. He said that he'd seen four doctors who diagnosed three bone bruises and no breaks, and that they all prescribed rest, rest, and more rest.

Now Sebastian wanted to rest his legs through the Christmas and New Year's holidays. He wanted to make certain he was healthy for the big day at UCLA on January 3rd. NBA executives and scouts would be all over Pauley Pavilion for that one, and Telfair didn't want to attack a make-or-break opportunity at half speed.

But the showman in Telfair didn't want to disappoint in Philly, either. While the point guard waged his own internal battle between the pros and the cons of playing, Treatman was just realizing the extent of an injury he didn't even know Telfair had. That was the bad news. The worse news? Some 2,500 people were in the Palestra stands, 500 shy of the break-even line.

Telfair was happy only that the small crowd included one special guest. Sylvester Telfair was seeing his first game of the year. Sebastian's 23-year-old brother had been released from Sing Sing the day before, this after serving a 3-year sentence on a gun conviction. He declined to talk about his confinement, and the case records were sealed. All Sylvester cared to discuss was the chance to see Sebastian play, and his own visions of deferred athletic glory.

"I'm a baseball player," he told me. "I'm trying to get a tryout in Pawtucket, with the Red Sox farm team."

He had the look of a second baseman, but his odds of going from jail to Fenway Park were a tad longer than his younger brother's odds of going from Lincoln to the NBA.

As it turned out, Sebastian couldn't even make it to halftime. His ankle was on fire, Lowry was even hotter, and so the Lincoln star limped over to the bench and away from a losing proposition.

There would be a price to pay for this surrender. Nobody gets out alive in Philly. Telfair didn't just watch Lincoln lose another game in the second half; he sat and absorbed a relentless verbal assault. Two fans seated a half-dozen rows behind the Lincoln bench started in on him, their mocking voices bouncing off the Palestra's pale blue rafters as the blowout thinned the crowd.

Eventually, one college-age fan assumed the responsibility of driving Telfair mad. His booming voice could have easily been heard above the din of a Super Bowl crowd.

"Kyle is way better than you. . . . You're supposed to be the best. . . . He's scared of Kyle. . . . You should get an award for acting."

Sitting right behind the Lincoln bench, Sylvester faced the fan and said, "You need attention, don't you?" The heckler didn't know about Sylvester's past; he wasn't to be intimidated or denied. Telfair never acknowledged the fan. As the Lincoln point guard sat there and took it with his S31T Adidas sneakers unlaced, the fan turned up the volume.

"Finish him off, Kyle. . . . Kyle should be on ESPN. . . . (Telfair's) going to the league? Kyle should be the number one fucking pick then. . . . They say he run up and down the stairs on ESPN? Kyle, you going to take this shit to Rucker next summer. . . . Pitino's going to be as disappointed as a motherfucker when you get out there. . . . Hey Kyle, I just got off the phone with Rick Pitino. He wants you."

On the losing side, Morton gathered his team in a locker room littered with shredded ankle tape and tattered goals. "That's the first time I ever didn't score in a game in my life," Telfair sighed. Lowry finished with 21 points, 6 rebounds, and 4 steals.

"I hope I get to play him in the tournament in college when I'm healthy," Telfair said. College? It was looking more and more like a viable option. In the Palestra, that multimillion-dollar NBA contract seemed as far away as Prague.

Telfair apologized to Treatman for showing up in no condition to play. "I just told him to get healthy," the promoter said. "We had 9,000 for LeBron's game last year—more people than at any moment in the history of that building. I think Sebastian figured there would be 8,000 people here and mass hysteria, and there wasn't."

Telfair found only unwelcome sentiment in too many places. "Everybody had a sad face on," he said, "like it was my fault."

The same night Telfair and thousands of expected fans were no-shows in the Palestra, LeBron James had 32 points, 10 rebounds, and 6 assists in a victory over the Chicago Bulls for Cleveland's second straight road victory. LeBron and Telfair, the most hyped players in the classes of 2003 and 2004, were living on opposite ends of the basketball spectrum, and this was hardly what Telfair had in mind.

"I need to get better now," he said before leaving Philadelphia. Only Treatman had another Lincoln-led tournament scheduled for the following weekend, a post-Christmas show in the Bronx, and Telfair was back in the same old spot, caught between a promoter's need to sell tickets and a playmaker's desire to strike gold.

      o o o o o

The black bus parked outside the South Bronx gym that belonged to the Gauchos wasn't your average ride for high school teams being ferried from one holiday jamboree to the next. This was Nike's King James bus, complete with portraits of LeBron sitting on a throne with a large crucifix dangling from his neck and three large lions resting at his feet.

With a white mink coat draped over the left arm of his chair, LeBron cut a thinking man's pose on the throne. "Air Zoom Generation," read the back bumper, between the swooshes. Rap music raged from the rear of the bus. Sneakers were on display inside, and small television monitors played the LeBron commercial that showed him entering a church revival and throwing passes to a series of high-flying dunkers. Potential sneaker buyers invited inside by a Nike rep were greeted by barely dressed hotties who did nothing more than sit around and look like barely dressed hotties.

It was a Friday night on Gerard Avenue, December 26th, with little Christmas spirit in sight. This was a dark and desolate place in the shadows of Yankee Stadium, the gym wedged between warehouses and auto wreck shops ringed with rusted barbed wire fences. But the home of the Gauchos was the home of the only game in town on this cold and clear night, a rematch of the previous season's PSAL city championship game between Lincoln and Banneker.

Jeremy Treatman was working the door of his Big Apple Holiday Classic. This time around, Treatman wasn't harboring any false hopes over the participation of Lincoln's franchise star. Sebastian Telfair wasn't about to put his ankle to the test until the following Saturday's NBA festival at UCLA, where he hoped to be 80 to 90 percent. "I've got two pair of LeBron's sneakers, Air Zoom, that I might wear at UCLA," Telfair said. His mother had bought him an ankle boot for Christmas to promote the healing of his injury.

The gym was decorated with pennants marking the Gauchos' Amateur Athletic Union national championships, and in a large orange banner carrying the image of a black bull blowing gray clouds of smoke from his nostrils. The same image was painted above the main entrance and across the peeling white paint retreating from the gym's brick facade.

A shallow fly ball removed from the House That Ruth Built, this was the House That Lou Built. Lou d'Almeida, the Argentine businessman and self-styled philanthropist. He found his calling through inner city basketball, through being friend and benefactor to poor New York kids who also happened to be major Division I prospects, including Stephon Marbury.

For them d'Almeida built this $2.5 million arena in 1986, a basketball temple in the middle of all that South Bronx blight. Ultimately, the place would carry the Nike label. The Gauchos were a Nike team. And under the Gauchos Gym roof, Lincoln coach Tiny Morton took the battle for young athletes' hearts and soles to a preposterous level. In the pregame locker room, Morton spotted Nyan Boateng wearing a white sweatband around his right leg with gold lettering that spelled "Reebok."

"Take it off," Morton said.

"It's my good luck charm," Boateng responded.

"Take it off."

Boateng turned it inside out instead. For the first time in recorded history, an Adidas coach had banned a Reebok logo in a Nike gym.

Without Telfair, Lincoln beat Banneker in the first game and then lost to Cardozo in the second. Before the second game, Cardozo coach Ron Naclerio sat on the end of his bench and wished aloud that his team could face a truer test. "I wish he was playing," Naclerio said as he pointed toward Telfair. "I want to beat them once with that fucker."

"What would be good for the city is if we win one regular-season game against them, Lincoln wins one against us, and then we play for it all in March in Madison Square Garden. We'd get 15,000 in the Garden for that. That would be crazy."

That would be Telfair against a well-balanced Cardozo team. That would be Brooklyn versus Queens on the night of St. Patrick's Day. "Brooklyn kids think Queens kids are soft," Naclerio said. "We're really good, but we don't come to play. We're a bunch of soft Queens pussies."

Near the end of the Cardozo loss, Telfair didn't bother joining a Lincoln huddle. He already had on his black winter jacket. His head was down, and his season was passing before his eyes. At the buzzer, Telfair headed for the exit with his brother, Sylvester, by his side.

Out on Gerard Avenue, Nike people were handing out cards and asking fans to step on the King James bus to survey the merchandise. The rap music was still blaring as Lincoln's point guard walked on by.

Sebastian Telfair knew if he didn't put on a Hollywood show in California, that LeBron James bus would be leaving him in the dust for good.

○ ○ ○ ○ ○

Clark Francis stood in a corner of a Beverly Hills restaurant and confirmed that he planted the first seed for a tree that grew in Brooklyn. Francis beat his fellow talent evaluators in the rush to declare Sebastian Telfair the number one basketball player in his American class, and he saw no need to apologize for making this declaration when Telfair was 10 years old.

That was the business. Legends weren't born until someone said they were, and, in Telfair's case, Francis was that someone. He fielded calls from New York contacts, one of them Ziggy Sicignano, the Brooklyn USA coach. Sicignano told Francis that his new point guard was touched by stardust. Sight unseen, Francis used his *Hoop Scoop* publication to spread word of a child playmaker with an NBA handle.

But that was then and this was most definitely now. Eight years later, with Lincoln High preparing to play in the Pangos Dream Classic at UCLA, Telfair found himself across from Francis in a news conference above Rodeo Drive, a whole nation away from the Coney Island projects and the number one seed in Francis's imaginary tournament field.

The lord of *Hoop Scoop* had dropped Telfair all the way to number nine in his senior class.

"Listen," Francis said, "pound for pound, inch for inch, Sebastian might be the best player ever to come out of New York City. He's as good at the stop and go, at changing directions, and at throwing the phenomenal pass as any player you'll ever find.

"But the problem comes when he tries to take the team on his shoulders; he can shoot you out of the game. I still think if he goes to college next year, Louisville wins the national championship."

Only Sebastian hadn't come to California dreaming of the Final Four. Some 15 NBA general managers were expected to attend the five-game, one-day Dream Classic festival, along with dozens of NBA scouts. The GMs were the draft-day decision makers. They'd already seen Telfair in his TV game in December, but there was no substitute for studying a prospect in the flesh.

Telfair's opponent would be Harvard-Westlake of North Hollywood, a good California team but no powerhouse. Zach Woolridge, the 6-foot-5 son of the former NBA and Notre Dame star, Orlando Woolridge, would be assigned to Lincoln's point guard.

Good ankle or bad ankle, Telfair had to prove to NBA executives and scouts that he could "get his game off" against a taller, longer defender. This was his life as an Everyman-size playmaker.

If nothing else, Telfair was smart enough to stay as close as he could to LeBron James and Dwight Howard, the first pick in the 2003 draft and likely first pick in the 2004 draft. Howard was in the 2004 Dream Classic lineup a year after LeBron was the Pauley Pavilion headliner, with Telfair as the lounge act.

LeBron was matched against D.J. Strawberry, son of the tortured former slugger, Darryl, and the kid who would play the St. Vincent-St. Mary phenom tougher than any defender would all year. "But it didn't matter," said Dinos Trigonis, founder of the Dream Classic. "LeBron did something at Pauley that the UCLA team couldn't do: He sold it out."

Some 12,500 fans paid to see LeBron's L.A. stop. They didn't get to see James at his skywalking apex, but the 6,000 who hung around to watch Lincoln High play Vallejo High in the nightcap saw Telfair at his show-stealing best.

"We were in LeBron's postgame press conference," Trigonis recalled, "and we heard all these ooohs and aaahs outside."

Telfair put on a show and Lincoln won big. Trigonis invited back the Railsplitters, and everything was in place for Telfair's final Dream Classic—everything but LeBron and the white limos. Trigonis caused quite a stir in 2003 by shepherding around LeBron, Telfair, and friends in white limousines, a mode of teenage transportation that served as the flash point for critics who yearned for the days of yellow school buses and 400-seat high school gyms.

Trigonis paid St. Vincent-St. Mary of Akron a $15,000 appearance fee in 2003. This time around, Trigonis said, no participating school requested an appearance fee.

For his 2004 Dream Classic, Trigonis landed Telfair from Brooklyn,

Dwight Howard from Atlanta, and Robert Swift from Bakersfield, the seven-footer who was telling friends he wanted to become the first white American high schooler to leap onto David Stern's stage.

All three were strong candidates to skip college, with Howard a lock. Swift was scheduled to play at 4:00 P.M., Howard was scheduled to play at 7:00, and Telfair was scheduled to be sandwiched in between.

"Is your ankle about 80 percent?" I asked Telfair.

"I hope," he said.

When the Dream Classic news conference was complete, Telfair and his teammates headed downstairs to find the bus that was supposed to meet them on Rodeo Drive. The kids stopped at the store windows and gawked at the $10,000 necklaces on the other side. "This is Tiffany's," Danny Turner shouted. "The real Tiffany's."

Only a sheet of alarm-rigged glass separated Coney Island from another universe, but Telfair was the one Railsplitter as close to the gold as his eyes were telling him. If his ankle would let him play the game of his life at UCLA the following day, that Beverly Hills lifestyle would be well within reach.

o　　o　　o　　o　　o

Danny Ainge was the first executive to arrive at Pauley Pavilion, the first by a good hour. With fewer than 200 fans in the building, the new lord of the Boston Celtics settled into a courtside chair with UCLA seat cushions and began picking as many brains as he could about the teenagers likely to show up on his June draft board.

I introduced myself, explained my presence, and asked a few questions about high school stars and the choices they faced. Fifteen minutes later, Ainge called me back and motioned for me to fill the courtside seat next to him. Against all odds, he'd decided I might be of some assistance. He wanted to ask about Telfair, Howard, and the other players I'd watched at ABCD.

We talked about Swift. "I heard he's not all that," Ainge said. I agreed.

"I heard he's probably going to college for a year," Ainge said. I told him I'd heard otherwise.

On the subject of Howard, I told Ainge I'd seen a whale of a talent, a big, long kid with an amazing ability to quarterback the fast break with a point guard's vision and handle. "Yeah," Ainge said. "My people told me the six sure things who make people go, 'Wow,' are Howard, Josh Smith, Marvin Williams, Shaun Livingston, LaMarcus Aldridge, and Al Jefferson."

I mentioned to Ainge that he didn't include Telfair in his list of can't-miss prospects.

"I do think he's great," he said. "I saw him twice, once on TV. I think a young Isiah is a good comparison. He knows how to play the game. Man, I think he's just great, but some other people are a little down on him."

When I told Ainge that Telfair was worried he might slip into the second round, à la Omar Cook, he said, "Don't worry, that's not going to happen. I think he's got a better jump shot than people give him credit for."

Ainge made the most of this time. Within a half-hour after our second talk ended, the Celtics' executive had filled my seat with someone who could offer a much better perspective on the Robert Swifts of the world—Robert Swift himself. I was surprised at the public nature of this meeting, and I wasn't alone. One Eastern Conference official in attendance saw Ainge talking to Swift and later told me he realized instantly it was a violation of league policy.

"But nobody made a big deal of it," said the official. "Danny probably just didn't know the rule."

Under David Stern's law, NBA executives and scouts weren't supposed to have contact with high school players until and unless they'd formally applied for the draft. Ainge had been on the job in Boston for 8 months, and he'd been an NBA head coach and broadcaster. If he didn't know that the rules prohibited him from speaking with Swift, he should have known.

Ainge spoke to Swift for 15 minutes as an undercard game went on without their attention. When they were done, I approached the Bakersfield center and asked if Ainge had inquired about his intentions regarding the draft.

"Yeah, I told him what I'm doing," Swift said.

"What are you doing?" I asked.

"I'm just going to look forward to my senior season and then see," Swift said. "Danny was asking me about other players from around the country, about what I thought of them." I asked Swift about Sebastian Telfair. "I played against him a few times," he said. "I think he's a great high school player, but Shaun Livingston is better, taller, and sees the court better. I like Shaun a lot better."

Swift would excuse himself and head for the locker room to suit up for his game against Seattle's Rainier Beach. It was a big day for him, just not as big as it was for the point guard who would follow him onto the Pauley court. Telfair might not have been Swift's idea of an elite playmaker, but he was the Dream Classic's main attraction in the game-day edition of the *Los Angeles Times*.

"Hype Machine Revs Up for Telfair," read the headline. Hype wasn't going to do him any good now. Telfair would have to do something about as special against Zach Woolridge as Danny Ainge once did against Woolridge's father, Orlando, in that indelible NCAA Tournament holy war waged between Brigham Young and Notre Dame, a game decided by Ainge's coast-to-coast layup.

But that was way back when the best high school players went to college. Telfair didn't expect to attend Louisville for even one year, never mind four. He wanted to make this appearance on John Wooden's hallowed floor the closest he'd ever get to big-time Division I ball.

o   o   o   o   o

The NBA executives filed in one by one. Mitch Kupchak of the Lakers. Elgin Baylor of the Clippers. Kiki Vandeweghe of the Nuggets. Ernie Grunfeld of the Wizards. John Nash of the Trail Blazers. They were among the decision makers to join Danny Ainge, who had just watched Robert Swift confirm everyone's worst fears about him.

"Did that guy look like an NBA player to you?" Ainge asked me. No, I said, he most certainly did not. Swift did manage 14 points, 11 rebounds, and 4 blocks in a loss to Rainier Beach but generally looked slow and soft in the process.

"(Swift) needs to go to college," Ainge said. "Somebody better tell that kid to get real."

Inside the Lincoln locker room, this was sweet music to Sebastian Telfair's ears. Swift had hand-wrapped him a perfect act to follow.

"Who's out there?" Telfair asked me after he slid the headphones off his ears.

"The entire NBA," I said.

"Like who?"

"Lakers, Clippers, Celtics, Wizards, you name it."

Telfair smiled and slid his headphones back on, losing himself in some Jay-Z rap. The setting made it impossible to remain in the moment. In addition to the NBA people, reps from the Big Three sneaker companies were all over the place. George Raveling led the Nike contingent. His former best friend and current sworn enemy, Sonny Vaccaro, led the Reebok group, with lieutenant Chris Rivers at his side. Adidas had its post-Sonny management team in the house.

Everyone was working an angle. Rob Pelinka, agent for free-agent-to-be Kobe Bryant, was chatting up a couple of team executives. Bryant was the most successful high school player to turn pro, after all, and word was he wanted to get as far away from Phil Jackson and Shaquille O'Neal as he possibly could.

Of course, Bryant had to stay out of jail first. His sexual assault case was the source of much locker-room chatter on the big-time high school circuit, but Bryant's troubles weren't about to convince the members of Telfair's class that one should bypass college's formative years at his own peril.

Back in the Lincoln locker room, Telfair was back to his lively pre-injury self, bobbing and rapping to his headphone beat. Soon enough, the public address announcer gave him the kind of drumroll-please introduction Michael Jordan used to get in Chicago. "And a 6-foot senior, Slick Sebaaaaaaaastian Telfaaaaaaaair."

The fans responded to the introduction, though this tripleheader of Swift, Telfair, and Howard drew only one-third the crowd that LeBron brought to Pauley. Telfair didn't care. He wasn't playing this one for the people who paid to see him, but for the people who might draft him in June.

Telfair started with a nice kick to Eugene Lawrence, who buried the 3-pointer. Telfair followed with a better pass to Antonio Pena in the blocks, and then with a teardrop floater to give Lincoln a 9–5 lead. Even with a slight limp, with his ankle wrapped up tight, Telfair was settling into a perfect early rhythm. Soon he hit a bank shot over Princeton-bound Zach Woolridge, and then a 3-pointer that signaled to the ooohing and aaahing crowd that this had the potential to be a memorable performance.

The GMs and scouts noted that Telfair was having no trouble operating against a defender who had a half foot on him. This was important. Very important. In the NBA, Telfair would have to face a wave of bigger guards. He had to prove he could take and make shots over opponents as tall as, say, Jason Kidd.

Telfair had to do this while also revealing his selfless side. So he fired a perfect pass to Pena off the pick-and-roll, a pass Pena fumbled. He hit Pena again, this time for a basket giving Lincoln a 16–8 lead. Telfair drained a 3-pointer from out near Burbank, made a layup, and then blew into the lane and finished on a twisting, turning banker before the first-quarter horn to make it 25–14.

Wow. That's what the fans were saying, what the GMs and scouts were thinking. Telfair was doing precisely what he had to do, grabbing Pauley Pavilion by the throat. He didn't let up in the second quarter, either, throwing no-look passes and showing the 3-point range he wasn't supposed to have. Telfair sank a 3, a pull-up jumper, and then another 3 while being fouled by Westlake's 6-foot-5 Bryce Taylor, the Oregon recruit, turning the crowd on its ear before completing the 4-point play.

Telfair hit Nyan Boateng with a behind-the-back look-away dish on the break, again firing up the crowd. Telfair then found Yuriy Matsakov underneath with one of his Linda Blair assists—the trademark pass he'd throw toward one baseline while somehow spinning his head so it faced the other—and extended the Lincoln lead to 48–28. With 1.3 seconds left in the half, Telfair came to the bench with 23 points in his pocket and the NBA at his feet. The fans gave him a rousing ovation. The place wouldn't have been any louder had Old Man Wooden just walked through the door.

Telfair slowed down in the third quarter as his hobble became more pronounced, as if to remind the NBA reps that they weren't observing him at full health. After Westlake made a dramatic comeback to tie the game, Telfair missed two shots in the final seconds of regulation. The horn sounded, and Telfair flashed the smile of someone who knew something you didn't. He knew he'd become a different player in overtime. His hot hand had cooled. Like any great quarterback who had lost his touch, Telfair had already decided to attack Westlake with the ground game.

He started his overtime session with a bounce pass to Pena for a layup and an 80–78 lead, a lead Lincoln wouldn't relinquish. Telfair took care of the ball, Lawrence made a couple of big free throws, the Lincoln defense put the brakes on Taylor, and the NBA people had themselves something heavy to talk about before Dwight Howard took the floor.

Telfair had finished with 37 points and 6 assists.

"Oh man, he's really, really good," Ainge said. "And you could tell his ankle was bothering him all game. . . . He'll be a first-round pick for sure."

Vandeweghe was overheard saying Telfair would be a first-round pick, "but a lottery pick if he goes to Louisville for a year." Grunfeld wasn't as impressed with the 37 points as he was with Telfair's passing. "If his teammates caught the ball and finished," the Wizards' GM said, "Sebastian would've had 13 or 14 assists. He's got it."

Telfair wanted everyone to see that he gets it, too. So he took a postgame romp off the court, into the stands, and set up his own autograph table. In his sweat-drenched uniform, Telfair sat and signed for a good 50 minutes.

Meanwhile, Howard's Southwest Atlanta Christian Academy team was busy playing Dominguez of Compton, and Howard's name hadn't come across the loudspeakers in the longest time. "Is he doing anything?" Telfair asked as he kept his head down and signed away.

Howard had picked up three early fouls and was threatening to make Robert Swift's performance look Telfairesque. Compton ran the Atlanta team out of the gym. Howard finished with 2 points in the first half, racked up some garbage-time numbers in the second, and left behind a disappointing effort that only magnified what Telfair had pulled off.

"How does it feel to finally be back to your old self?" I asked the Lincoln star as he limped away from his completed autograph rounds.

"I'm not back to my old self," he said.

"Did you see the looks on any of the GMs' faces while you had it going?" I asked.

"I don't really know their faces," he said.

No, Telfair couldn't have told you Ernie Grunfeld from Ernie Banks. But he fully understood what he'd just accomplished: Telfair had sent a lightning bolt through NBA offices across the entire league.

"I prayed for this," Tiny Morton said.

One year after outplaying the number one pick in the 2003 draft, LeBron, Telfair had outplayed the likely number one pick in the 2004 draft, Howard, and the sneaker men were eating it up. "Sebastian owns this court," Sonny Vaccaro said as he stood behind one UCLA basket with his wife, Pam. "Pitino should get a game with the Bruins next year."

Chris Rivers was thinking that Pitino shouldn't bother. "You have to give Sebastian a real chance to play in the league now," he said. The league? Rivers wasn't talking about Conference USA or the Pac-10, nor were the other sneaker reps in attendance.

"We're very interested in Sebastian," Nike's George Raveling said. "I think he's a guy that has multiple skills, and a personality for the game. I think he would connect with young people from a marketing standpoint. I think he's an attractive type of guy that we'd want in our stable."

Adidas felt very much the same. "Sebastian's a very charismatic player," said Adidas's Daren Kalish. "My gut feeling is if he can (go pro), he will."

Telfair had finally overcome his injury, and before he left Pauley Pavilion, he said he felt sorry for the teams that had taken advantage of Lincoln in his absence.

But he had bigger targets in mind than Cardozo and Sheepshead Bay.

"How much do you think I helped myself?" he asked me.

"A ton," I said.

Soon he was heading toward his airport hotel, heading toward the LAX radio billboard that read, "KOBE" in big yellow letters, and "What's Next?" in smaller white ones.

Mystery was trailing basketball's teen wonders past and present. Sebastian Telfair flew back to Brooklyn with the NBA's undivided attention stuffed inside his suitcase, but his destination remained unknown.

10

Most of the oversize trophies cluttering up the Telfair living room were claimed at Stephon Marbury's annual summer tournament. They were wedged against walls, between couches, wherever they could be displayed for guests of the Telfairs' third-floor apartment, home of the point guard who had defeated the great Marbury in a playground game that helped sever the bond connecting one side of the family to the other.

Actually, Sebastian Telfair beat his cousin in two games. One was held at Surf Playground, where a full-court run among friends and neighbors was interrupted by the arrival of a big NBA star.

"Stephon jumped out of his Range Rover shirtless, all buffed up, like he was some tough guy," recalled Danny Turner. Stephon shouted, "I got next."

By the time Marbury got Telfair, word had whipped through Coney Island like an angry Atlantic gust. This was the summer before Telfair's junior year at Lincoln, and Marbury had just finished averaging more than 20 points and eight assists for the Phoenix Suns.

Telfair wasn't just the new kid on the block; he was family, Marbury's younger cousin by more than 8 years. Telfair's maternal grandmother and Marbury's mother were sisters. The Telfairs and Marburys had grown up together, one flight apart at Surfside Gardens. The Marburys lived on the fourth floor, the Telfairs just below, and they shared each other's clothing and food and took turns hosting sleepovers. Sometimes Stephon and the older boys would go down to the beach and put Sebastian or one of the other little ones on a bedsheet and hurl him into the air.

Money changed all that. NBA money. The Marburys had it, the Telfairs didn't, and so one side of the family moved out of the projects and left the other side behind.

"And Stephon never gave us anything after he left," Turner said.

The Marburys and Telfairs weren't on speaking terms by the time their chosen ones went head to head, crossover to crossover. "More than 100 people came to watch us play," Sebastian recalled one day while standing on the Surf asphalt.

Marbury was 25, and Telfair had just turned 17. It was man against boy. It was a five-on-five game, but a one-on-one event all the way.

"Stephon stole the ball from Sebastian on the first possession," recalled Turner, who played on Sebastian's side. Stephon would convert the turnover into a basket and tell Sebastian, "You need 5 years before you come see me in the NBA."

Sebastian would answer with a three and respond, "I'm thinking about 2 years."

Sebastian made some more threes and put a defensive choke hold on Stephon. "Is that all you can do, shoot the three?" Stephon asked him. Sebastian answered by going hard to the basket. Turner kept throwing him the ball so he would keep the pressure on Stephon. Sebastian made one move with the ball that nearly made Stephon fall. "And the crowd went crazy," Turner said.

Stephon tried to back down Sebastian, and the kid held his ground. "I'm not a little boy anymore," Sebastian said. "You can't do that to me." With Sebastian's team on game point, Stephon told his cousin, "You ain't scoring this one." Sebastian drained a step-back three for the win, and the crowd went wild. Stephon immediately asked for a rematch, but Sebastian and Turner said they were tired after playing four games to Stephon's one.

Stephon sought retribution in other ways, according to Turner. "So then Stephon says, 'I've got $5 million in the bank.' Bassy said, 'You're the only one in the park talking about money. We're all broke here.'"

The discourse wasn't any deeper when they played their one-on-one at the Garden, the Surfside playground court named for the Knicks' home. Right outside the building where they were raised, Telfair and Marbury squared off as dozens of locals gathered around the court. This time, there was nobody else to pass to. Nobody else to set picks. Nobody else to rebound. The rules of engagement were clear: one ball, one basket, and two extraordinary point guards vying for the title tattooed across Marbury's left arm.

Coney Island's Finest.

Telfair took the early lead, and protected it with his wide range of spin moves. "He'd go one way," Turner recalled, "and Stephon would go another. Sebastian busted him." Stephon turned up the physical intensity and pushed Sebastian into the fence. "Eventually, we had to stop it because it was getting too rough," Turner said.

The unofficial final was 11–7, Sebastian. Their mano a mano would instantly belong to Coney Island legend. Spike Lee, whose film, *He Got Game*, revolved around a Marbury-esque prospect out of Lincoln High (ironically played by the guard dealt for Marbury on draft night, Ray Allen), would be among the basketball-mad fans of Brooklyn to pass along unconfirmed tales of Telfair's conquest. "I don't know if it's true," Lee said, "but I heard Stephon quit in the middle of the game. I heard he was saying, 'I don't have my right sneakers. Let me go upstairs.' I heard he quit or something, because Sebastian put it on him."

Turner said a nasty exchange punctuated this latest family feud. "You're a spineless jellyfish," Stephon told Sebastian. "I'm the one who takes care of your family."

"You don't take care of us," Sebastian replied. "Giving us a couple of dollars here and there is taking care of us?"

Yes, money had divided this house. Marbury was the number four overall pick of the 1996 draft, and he would grow into a big enough star in Minnesota, New Jersey, and Phoenix that he scored more than $100 million in contracts before he was dealt to his hometown Knicks on January 5, 2004, the day after Telfair returned from his breakthrough game at UCLA.

The Telfairs were still living one floor down from the projects apartment the Marburys had left for green lawns and white picket fences. Stephon had bought his parents a large home in Maryland. He'd helped his four brothers move out and up in life. Meanwhile, the Telfairs were still getting by on Otis's disability checks, on food stamps, and on the leftover money Jamel Thomas sent from Europe.

The point guards' lives had become as different as their images— Telfair was the choirboy, Marbury was one big preening tattoo covered in bling and appearing in ads that said, "Before you can have the cribs, cars, and crew, you gotta have the moves."

Telfair was the point guard who patted a teammate on the ass when that teammate dropped one of his passes. Marbury was the point guard who met a drop with an eye-roll or a scowl, the reaction that broke down Keith Van Horn, the kind of fragile player Telfair would have built up.

Telfair talked of Marbury's image as being "all messed up," which was a fitting way to describe their relationship. "Sebastian really loved Stephon, so this hurts him," said Bubba Barker, Telfair's best friend. "It hurts him in his heart. . . . Me and Sebastian, we didn't care about the money. That's the sad part. We still looked at Stephon as Stephon, but he didn't see it that way."

Marbury shared his wealth with his immediate family, so he understood what Erica Telfair always told her six boys: You are your brother's keeper.

But are you your cousin's keeper?

Around Surfside Gardens, everyone knew that question met a unanimous response inside one third-floor apartment.

o   o   o   o   o

The Telfair home didn't meet anyone's preconceived notion of a public housing hellhole, at least after you escaped the smell of stale piss in the hallway and arrived at a front door graced by Sebastian's autograph and number, 31, and a sticker that read, "My Neighborhood Supports Our Troops."

The Telfair unit was good for five bedrooms, two baths, a walk-in kitchen, a microwave, air conditioners, a living room bordered by a wraparound blue couch, and a dining room highlighted by two glass swans for table legs and a chandelier made up of dozens of tiny transparent balls.

The living room walls displayed framed photos of Sebastian in Madison Square Garden, and Jamel Thomas in the colors of the Providence Friars. To get to Sebastian's mid-size bedroom, you had to take the narrow hallway on the left side of the unit until it T'd off, making a left after passing the rooms belonging to Sebastian's older sister, Sylvia, his younger sister, Octavia, his younger brother, Ethan, and his parents, Otis and Erica. Sebastian's TV was on a dresser beyond the foot of his bed, and his desktop computer rested on a nightstand to the left of his headboard. The room was decorated by a picture of Ethan and Jamel, a poster of Magic Johnson, Larry Bird, and Dr. J, and a taped-up television cable that ran up a wall and drooped from the ceiling.

If it wasn't the Ritz, it wasn't the pits, either. "Outside your front door is the projects," Danny Turner said. "But once you're inside your home, it's a different world."

Turner was inside the different world on this day, a world his stepfather was fond of calling "one of the biggest apartments in all of Coney Island." Otis and Erica were home, as were Sylvia and Jerry Ferguson, a cousin Otis said he treated like a son. Sitting in a semicircle with the Telfairs, Jerry was decked out in a John Elway throwback jersey.

Today's 2-minute drill amounted to a 100-yard dissection of Stephon Marbury.

I had given Sebastian a lift to the Garden for Marbury's first home game as a Knick, this after Isiah Thomas acquired Marbury in a blockbuster trade with the Suns. On the ride there, when he was done telling me he couldn't wait to get a credit card so he could use the E-ZPass lane at the Battery Tunnel, Telfair said he'd let out a loud yelp when his cell phone rang in class and the caller informed him Marbury had been dealt to the Knicks. "I was so happy," Telfair said, "and everybody was just looking at me. I said, 'Stephon's coming to the Knicks.'

"I was happy even though in my heart, I always thought I was going to be a Knick. Somebody close to the Knicks told me before the season that they were going to be looking real close at me."

That person wasn't Jeff Nix, New York's assistant GM. While Telfair was visiting LeBron James at the Knicks' practice facility during the NBA's rookie orientation, Nix walked into the gym to find Telfair and his friend and trainer, Andrew Amigo, shooting around.

Nix shouted Telfair and Amigo off the court, telling them their presence was in violation of league rules. Sebastian was pissed off. Amigo told him not to worry. "You're a point guard," Amigo said. "He'll be back."

Sure enough, Nix returned to apologize. "I didn't mean to sound like that," Nix said, "but I'd rather draft somebody and pay them a million dollars than get fined a million dollars because you're working out here."

Telfair got in the car and told his trainer he still felt dissed. "Well, you got something out of it," Amigo said. "He knew your name."

Now everybody knew Sebastian Telfair's name, even the armed female cop at the Battery Tunnel who once stopped the truck Sebastian was riding in—Jamel's—because it had tinted windows. "As soon as I rolled down the window," Telfair said, "no lie, she shouted, 'Sebaaaaaaaastian.' And she waved us right through."

New York was his home court, after all. "I'm definitely applying for the draft, and I definitely still want to be a Knick," Telfair said. "But now they have Stephon and no (first-round) pick. My father wasn't too happy about that."

No, he wasn't. In the Telfair apartment, with Barry White playing on the radio, the conversation that would make an inevitable beeline for Stephon started out harmlessly enough. The Telfairs introduced their cat, Goldie, who liked to chase dogs. Otis talked about the benefits of living on the ocean, near the amusement parks. He rummaged through the different reasons he named his golden child Sebastian—"The Catholic Church has a Sebastian"—while his wife enjoyed a private laugh. Erica had her own story—she named Sebastian after Sebastian Cabot from the old *Family Affair* show.

Otis showed a picture of himself as a young man in sweatpants and a shirt worn tight enough to show off his V-shaped upper body and powerfully built arms. "On draft night," he said, "this is how Sebastian should look." The photo was taken when Otis was busy doing time upstate.

Soon enough, Erica got the ball rolling. Draped in an oversize T-shirt, she looked at me from across the *Post* and *Daily News* that sat on her glass dining table and asked, "Is Marbury going to be in this book?" I confirmed that Marbury would indeed be in the book. Jerry Ferguson, in his Elway jersey, proceeded to fire the first spiral. "He should've given us tickets, man," Ferguson said. Cousin Jerry wouldn't be heard from again.

The march to pay dirt was on.

"We haven't called and asked for tickets, either," Erica said. "Stephon didn't offer and I didn't call. If I'd called and asked, they'd probably give them. But I didn't call. I don't know, I still love Stephon. He's my blood."

"Make sure you put this in the book," Otis said. "Stephon's been in the league 8 years, and none of us has seen him play live, except for Bassy when Jay-Z took him. Not one person in this family has seen him play live. None of us has been to his house."

Isiah Thomas, Knicks executive and Stephon's boss, had told me he had some interest in Sebastian. The notion of a future Stephon-Sebastian pairing in the Garden raced into the conversation like a flame chasing a trail of gasoline. "That would be the worst thing for Sebastian," Erica said.

"Sebastian and Stephon would make more money together than they'd make apart," Turner said.

"They'd have the fastest backcourt in the NBA," Otis said. "Business is business. You have to put personal feelings aside."

"They could play in Africa and it would be sold out," Turner said, "because of two Coney Island kids."

"They could move Stephon to the two," Otis said. "Fastest backcourt in the league."

"You listen to me," Erica ordered. "Number one, Stephon won't let that happen. Two, Sebastian would get hurt following behind Stephon.

It won't work. . . . He should never go with Stephon, never, because Stephon is not going to look out for him. And the truth is, Stephon is the king. He feels like, 'I don't want you here on my throne.' He is the king of Coney Island."

"No he's not," Otis barked. "Where you been at? Bassy busted him down twice. Go out there in the street and ask anybody."

"Yeah," Danny said. "If you don't have street credibility, you don't have any credibility."

"They hate (Stephon) in Coney Island," Otis said.

"They don't hate him out here," Erica answered.

"Okay, hate is a strong word," Otis allowed. "They're not feeling him, just put it like that. . . . I've got a feeling Sebastian's going to wind up with (the Knicks)."

"He should end up in Cleveland with LeBron," Danny said.

"Stephon and Sebastian," Erica said, "I wouldn't want that at all. That would be very bad."

"Business is business," Otis said, "and personal feelings are personal feelings."

"Sebastian's going to look at it as a business deal," Erica said, "but Stephon's going to sabotage it any way he can."

"I don't think Isiah Thomas is going to let that happen," Otis said of the Knicks' newly anointed president.

Thomas knew all about Telfair, and how Rick Pitino and others called the Lincoln star a "young Isiah." The Knicks would have had to trade back into the first round to get Telfair. When I reminded Thomas that he already employed a Coney Island point guard, he said, "That's okay. I'd take another one. I don't think you can have too many. In this league, you can have great success with two point guards, the way Sacramento uses Mike Bibby and Bobby Jackson at times."

I informed the Telfairs of Isiah's remarks and offered the opinion that the team president wouldn't stand for one Knick sabotaging another.

"Then that would be a problem," Erica said. "It would be a problem if they tried to move Stephon to help Sebastian."

"I'm just calling it the way I see it," Otis said as he dragged slowly on one of his Newports. "With every team, Stephon gets there and he lets them falter. He left the Timberwolves. He gave the Nets one of their worst losing seasons in their history. Phoenix hadn't missed the play-offs in (13) years until he got there. If he doesn't bring the Knicks to something, then his whole career has been like that."

The conversation turned to Marbury's relationship with his teammates. He'd walked out on Kevin Garnett in Minnesota—a disastrous move—and then tormented Keith Van Horn in New Jersey before getting shipped out to Phoenix in the Jason Kidd trade. On arrival in New York, where Van Horn was already in place, Marbury put a smiling public face on what he said would be a new beginning with the 6-foot-10 forward he couldn't stand in Jersey.

When Van Horn was traded for Tim Thomas, Marbury swore he had nothing to do with it. But Turner said Marbury had told him in two different phone calls that he had pushed Isiah to deal Van Horn. "Stephon told me that," Turner said. "He said, 'Yo, I got Van Horn.'"

"And that was the worst thing the Knicks did," Otis said. "Everybody knows Stephon was involved in that. I told you all, when Stephon came to the Knicks. Didn't I say Van Horn was on his way out?"

The subject of Sebastian's draft possibilities came up, and the chance—however remote—that the family was being set up for another devastating fall. Five years earlier, Jamel Thomas had been shut out after leading the Big East in scoring.

"Nothing's guaranteed," Erica said. "Jamel got messed up. We really don't talk about that no more. I just don't want Sebastian to get hurt. . . . Jamel's a remarkable person. He's a man among men. He takes a licking but keeps on ticking. But what he's doing now, playing pro ball in Greece, that's not his dream. His dream's to be in the NBA. That's what these kids around here are struggling for. They want to get to the NBA, not Europe."

Turner said he'd heard Sebastian might go between numbers four and eight in the draft lottery. Otis declared that he'd like to see his son play

Courtesy, Otis Telfair

A child shall lead them: The boy wonder, Sebastian, became his family's hope.

No place like home: The Surfside Gardens projects produced two lottery picks—
Stephon Marbury and Sebastian Telfair.

Otis Telfair in Vietnam: "I was 19, and suddenly I was being trained how to kill."

Tiny Morton and the Lincoln Railsplitters

Sebastian's name was a bull's-eye. "You're going to be like a gun-slinger walking into a bar now," Ziggy Sicignano told him. "Every-body will want to take you on."

©David Saffran

Courtesy, Lincoln High, Renan Ebeid

The Lady is a Champ: Renan Ebeid, Lincoln AD, demanded respect in a male-dominated world.

Ziggy Sicignano, Sebastian's former summer coach, tried to ruin Tiny Morton for taking away the point guard.

Courtesy, Ziggy Sicignano

©Danny Turner

Bassy learns the summer-circuit alphabet at Sonny Vaccaro's ABCD Camp.

Sebastian Telfair, friend Omar Rodriguez, and LeBron James, with a broken wrist, at ABCD Camp.

©Omar Rodriguez, Jr.

Sneaker maven Sonny Vaccaro spends hang time with Lincoln's high-jumping Nyan Boateng.

"Sebastian has the best crossover since Columbus left Spain," said Tom Konchalski, recruiting analyst.

Sebastian Telfair always looked up to LeBron James, the teen wonder who paved his way.

©David Saffran

NBA executives had doubts about Sebastian Telfair's jump shot.

©David Saffran

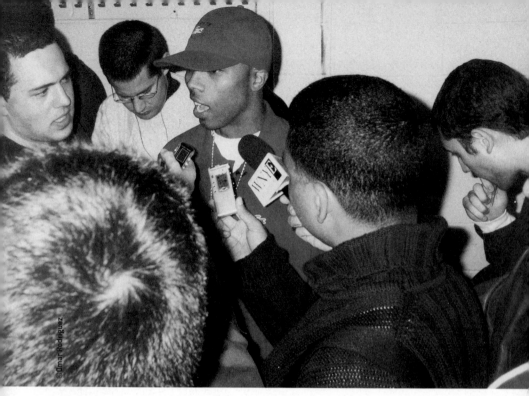

©Omar Rodriguez

Media magnet: Sebastian handled the New York press as if he were a seasoned NBA star.

It's gotta be the shoes—Adidas gives Sebastian sneakers bearing his initials and number.

©David Saffran

Sebastian and Danny Turner put their heads together on the road to the NBA draft.

Kissing cousins: Sebastian and his cousin and rival, Stephon Marbury, brought together for a rare family photo op.

Sebastian was never afraid to take the ball, and his 5-foot-11 body, to the hole.

©David Saffran

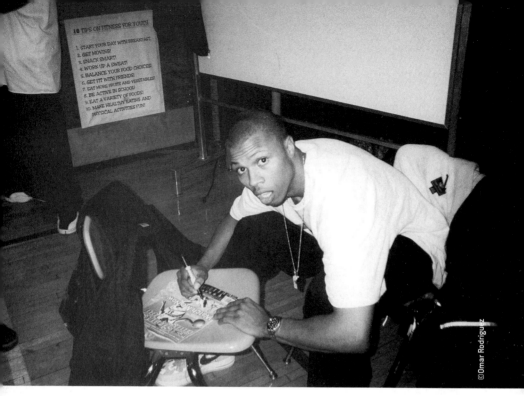

Sports Illustrated jinx? Sebastian signs the *SI* cover that bears his smiling face.

Nyan Boateng and Sebastian prepare to win their third straight city title in the Garden.

©Omar Rodriguez

Jay-Z gave Lincoln a pregame pep talk before the city title game against Cardozo.

You're hired: In his Trump Tower suite, Sebastian puts down his Trump water bottle and explodes from his seat the second David Stern calls his name at the NBA draft.

Secret agent: Andy Miller in the Trump hideaway, with his just-drafted client on the tube.

Soaked with champagne on draft night, Erica and Otis Telfair celebrate their son's LeBron moment inside Jay-Z's 40/40 club.

Out front and center: Sebastian begins his NBA life as a Portland Trail Blazer.

©Bruce Ely, *The Oregonian*

©Bruce Ely, *The Oregonian*

Sebastian at a Portland Boys and Girls Club: The team was desperate to change its "Jail Blazer" image.

Passing fancy: Trail Blazers officials thought Telfair was one of the best young passers they'd ever seen.

©Bruce Ely, *The Oregonian*

with Tracy McGrady in Orlando. He wondered if LeBron James would push to get Sebastian in Cleveland.

"Jeff McInnis is a backup point guard," Turner said. "Everybody knows that. And look around the league. Earl Boykins can play and start in the league, and Sebastian is 10 times better than him."

"But there's no guarantee until they call that day and say Bassy's in the draft," Erica said. "They said the same exact thing about Jamel. They said he was going to be a lottery pick. They said this and they said that. We were all so excited with this and that, I almost had a heart attack when he didn't get picked."

"That night tore up my whole family," Otis said. "What hurt me more, Stephon must've been watching. After they called the last name (in the draft), the phone rang and guess who it was. Stephon. Erica gets on the phone and he tells her, 'I don't know why everybody's upset. I'll be there in the morning. Don't worry about nothing.'"

Otis then slowly lifted his left arm within inches of his nose and studied his wristwatch. "We're still waiting," he said.

"Stephon was so close to Jamel, too, before they were even in high school," Otis continued. "One night they sat here and made a deal. Stephon said, 'The first one of us to sign with an NBA team will buy the other one a car.' We still haven't seen that car."

Jamel made a good living playing ball in Europe and getting temporary NBA work with Boston, Golden State, Portland, and New Jersey. But Erica felt so betrayed by Thomas's draft snub that she attended only a couple of Sebastian's games. She was too afraid to buy back in. When Erica did attend a game, she'd spend half of it in the bathroom, too nervous to watch Sebastian make or miss the big shot.

But Sebastian made enough of them to put his family back in a position to challenge King Stephon for his Coney Island throne. "Stephon thought that once the Jamel era was over, 'I'm the king. I'm filthy rich. I ain't got to worry about nothing,'" Otis said. "He never dreamt of this. He thought Bassy was going to be fly-by-night. He had no idea that Bassy was going to do what he has done."

Stephon Marbury had his back against the wall. He was standing with me in an otherwise empty Knicks practice facility in Westchester County, New York, and he was about to speak publicly for the first time about the compound fractures in his family caused by—what else?—money.

Like millions of fortunate souls before them, the Marburys stood accused of being changed by money. At least one person who knew the Marbury and Telfair families saw it as a bogus charge. "I never saw Mr. Marbury or his kids change, as far as their attitudes," said Ziggy Sicignano, who coached Stephon and Sebastian for Brooklyn USA. "Donnie and Eric never came off any different than before, and Stephon is still Stephon. He's worth $100 million now, but as far as giving a handshake and a hug and being appreciative, he's still a sweet kid."

But Stephon's name was still mud inside one Surfside Gardens apartment because he didn't share his fabulous wealth to the Telfairs' satisfaction.

"Bassy killed him, embarrassed him, destroyed him, made him fall down," Otis delighted in saying of the playground duels won by his son. "People were saying, 'oooh and aaah,' and Stephon said some hateful shit after that. You're not supposed to do that. You're supposed to help."

Marbury was a proud, defiant NBA star, a projects kid who beat million-to-one odds. He rose long before classes started at Lincoln so he could do all the drills his cousin, Sebastian, used years later. Marbury ran up and down 15 flights of stairs. He sprinted through the heavy beach sand. He took 500 jump shots in the Lincoln gym before the first bell rang.

Bobby Hartstein coached him, just like he'd coached the three older Marbury boys, Eric, Donnie, and Norman. Eric was an explosive leaper who played with Dominique Wilkins at Georgia. Don was a pure shooting guard who starred at Texas A&M University. Norman was a highly regarded prospect who originally signed with the University of Tennessee and, after failing to meet academic requirements, emerged at St. Francis College of Brooklyn.

But Stephon was different. He was John Fitzgerald Kennedy, and everyone else was Bobby and Ted. Nothing could stop Stephon's rise to the top. Not poverty, not crime, not even teenage fatherhood.

Marbury had a daughter days before he won his New York City high school championship. He spent 1 year at Georgia Tech, then used his sturdy 6-foot-2 body and nasty jumper to ascend to NBA stardom. But back home, in the 'hood, Marbury was largely seen as a distant figure. At least that was the majority view at Lincoln High.

"The community turned away from Stephon because Stephon never gave anything back to the school," said Lincoln athletic director Renan Ebeid. "Not that we want anything back. Just come back and promote the neighborhood in a positive way. Show kids that you can make it from here."

Corinne Heslin said Marbury hadn't made a donation to Lincoln. Tiny Morton said Marbury "wasn't the people person that Sebastian is. . . . Stephon never gave back enough." Morton's brother, Jeff, who was close enough to Marbury to live with him during his rookie NBA season in Minnesota, said he busied himself writing a book proposal titled *Money, Power, but No Loyalty*, with Marbury as the main character.

Spike Lee, who attended an occasional Lincoln game, would speak for the masses when he said, "In Coney Island, Sebastian is more loved than Stephon."

The Marburys didn't understand this dynamic. Stephon's annual basketball tournament provided scholarship money to a fortunate few. Stephon presided over a Thanksgiving turkey drive that provided 2,000 free turkeys to needy locals. Stephon created a Christmastime toy drive, which allowed 400 kids to pick up $50 certificates at Donnie's hair salon. Stephon ran an all-expenses-paid camp in the Poconos for promising Coney Island students. Stephon was given the NBA's Hometown Hero Award in August of 2001 for his community outreach work that month.

Stephon handed out free NBA gear to kids. He paid for the glass backboards hanging outside Surfside Gardens. "And I know he gave (the Telfairs) money," Donnie said. "What they're saying isn't true. I know Stephon gave Sebastian money. We were a very close family. A lot of things Stephon does people don't hear about. You don't do things from your heart and then look for publicity for it. We were taught to share. I think Stephon's done a great job doing things in the community."

Don Sr. saw it the same way. In fact, Don Sr. actually claimed to be unaware of existing tension between the Marburys and Telfairs. "I never sensed a split," he said. "I don't think it was like that. It wasn't like Stephon stepped away. Stephon came from an extremely large family, and giving has always been a part of his family life. I don't understand why some wouldn't appreciate that. I guess you can please some of the people some of the time, but not all of the people all of the time."

It appeared Stephon couldn't please any of the Telfairs any of the time. And so there he was in his white Knicks practice jersey, back to the wall, answering the $100 million question: Are you your cousin's keeper?

"You can't get mad at ignorance," Marbury said. "Ignorance is not a bad thing."

Marbury stopped me when I tried to rattle off a list of Telfair family grievances. "I really don't care," he said. "I already know how they think. It's tough when you don't know something. When you don't know two plus two is four, when you're saying it's five, I can't argue with you. . . . So you just don't say anything. You stay quiet."

Marbury said he wasn't interested in refuting anything the Telfairs had told me. "I'm not going to sound like them," he said. "I'm not putting myself there. They will see soon enough. They will understand what the NBA game is really all about. They think it's just money and cars and houses, and it's really a billion different things you have to go through. They have no idea about this life."

I told Marbury that the Telfairs apparently believe he should have offered them some form of support, at least until Sebastian made his own first-round NBA way. "That's their mentality," he said. "It's okay for me to work hard and do what I do. Forget about me having a big family. Forget that I take care of 25 people. They don't understand that, in regular society in this world, people work for their families. I have a wife, kids, a mother, a father, brothers and sisters, nieces and nephews."

"You bought your parents a home in Maryland, right?" I said.

"Yeah," he said. "So I mean, I don't work and I don't play ball for (the Telfairs). I play basketball and work hard for my immediate family, and whatever I can do to help sometimes, then I do that. But (Sebastian) doesn't owe anybody . . . in Coney Island nothing. If he wants to do something for somebody, he should do it because he wants to. If he tries to take care of everybody in Coney Island, he'll be broke. He'll have nothing. Once he understands and sees that life is not what everyone tries to make it to be, and once he goes through the experiences in the NBA, he'll learn.

"I once gave him a lecture, a 3-hour lecture about that. He was a sophomore in high school. I said, 'Yo, let me tell you about the NBA. If you're drafted number one, you're going to make $4 million. Of that $4 million, $2 million is automatically gone to the government. Then you've got to pay your agent. Then you've got to give your financial planner something. . . . Then you've got to pay insurance for your family. You've got to get your own life insurance. You've got to get insurance for yourself because you're only 18. Then your mother wants a car, your brother wants a car, and you've got to get their insurance.'

"I told him, 'Now you want to get some jewelry. Now you've got to get clothes. Now you want to get a house. Who's going to get a house, you or your mother? Are you going to live in an apartment and let her have a house? There's seven of us in my family, with my mother and father making nine. I've got a wife, two kids, two nieces, and four nephews. People think you've got a $100 million contract, but it's not $100 million. It's $50 million over a number of years. People don't understand that.'

"To me, I don't live the way I want to live because I'd rather take care of my family. I love doing it. I would love to have a yacht and to charter planes, but I can't do that. I've got to take care of my family. That's the reason I play basketball. I love basketball. It's fun. But the money that I make is to make sure everyone is comfortable. Like I said, (the Telfairs) will see. They will find out."

155

Fair enough. But I also wanted to know what Sebastian would find out about the basketball side of NBA life.

"He can play in the NBA," Marbury said. "But it's not about just playing in the NBA at that position. There's so many other things you've got to do to play in the NBA. Then on top of it, he's only 5-11. I mean, 5-11, and he can't really shoot from deep. He doesn't dunk. He's got so many different things against him.

"I figured out the game only 3 or 4 years ago. It's hard. Point guard is not just another position to be coming to right out of high school. I probably could've jumped right from Lincoln to the NBA, but I knew in order for me to play at the level I wanted to play at, I had to go through some type of structure, some type of discipline. I played for one of the best coaches in high school basketball in Bobby Hartstein. I got all of my fundamentals.

"And when I came out, I viewed tape and broke down who was coming out of school. With Sebastian, you've got the kid from Connecticut (Ben Gordon) coming out. You've got Jameer Nelson coming out. You've got all these guards who have proven themselves in college, at a high level, in front of big-time crowds and against players who can play. When I came out, it was the perfect time to come out. This is not the perfect time to come out for my cousin.

"I wish he could go number one, but I know that's not going to happen. Maybe something will change, but I like dealing with knowing. I can't deal with not knowing. And these dudes in the NBA are nice. You're playing against somebody nice every night. He has to be able to dominate Earl Boykins, and Earl Boykins isn't no slouch. He's got to play with that same type of intensity every night that Earl Boykins plays with because Sebastian's only 5-11."

Gingerly, I asked about the intensity Sebastian showed when he beat his older cousin in those two playground games.

"Man, I had just gotten off surgery and . . . well . . . if that gave him confidence, then good," Stephon said. "But it's a whole different thing when you get on the basketball court in the NBA as opposed to playing in the park. That's a whole different world. That's got nothing to do with family, none of that shit. He's going to get his ass busted, and I think he knows he's going to have to go through his growing pains first, then maybe it will be his time to shine.

"He has to understand that everyone's mentality every time they step on the court is to kill him. Man, if you go to a team that's got an asshole point guard, and they're killing you in practice, he's not helping you. I was fortunate because I had Terry Porter and Micheal Williams in Minnesota. I had two guys who wanted to help, two good people. And I was more prepared to go to the NBA than (Sebastian). He don't even dunk. He can't even dunk.

"He says, 'I don't need to dunk.' You've got to be able to dunk in the NBA. I mean, T.J. Ford can dunk. If you don't play above the rim in the NBA, your shit is getting beat up. . . . And Sebastian doesn't love basketball yet. He really doesn't understand what the game really is. He likes basketball, but he doesn't love basketball. I'm a big student of the game. I eat up all facets of 94 feet. Like, I can watch anybody play basketball. I can watch little kids play basketball and be into the game and pick up stuff from them. His focus isn't there yet. He's not that basketball savvy yet."

I told Marbury that a shoe company, probably Adidas, was likely to bet millions upon millions—and much more than Stephon ever got in a shoe deal—on Sebastian's savvy.

"When you're on the basketball court," Marbury said, "if you're not playing well, that money won't do shit for you. . . . It solves a lot of problems, but money doesn't make you happy.

"But my little cousin, he'll be okay. He's got to go through some trials and tribulations in order for him to get where he's going. . . . And if you can't go through something to become something, you're basically like a dead plant. You're not growing.

"I think my little cousin will grow."

o   o   o   o   o

Sebastian Telfair was in the Lincoln gym, arguing with Tiny Morton over Isiah Thomas's place in point guard history. "He was better than

Stephon?" Telfair asked with more than a trace of incredulity. "Better than Stephon?"

Deep down, Telfair saw his older cousin as a ballplayer almost without peer. Heck, Willis Reed, the captain, said that Marbury was the first point guard the Knicks had employed since Clyde Frazier who could compare to Clyde Frazier.

Telfair admired Marbury's talent and respected his place among the NBA elite. But in the end, Telfair and Marbury were cousins defined by their differences. Marbury was a score-first point guard with reliable 3-point range. Telfair was a pass-first point guard with an inconsistent jumper. Marbury could start or finish a nasty alley-oop dunk. Telfair was sensitive about the fact that he never tried to dunk in games, and struggled to dunk in practice.

Different people, different players, same blood.

"Sebastian is better than Stephon was at the same stage," said Bob Gibbons, the recruiting analyst.

"Stephon is bigger and shoots it a little better than Sebastian," Jim Boeheim said. "Stephon's the best point guard I've ever seen come out of New York."

Comments like Boeheim's lit a fire under Telfair, inspired him to smash Marbury's records at Lincoln and to give the Railsplitters multiple city titles after Stephon merely delivered one.

Still, Telfair was reluctant to join the family bashing of Marbury; he didn't need the headache. "I don't want to be quoted much tearing up my cousin," Telfair would say, "but he . . . doesn't talk to Jamel anymore, and they were best friends. I've never seen a quote from him about me in the paper. His parents have never had my mother over to their new home. I mean, we lived one floor apart, and now it's like we're not good enough for him anymore.

"It's not like I'm mad at Stephon. He probably thinks we're mad because he didn't give us money. It's not that. It's just that he and his family weren't nice to my mother and family after my mom was very nice to them."

Telfair and Marbury did embrace at the one game Marbury's little cousin attended with Spike Lee. "Every family has shit going on," Lee said, "and I still think Stephon and Sebastian love each other despite their differences." Telfair and Marbury engaged in a less enthusiastic embrace at another game Telfair attended in the company of Jay-Z.

Telfair felt Marbury came over only because Jay-Z was sitting next to him.

Over and over, Marbury would say his job with the Knicks amounted to his dream come true. The Telfairs didn't see it quite the same way. They knew the Knicks forever seemed to have a void at point guard, and they knew Isiah Thomas wasn't about to let that continue. They knew Thomas had heard that Telfair was being compared to a young Isiah.

"I could end up anywhere in the NBA," Telfair said after Marbury was traded to New York. "But I had a gut feeling that I was going to be a Knick."

Telfair's gut feeling was wrong. His spot was filled. His cousin had beaten the Telfairs to the punch for the sake of old times.

11

The coach bus pulled up to Tailgaters Sports Bar and Grill, and out into the chilled Kentucky morning spilled a groggy crew of ballplayers too young to order a Bud. The Lincoln Railsplitters had touched down on a snow-kissed January day, no small victory to the man who had arranged their flight. Mike Pitino would see Sebastian Telfair play a basketball game in Louisville when there was a fairly strong chance Pitino's famous father never would.

"Are we really doing this press conference in a bar?" sighed Pat Forde, columnist for the *Courier-Journal* of Louisville. Telfair was seated on a small stage in the back corner, positioned between his coach, Tiny Morton, and Telfair's local opponent for the weekend, 6-foot-10 Terrance Farley, a low-profile member of the same Louisville recruiting class that had Telfair on the marquee.

Four TV stations had cameras aimed at the participants. Print guys, Internet guys, photographers, and fans stood at the edge of the stage while the jukebox music and lunch-crowd prattle drowned out the small talk between Telfair and Farley. When the press conference began, the principal at Pleasure Ridge Park High (PRP) made it clear the host school was accepting its sparring-partner role. "We're honored to be on the floor with such a talented player," he said of Telfair, not Farley. "I'm glad Mr. Pitino could set this up."

That would be Mike, not Rick. Rick Pitino would say he was hardly comfortable with the fact that his sons Mike and Chris helped "set this up." Kentucky fans were busy trying to turn in their former coach, loved in Wildcat blue and loathed in Cardinal red. Those fans wanted to know how the NCAA could allow Pitino's family to promote a high school game involving Louisville's top recruit, a game that would earn Telfair's team a $5,000 appearance fee on top of an all-expenses-paid trip out of class.

"I actually didn't want this game," Rick Pitino said in his office, hours before he'd take his white-hot Cardinals to the University of South Florida. "I'd like to control the environment more."

Mike Pitino had a different recollection of his father's sentiment. Asked if the Louisville coach was happy his sons had pulled Telfair's big day from the ashes, Mike said: "Definitely. He knew how Louisville fans feel about basketball and how badly they wanted to see Sebastian play. He's just upset he won't be back in time from South Florida to see it."

Rick Pitino had asked his son to push back the 5:00 P.M. start to 7:00 P.M., so he could return from his day game at South Florida in time to watch Telfair. Mike rejected his father's request because Kentucky was playing that same night. "I told my father I wasn't going head-to-head against Kentucky just so he could see Sebastian," Mike said.

So the Lincoln-PRP game would be played at 5:00 P.M. on January 10th, with the Louisville coach out of sight, out of mind, and out of town. Mike and Chris Pitino and their company, Game Seven Sports Marketing, were running the show. It was a show that almost didn't come off.

In fact, the Philadelphia-based promoter who ran the Palestra and Bronx tournaments spoiled by Telfair's injury had originally booked this event. "It's the first time in 5 years I've had to cancel anything," Jeremy Treatman said. He'd lost money on the three Lincoln games he'd promoted. "I was selling the next Isiah Thomas," Treatman said, "and it didn't work."

Treatman laughed when informed that Pitino's sons were the ones who had salvaged the Louisville game. "Man," he said, "the things you see in this business. Maybe they'll sell out; it's all timing. If they've got their dad behind them, they can do anything they want."

The Pitino boys said they wanted to go it alone. Mike was the 26-year-old former Wall Street trader and current Game Seven senior vice president. Chris was the 23-year-old Georgetown graduate and Game Seven account executive. To their father's credit, Mike and Chris didn't carry themselves with the air of royalty. They came across as nice kids. In a jacket and tie, Mike almost looked ready to make his First Communion.

Brooks Downing, Pitino's sports information director at Kentucky, was Game Seven's executive vice president. The company had marketed

Pitino's instructional basketball video—former Pitino players Reece Gaines of Louisville and Walter McCarty of Kentucky appeared on the tape—and represented Pitino's friend and colleague, Louisville football coach Bobby Petrino. Jamal Mashburn, another former Pitino star at Kentucky, was an investor in Game Seven, which was a division of Ott Communications, which was owned by MAP—Mashburn, Avare, and Pitino (Avare would be Rick, as in Pitino's business manager).

"Conference USA has already called us to check this out," Rick Pitino said. "Kentucky fans had called to complain, thinking I had something to do with Game Seven. The only thing my sons promoted with me was my video, so they could do whatever they wanted with (the Lincoln-PRP) game. It's clear I had nothing to do with it, but that's the way it is here. There's maybe 50 Louisville fans in Lexington, but 50,000 Kentucky fans in Louisville. Then there's all that shit you see on the Internet. So it's a lot worse for us."

Pitino grumbled some more about the imbalance, and added through a half smile that Kentucky's players drove nicer cars than Louisville's.

"If Kentucky can do anything to get us in trouble," Mike Pitino said, "they will."

Life was easier—if less interesting—when the Pitino boys were staging an exhibition tennis match between Andy Roddick and James Blake. But when they read on InsideTheVille.com that Telfair's scheduled appearance in Louisville was suddenly in ruins, Mike and Chris couldn't resist.

"Louisville basketball fans are fanatics," Mike said. He didn't see any problem finding 5,071 fanatics to fill the Louisville Gardens, a charming old arena that had once been a stage for the likes of Elvis, Martin Luther King Jr., and Harry Truman.

The Pitinos came up with the ticket price of $10 a pop, and gave naming rights to Tailgaters in exchange for feeding the Railsplitters. Fans would have to buy their tickets at Tailgaters, across the street from Louisville's Papa John's Cardinal Stadium, and they would need cash. Tickets went on sale 4 days before the game, and when Mike Pitino stopped by to gauge the early interest, he found a line snaking its way outside the bar's door.

"Those fans are all praying Sebastian doesn't go to the NBA," Mike said.

Those prayers were falling on deaf ears. Telfair had followed up his 37-point game at UCLA by dropping 55 points on Lafayette High and 48 on New Utrecht High, this after Stephon Marbury was traded from the Suns to his hometown Knicks. Most observers figured the news of his cousin's trade had lit a fire under Telfair; in fact Sylvester Telfair, just released from prison, was the motivational source. Sylvester kept telling his kid brother he had to dominate in the second half of the season, and Sebastian said he was only following orders.

The NBA certainly noticed, and Louisville fans were buying up these Tailgaters tickets just in case. By the time Lincoln showed up for its Friday press conference at Tailgaters, the Pitino boys were wishing the Gardens could accommodate 7,000 fans.

Telfair was an easy sell. Morton made the Louisville deal with Treatman before Mike and Chris Pitino swooped in with an offer to cover Lincoln's airfare, lodging, transportation, and meals, to give Morton 100 complimentary tickets to the game, and to throw in $5,000 as a reward for filling the house.

Morton declined the 100 tickets; he said he didn't know anyone in Kentucky. Morton accepted the rest of the deal. "(Morton) knows we've had less than a week to put this together, so he hasn't been demanding," Mike said. "We're giving Pleasure Ridge Park an appearance fee, so Lincoln has to get one. Lincoln could play the worst high school team in Louisville, and we'd still sell out."

PRP was the best high school team in Louisville, a distinction earning it $3,000 and 100 tickets from the Pitinos. The host school wasn't moved to complain about Lincoln's fee. On the street outside the Gardens' front door, Muhammad Ali Boulevard, everyone understood that greatness commanded the biggest purse.

o   o   o   o   o

The press conference site, Tailgaters, was everything you'd expect in a college sports bar. Dark and loud. Louisville banners and pictures everywhere. Pool tables and video games at one end, the small stage at the other. Townies and students in between, hunched over bacon cheese-burgers and salsa chips.

Reporters pressed Telfair about everything from his ankle to his intentions. When someone asked if he was sure he'd attend Louisville, Telfair answered, "If I'm alive."

But Telfair was alive when he refused to say whether he'd enter his name in the NBA draft. The kid was too smart to kill the drama that made him hot copy. "In the history of basketball," Forde wrote in his game-day column, "there never has been this big a deal made of this small a player at this young an age."

Telfair signed autographs at Tailgaters when fans approached with shirts, caps, or the front page with the giant "Telfair Picks U of L" headline in the *Courier-Journal*. Danny Turner brought boxes of T-shirts to sell at the game, the same "NBA or College?" T-shirts Lincoln players wore at Telfair's I'm-going-to-Louisville news conference in October. Only these shirts carried the black Adidas name and logo and would sell for $15.

Business was business, and on this day the product would point a toy rifle at a video machine so he could fire away at animated turkeys. Telfair was being a kid, acting his age. The Lincoln players were done with their burgers and were passing their pre-practice time in the bar's game room, when Telfair grew frustrated with his wayward aim, put down the toy rifle, pulled up a chair, and began a conversation with me about business. His business. The market for teenage basketball stars, where rules were made to be broken.

He slid down his sleeve to expose his shiny new Iceman watch, with its thick black band and giant face. "Jay-Z gave it to me," Telfair said. Jay-Z, king of rap and de facto general manager of the S. Carter summer league team Telfair ran at the Rucker.

Iceman watches ran between $995 and $5,000, and this one looked closer to the high end than the low. That gift might have jeopardized Telfair's amateur eligibility—"A gift from a summer coach could potentially put your eligibility at risk," said Bill Saum of the NCAA. But Jay-Z wasn't your typical summer league figure. He wasn't a representative of any university's athletic interests, and he was said to have had a friendship with Telfair that predated the point guard's appearance on his team—facts that might have put Telfair in the clear. The point guard would often visit Jay-Z's new club, 40/40, though he never drank alcohol.

"I really didn't give Sebastian any gifts," Jay-Z maintained when I approached him at a Nets game. "Just support."

At an earlier Knicks game, the rapper told me he'd met Telfair through mutual friends. "He's amazing," Jay-Z said. "He's got that heart of Brooklyn, the heart of Coney Island. He's going to play for me forever. We have a Brooklyn bond. I'm going to be like a mentor to him, do anything I can to help. . . . He's definitely ready for the NBA. They've got to fix the college system, anyway. There's a lot of money being made in college from the kids; they should be paid something."

Another of Telfair's heavyweight friends, Spike Lee, shared Jay-Z's view. "Sebastian should go pro," Lee said, "because I think the NCAA guys are pimps. Just saying the players are getting free tuition and board, that's a crock. Why would these guys continue to make billions for these schools without getting paid?"

But the issue of monthly stipends for college athletes wasn't weighing heavily on Telfair's mind. When I asked him why he'd just told the Louisville media he'd play for the Cardinals the following year as long as he was breathing, the point guard said, "I don't want to burn any bridges. I've got to keep saying the right things."

A young waitress who had been flirting with Telfair interrupted to make small talk. In the background, Telfair's pool-playing teammates, Nich Leon and Yuriy Matsakov, were locked in a heated eight-ball debate.

Our conversation rose above the din and veered back to the offers of gifts and cash forever made on the big-time high school and summer circuit. "You know," Telfair said, "Louisville hasn't offered me anything illegal. Zippo. Coach Pitino just doesn't do that."

"What's the biggest offer you ever received from a school?" I asked.

"$250,000," Telfair answered.

"From what school?" I asked.

Telfair would say only that the offer came from a prominent Division I program in the East. I figured I'd come back to that issue at a later date.

"I turned it down," he said of the offer. "It wasn't worth it for me to get in trouble over. I had other big offers, too, one for $150,000. I think if it wasn't for my brother, Jamel, and the way he takes care of me and my family with the money he's making (playing pro ball) in Greece, I'd probably have gotten in trouble. I probably would've gotten caught taking something. Jamel would be rich if he didn't take care of our family. That's why when I make $2 million, I'm going to give him $1 million because me and my family need to pay him back."

Money was a sensitive subject to Telfair, if only because nobody in Coney Island seemed to have any.

"I grew up with people now called drug dealers because that's what they do," Telfair said. "But they're my friends. Those guys looked after me and got me something to eat when I had nothing. The dealers won't hang around you; they'll stay away from me or protect me. They don't give me money to put in my pocket, but they'll buy me Chinese food or make sure I've got something to drink. People don't know how it feels to play basketball for 6 hours and after the game have nothing to eat or drink.

"I mean, every player is taking something out there. Everybody. . . . Kids out there are starving. We're starving. We've got nothing, and people are making all this money off of us. Maybe I want to buy my mother something for Christmas. She told me, 'They make all this money. They sell all these pictures of you, and nobody gives anything to our family.' When I was younger, I used to have to borrow sneakers to play ball, but nobody cares. Nobody knows what's going on in our household. They just make their money and move on. Hopefully, I'll make it to the NBA. If I don't, well, I guess that's our problem."

Telfair wanted to make sure it wasn't a problem. A half-hour after declaring on the stage side of Tailgaters that he would definitely play at Louisville, he declared on the game room side that he was as good as gone. I asked him when he'd officially enter his name in the June draft.

"A-S-A-P," he answered.

Soon enough, Telfair and teammates were on a bus and off to the Cardinals' practice facility down the road, where Rick Pitino was putting his team through a workout. Morton and his assistants had beaten their players to the facility; after consulting with his NCAA compliance director, Pitino was told he could meet with the Lincoln coaches but not with Telfair and friends. So Pitino ran his Cardinals through drills while the Lincoln staff took mental notes. More than anything, Morton took note of Pitino's microphone and sound system that allowed him to speak at a conversational level and still fill the gymnasium with his commanding voice.

The microphone wasn't born of any egomaniacal whim, but of medical necessity. Pitino had a health scare the year before. He was coughing up blood when he checked into the hospital fearing he would be diagnosed with cancer. The doctor diagnosed Pitino as a serial screamer whose shouting would rupture blood vessels.

"I was very scared," the Louisville coach said, "and then very relieved."

Pitino's medical problems would continue during the 2003–04 season; ultimately he'd take an indefinite leave for urological pain that he'd call "excruciating." If Pitino was stepping away from the bench, his confidants said, this had to be serious. Some close friends had been concerned that Pitino was suffering from an eating disorder. They didn't like the way he looked. They spoke of his apparent preoccupation with his weight and the weight of others.

"I thought he might be anorexic," said one of those close friends. "Some of us were concerned enough to talk about it. I finally asked Rick, 'Are you eating?' It's the first time I ever had the nerve to ask him." Pitino assured his friend he was eating and feeling fine after a trip to the Cleveland Clinic ruled out cancer and other life-threatening possibilities. Pitino missed only one game.

But before this rare interruption, the Louisville coach courted Sebastian Telfair like he'd never courted another recruit. Back on campus, the day before Lincoln played Pleasure Ridge Park at the Gardens, Pitino asked me about Telfair while Tiny Morton was working his microphone in the gym and Sebastian and other Railsplitters were running on treadmills in the Cardinals' fitness room.

Pitino laughed over Morton's act—Lincoln might as well have been practicing in 18th-century France, as Tiny had morphed into Napoleon

Bonaparte. Pitino found little humor in the news of Telfair's 37-point game at UCLA, the performance that appeared to sell NBA executives on the playmaker's first-round skills.

"Was it against any competition?" Pitino asked me.

"He was going against Orlando Woolridge's son," I answered. "A 6-5 kid, good athlete. Sebastian had no trouble getting his shot off against him."

Pitino didn't really want to hear it. "Well, every pro scout tells me Sebastian's not ready," he said. "Every single one. Now, we all know it only takes one team to change that, and it looks like the Clippers are the one. Their scout, Evan Pickman, loves him, but he's biased. He's a Staten Island guy.

"The good thing for us is we are still recruiting other point guards."

Pitino mentioned Rajon Rondo, a Louisville kid lighting it up at Oak Hill Academy, ranked number one in the nation by *USA Today*. Rondo was a hell of an insurance policy to have against Telfair's NBA ambitions, but there was a problem: Tubby Smith's Wildcats, from Pitino's old Kentucky home, were all over Rondo, too.

Louisville was set to make a dramatic run at the Final Four in 2005, but the Cardinals needed a quarterback to make their 2005 vision complete. Taquan Dean was a good ballplayer, a combination guard squeezed into a vacant point guard hole. Only Dean wasn't the kind of talent who could inspire some overheated booster to offer him $250,000 in cold, tax-free cash.

I mentioned to Pitino that Telfair had said he'd rejected illicit cash offers before signing with Louisville, a school Telfair labeled "clean."

"Sebastian's got charisma and a million-dollar smile," Pitino said, "so why risk that? You never risk your reputation. . . . I think Sebastian's too smart to get involved in that."

Sebastian was smart enough to understand just how important he was to Pitino and the Cardinals. His commitment made national news. For the first time since the glory days of the 1980s, Louisville was the place for top-10 recruits to be.

Now came the hard part for Pitino: getting Telfair to show up.

THE JUMP

For the 5:00 P.M. tip-off, the Lincoln Railsplitters strolled into the Gardens at 4:55 LST (Lincoln Standard Time), 2 hours after the fans began lining up outside the Gardens and an hour after its doors were opened, unleashing a frantic flood of men, women, and children in Louisville jackets, pullovers, and caps.

One young father was wearing Telfair's number 31, the point guard's genuine Lincoln High jersey from his sophomore season. The man, Jason Redd of Owensboro, Kentucky, said he bought it on the Internet. "I don't want my wife to hear this," Redd joked, "but it cost me over $200. That's okay, it's a once-in-a-lifetime opportunity."

The same could be said for every other hopeful face in the sell-out crowd. Telfair's appearance had that one-and-done feel to it, so the Lincoln star was cheered as he and his tardy teammates walked past the stands on the way to their locker room, all of them still in street clothes.

For some unknown reason, Morton had run the Railsplitters through a 2½-hour morning workout. The spent players grabbed take-out lunches at Tailgaters, ate in their hotel rooms, and took a long winter's nap. "Guys overslept," Morton said. Shit happens.

Telfair made sure he was the last Railsplitter to dress. When he appeared on the court, 9 minutes after the scheduled tip, the crowd loosed a roar worthy of his last-man-into-the-ring status.

"This kind of hype surrounding a player is unprecedented at Louisville," said Mike Hughes, founder of InsideTheVille.com. "The day Sebastian made his commitment, we had more people on our message board than we did after Louisville got into the Big East and after Louisville beat Kentucky. It's the biggest day we've ever had in our chat room."

That mass appeal manifested itself in every conceivable form. A few fans were wearing T-shirts that read, "Got Bassy?" on the front and "Louisville does!" on the back. For those who hadn't come dressed in Telfair testaments, the public address man announced that Sebastian's "NBA or College?" Adidas T-shirts were on sale behind one of the

169

baskets. Fifteen bucks bought a fan the "Telfair Says Louisville" answer on the back of each shirt, a declaration the point guard was mocking in private.

Telfair was introduced last, of course, and to a standing ovation. The Gardens had that drafty auditorium feel to it. The seats were faded and the lights were dim. The only thing missing was a blue-white cloud of cigar smoke hanging low over the court.

Telfair burned to put on a show for the good people of Louisville who had afforded him so much love, people who figured to be heartbroken in June. He would shoot only 8 for 22 from the floor, but still contribute 27 points, 6 assists, 5 steals, and 5 rebounds to Lincoln's 77–68 victory. The Louisville fans were happy with the performance, yet unhappy that an early announcement promising Telfair would "sign autographs for everyone after the game" had been negated by a late announcement that Telfair would sign only the $15 T-shirts "due to time constraints."

When Telfair was done signing and posing with the budding local starlet who sang the national anthem, someone asked about the words Louisville autograph seekers had shared with him. "It was, 'national championship,'" he said. "Everyone wants to win a championship. That's what we have in common. I'm a winner, and that's what I want to do. That's why I'm coming to Louisville."

Nobody challenged his claim. Telfair answered a few more questions, briefly engaged the Owensboro, Kentucky, man wearing his old Lincoln jersey, then headed for the bus parked below the marquee that was still carrying the headliner's name in big, bright lights.

Telfair was going home, and the smart money said he wasn't ever coming back.

Sebastian Telfair was sitting in the Lincoln bleachers and handicapping the companies that were after his feet. Telfair had worn Adidas, Nike, and Reebok at different points in the season. He said Adidas was in the lead for his services, but that there was still time for the opposing teams to catch up.

We talked about money, and why amateur athletes were denied an opportunity to cash in on their talents. The system was set up so that the only way a high school or college player could profit from his or her skill was to take gifts or cash from people who weren't allowed to give them. It opened a door for me to ask Sebastian about the $250,000 offer he said he'd received as an underclassman from a man who claimed to be representing a major college in the East.

"I was at a game, another school's game, just watching," Telfair said. "It was an alumni, but I brushed it off. Certain schools are dirty, and certain schools are not dirty. Like Rick Pitino. He ain't doing nothing. Rick Pitino is not doing anything illegal. He's not buying you a drink. That's what I like about him."

I inquired about the man who made the alleged offer. "He asked me what school I was going to," Telfair said. "I didn't even know the guy at all. I knew the school he was from. . . . He said what school he was from. He was like, 'What school are you thinking about going to?' I was like, 'You know, I've got a couple of choices,' but I didn't say any names. He was like, 'If you come to this school, you'll get paid. I'm talking hundreds of thousands of dollars, $250,000.' And I was like, 'Oh yeah?'

"But it ain't worth it. If you do something stupid with a school and then after it happens, you get in trouble for it, you're like, 'Damn, I wish

I didn't do that. It wasn't worth it. I didn't get enough out of it for me to get in trouble.' If you've got a chance to be a millionaire in a couple of months or in a year, why take a couple hundred thousand when it's only going to hurt you and your family?

"But then, what if you do get hurt? What if you don't make it? Then you're like, 'Damn, I could've had that.' It's a risky situation, and nothing's guaranteed."

Back to the man who made the alleged $250,000 offer. I asked Telfair for a description, and he said the man was white. I asked if the man was old, young, or middle-age. "Middle," he said. "I don't know the guy's name. . . . The person that it was, I was in the gym of that school he said he was with."

Telfair wouldn't name the school the man said he represented. A person close to Telfair said the man claimed to represent the interests of Georgia Tech, the school that had landed two previous point-guard greats from New York, Kenny Anderson and Stephon Marbury.

Paul Hewitt, the Georgia Tech head coach, dismissed the possibility that any alum or fan at a Georgia Tech home game could have approached Telfair with an improper offer. "There's no way Telfair came to a game on our campus and didn't come into our locker room," Hewitt said. "If that happened, one of my assistants would've been fired. If he came to one of our games, it was an Elvis-like appearance. If he was down here, I didn't know it. I think somebody's trying to sex up the story."

Hewitt confirmed that Georgia Tech briefly recruited Telfair during his junior year. His assistant, Willie Reese, tried to convince Hewitt to go to Lincoln to see the point guard. Hewitt had seen Telfair as a sophomore and figured right then and there he would go straight to the NBA. "But I had Willie call Stephon and ask him if he thought Sebastian would go to school," Hewitt said. "We have these buses on campus that take you from one place to another, and we call them the Stinger. Stephon told Willie, 'You really think that kid's going to ride a Stinger bus when he can be driving a Mercedes? There's no way he's going to school.'"

Allison George, Georgia Tech's director of sports communications, said that she, too, never saw Telfair at a Georgia Tech game and reminded me that a player of Telfair's profile would have been almost impossible to miss. But Lincoln assistant Danny Turner said his brother did attend a Georgia Tech game, a claim Telfair declined to comment on. "It wasn't an official visit," Turner said. "He was down there for something else and just went to a game."

Bubba Barker, Telfair's best friend, confirmed Turner's account. "Yeah, he went to a Georgia Tech game," Barker said. "It was a brief visit, like in and out of there. He said he liked the people there a lot." Neither Turner nor Barker could recall which game Telfair attended.

Of course, someone could have made a $250,000 offer—and an empty one at that—without having any connection to Georgia Tech or its basketball program. Whether the alleged offer to Telfair was real or a hoax, this much was clear: The Lincoln star was forever in position to reject business propositions that could have landed him in trouble.

"I've turned down a lot of things over the years," he said.

"Sebastian's just too classy and too sophisticated to get bought by anyone," said Andy Miller, the agent hoping to represent him.

But Telfair was getting tired of the dance. A job in the NBA would end all that, and he would open February with another huge game to be witnessed by executives and scouts from every pro team.

Telfair would face Dwight Howard, the 6-foot-11 center from Southwest Atlanta Christian, in the Prime Time Shootout. This would be a battle between the most famous high school player in America and the best high school player in America. This would be a chance for Sebastian Telfair to prove that a 5-foot-11 teenager could survive and thrive in the land of the NBA giants.

o   o   o   o   o

The Prime Time could brag on two straight LeBron James appearances.

Jeff Hewitson, who ran the Prime Time, made sure he landed Dwight Howard the year after he was through with LeBron. The Prime Time would give Howard a chance to secure his position as the number one pick in the June draft.

The top player in the Class of 2004 didn't create half the stir caused by the top player in the Class of 2003—LeBron drove a brand-new Hummer, Howard a 1984 Ford Crown Victoria. But Howard was all Cadillac on the court. There wasn't an amateur player in America, maybe in the world, who looked so much like a center and handled the ball so much like a guard.

"There's no way you can take Emeka Okafor ahead of this kid," said one scout from an NBA Central Division team. "He can do everything, and you can tell he's a good kid. No tattoos, clean-cut, his dad's a state trooper, his uncle's a district attorney.

"Dwight's a slam dunk. He's got the whole package."

He also had braces. That's what struck me when I first met him: his youth. Howard was so big, so good, and so sure to be world famous, I'd forgotten that he was an 18-year-old *Finding Nemo* fan until he smiled and flashed those braces.

Howard had established goals of becoming the first black president of the United States, of convincing the NBA to make the crucifix part of its league logo, and of becoming a better player than LeBron James.

"I think I can surpass him," Howard said. He didn't sound inclined to waste any time trying.

"I always wanted to be the first pick in the draft," Howard said. "I've worked myself up to where I'm at the 5-yard line and David Stern is waving his hands saying, 'Come on in for a touchdown.' So I don't want to drop the ball."

◦　◦　◦　◦　◦

Sebastian Telfair hadn't dropped the ball after his Louisville trip; he spent the last 2 weeks of January breaking records and getting even. But

Telfair did open that stretch by shooting far too much in an overtime loss at Grady, scoring 11 of his 34 in the extra session and pissing off his teammates in the process.

"This NBA thing is killing us," Nyan Boateng told me. "We understood on the (UCLA) trip that Sebastian had to play for the NBA scouts, but he's got to play team ball in these games in our backyard, when there's no scouts here. That's how we won the state championship last year after he fouled out—by playing team ball."

The following day, Boateng had to be talked out of quitting the team by his football coach, Shawn O'Connor, who'd had this conversation with his wide receiver many times before. Boateng always seemed to get more love from the football coaches in his life. He said he received two calls on his cell from Greg Toal, coach of national powerhouse Don Bosco Prep in Ramsey, New Jersey, asking if he'd be interested in transferring to a school that would give him greater exposure. Those calls would be an obvious breach of high school rules on recruiting.

Toal denied making the calls. "We don't do business like that," he said. "I never met the kid. I wouldn't even know what he looks like. Where is he, in the Bronx? Brooklyn? That would be a 5-hour commute. Somebody's having fun with this. It sounds like *Fantasy Island*."

When told of Toal's remarks, Boateng said, "Really? He's bugging. I was with him at an awards dinner, and I know his son. He definitely called me twice. I guess he doesn't want to make a big deal out of it."

At Lincoln, Morton usually didn't want to make a big deal out of Boateng's desire to be a central part of Lincoln's offense. But this time around, Morton was on Boateng's side. He said he ripped into Telfair for playing selfishly and focusing too much on the UCLA and Louisville games.

In the get-even games with Cardozo and Sheepshead Bay high schools, Telfair returned to his playmaking roots to lead Lincoln to victory. It was a temporary adjustment. Aided by Morton's willingness to run up the score on hapless opponents, Telfair set a Lincoln single-game record with 61 points against the High School of Telecommunication

Arts and Technology, and then broke Kenny Anderson's New York career scoring record of 2,621 points by dropping 49 on Grand Street Campus, this while Morton put on a full-court press with the Railsplitters holding a 51-point lead.

Telfair was rising on everybody's draft board. Two days before the Prime Time game, the Los Angeles Clippers' director of player personnel, Barry Hecker, and their New York–based scout, Evan Pickman, dropped by Lincoln's practice to watch their potential point guard of the future.

Pickman was Telfair's biggest fan; Hecker was a skeptic who'd been won over at Pauley Pavilion. Telfair was aware of their presence. He acted like a playmaker possessed in the first half of practice, and when he fired a perfect one-handed bounce pass on the break to a streaking teammate, Hecker threw on his black parka and motioned to Pickman that it was time to go.

"He's seen enough," Pickman said through a smile.

The Clippers would see more in Trenton, where Telfair had put on some second-half show the year before against St. Anthony of Jersey City, ripping one of the nation's best teams, Jeff Hewitson recalled, "with a bone shooting out of his foot."

Rick Pitino sent his assistant, Reggie Theus, to monitor the Lincoln-Southwest Atlanta Christian game. Louisville had lost its Plan B at the point, Oak Hill's Rajon Rondo, to Kentucky, so the Cardinals were hanging on the thinnest hope that Telfair would crap out and crash-land in college. But Theus told me he wouldn't ask the Lincoln star if he was planning on entering the NBA draft.

"Why would I?" he said. "I don't want the kid to lie to me, and that's what he'd have to do."

o   o   o   o   o

Sebastian Telfair hit Dwight Howard with a first-quarter blitz of hesitation drives and jump shots. "He's quicker than Isiah Thomas," Theus said as he watched behind the baseline. "Quicker than anyone in the NBA?" I asked. "As quick," Theus answered. "It's like he's in fast-forward. You can't teach hesitation like that, dipping your shoulder. . . . Only the man upstairs can take credit for that."

Telfair completed a 3-point play with 34.2 seconds left to give Lincoln a 20–15 lead. Early in the second quarter, Telfair threw a no-look pass to Antonio Pena for a basket, then hit him again with one of his Linda Blairs to put Lincoln up by 8 and to leave the fans and the NBA executives buzzing in expectation of more.

"No way I'd put Jameer Nelson ahead of Telfair; Jameer doesn't have quickness like that," said John Nash, the Portland GM. "I have Telfair way ahead of him. Sebastian's already better than Damon Stoudamire."

"I just saw Jameer Nelson," Randy Pfund, the Miami GM, told another executive, "and he's the best point guard in college and he can't hold a candle to this kid. Sebastian runs the pick and roll better than most point guards in the NBA."

Telfair's quickness and verve would leave Howard appearing dizzy, at least until the Southwest Atlanta Christian center threw him down on a wild and vain left-handed attempt with 2:30 left in the first half. Only 20 seconds later, Telfair struck back with a hanging layup to punctuate a crossover so nasty it caused his defender to fall. With 5.5 seconds left and the entire place expecting Telfair to shoot, the Lincoln point guard used another brilliant hesitation drive to draw the defense and kick out the ball to reserve Jamel Jackson, who drained a 3-pointer to send the Prime Time crowd into a tizzy.

"Watching Sebastian in this game," said Jeff Lenchiner, CEO of InsideHoops.com, "was like watching a character in a video game. He just hit a thrust button and launched himself into warp speed."

Just like in Los Angeles, Telfair needed only one half to dazzle the entire NBA with his explosiveness, creativity, and vision. A year after watching from the front row while his friend, LeBron, dropped 52 on Westchester High, Telfair was planting his flag in the Trenton soil, encouraging the sneaker guys in attendance to drool just as much as the scouts.

"He's the people's player at this tournament," said Nike's George Raveling. "He was sitting in the stands before the game, and the whole section was filled with people trying to get his autograph or to just see what he looks like."

"He has all that drama about him that makes him special," said Reebok's Chris Rivers. "We want him. We can't get any closer on him without living on Coney Island. . . . But it's a business decision, and Nike gets who they want 95 percent of the time.

"I'd be surprised if he didn't go pro now, and that's going to open up dreams for other guys. There's a smaller eighth- or ninth-grader who's going to say, 'Shit, if he can do it, I can do it.'"

Telfair slowed down a touch in the third quarter as Howard moved his team into position to steal the game. With 1:56 left in the third, there was a moment of open-court truth that might have erased any doubt that Howard, and not UConn's Okafor, should be the first pick in the June draft. The Southwest Atlanta Christian center grabbed a rebound and started dribbling upcourt when Telfair came up to meet him inside the midcourt line.

With a simple change of gears and a subtle shift to his right, Howard kept his dribble and blew past the Lincoln point guard as if he weren't even there. The Warriors took their first lead in the fourth quarter, and Howard began to make his mark inside against the game Pena and the rugged reserve, Lawrence Alamilla, who hit their 6-foot-11 foe as much as possible to cover for their inability to see him eye to eye.

"We bodied him and collapsed on him," Alamilla said. "I took some elbows to the back, my face, my neck, and my arms, but I didn't back down. I was talking to him, saying, 'You're not going to the league. Stay here with me. You're not that good.' He didn't say anything, but his facial expression said it all."

As it did on Telfair's bold romp down the lane with 54 seconds to play and Southwest Atlanta Christian up by one. The Lincoln star took his dribble straight at Howard, launched himself into the air, switched the ball from his right hand to his left in a Jordanesque way, and made the acrobatic layup while Howard remained glued to the floor.

An exchange of free throws—one for Lincoln, two for Southwest Atlanta Christian—tied the score and set up the dramatic finish. Telfair smiled in anticipation of something he had never before experienced. Despite all the winning basketball he'd played in his life, Telfair's next buzzer-beater to give his team the victory would be his first.

But what about that smile? "It was like a dream," Telfair would say. "I knew a great moment was about to happen."

He was in the right corner, 20 feet from Theus, when that great moment left his hands from beyond the 3-point line with 5 seconds to play. The Southwest Atlanta Christian guards had made the lethal mistake of allowing Telfair to get the ball. Sebastian already had 27 points to go with his 9 assists. He had no time for his 10th assist, plenty of time for his 28th, 29th, and 30th points.

"Those are the moments that make you," Telfair would say. "You can't be scared of those moments."

Telfair hit the 3 and then watched Southwest Atlanta Christian hurry up an inbounds pass and a long and vain prayer. Telfair tilted his head forward, smiled, and gently wiggled his fingers as if telling his teammates to come smother him.

The Railsplitters mobbed Telfair before he went off in search of his mother, Erica, for the kind of postgame hug she hadn't received all season. Lincoln's last regular season game was the first attended by Erica, who felt so burned by the nondrafting of Jamel Thomas that she refused to take part in the winter-long celebration of her Bassy's ball-playing gifts.

"I didn't even see the shot," Erica said. She was in the bathroom when she heard the building quake. "I came out and asked a lady which team won," Erica said. "She said, 'Lincoln.' And I said, 'Okay.'"

Okay it was. Outside the locker room, Telfair said he knew his shot was good the second he released it. Felled by David's stone, the vanquished Goliath, Dwight Howard, had become a true believer.

"I think he's top 10, top 20 for sure," Howard said of Telfair. "Man, I've seen Sebastian play, but I've never seen him play like that. I was like, 'Wow.'"

The Telfair family was feeling the same vibe in the bowels of the arena, between the court and the loading dock. Telfair, Danny Turner, and their mother huddled with Andy Miller for a 15-minute strategy session.

The Telfairs asked Miller for direction, and the agent-to-be asked for a week or two to come up with a plan. "At first, I thought he was a 3- or 4-year college player," Miller said. "Now he's talked about as a possible lottery pick. It's amazing what momentum can do."

And what it can't. Erica emerged from this meeting hoping that her son had hit the lottery, but refusing to let herself believe it. The pot of gold had been within reach before, only to be yanked away like a carrot on a string. She wasn't about to get hurt again.

"It's a tough decision," Erica said, "but I believe it would be better for Sebastian to go to Louisville. Give him a chance to grow a little more. But if (the NBA) is the Lord's plan, what can I say?"

What could Theus say to his boss, Pitino, when he delivered the awful news that Telfair was so good at the Prime Time Shootout that there was virtually no chance he'd play for Louisville? Pitino had been talking by phone to his top recruit on a regular basis. He was feeling his own hopes dim with every call.

But the Prime Time performance was the clincher. Those 95-to-5 odds Pitino gave in December, when he was almost smug in his belief that Telfair would be his point guard, had turned all the way against him.

"Sebastian's going pro," Pitino said, "and we're resigned to that. I don't mean to sound corny, but you're in this business to see young people fulfill their dreams. So I still feel very good about Sebastian. He was worth the gamble, because no point guard had ever made the jump.

"We're not holding out hope now; I seriously do wish him the best. But until he has to declare, you never know what's going to happen. A turned ankle, a bad workout, whatever. I told Sebastian, 'Let's hope for the best. Let's hope you go in the lottery, but let's keep all our options open.'"

◦   ◦   ◦   ◦   ◦

Get Tiny. Tiny Morton hadn't seen the movie *Get Shorty*, so he didn't understand the headline in the Sunday morning *Daily News*, above the image of the Lincoln coach set against a bull's-eye. The man who had just won a big game on the YES Network the night before, who had just conquered Dwight Howard, was back in the crosshairs of the Brooklyn summer coach bent on destroying him, Ziggy Sicignano.

"I was the author of that story," Ziggy boasted.

Anonymous sources don't often throw news conferences after the fact, but Ziggy was proud that he had delivered on his pledge to set a moving screen on Morton's run at history. Ziggy had gone to the Department of Education and the NCAA with allegations that Morton had violated their rules, and both governing bodies were investigating those allegations.

Ziggy claimed the Lincoln coach had violated recruiting rules and had improper contact with agents, virtually the same claims he had used to fuel a Department of Education investigation of Morton 2 years earlier. This two-page story mentioned the coach's new Escalade before it hit the second paragraph.

At the start of the following practice, Morton was nowhere to be found. He was meeting with Corinne Heslin while his players gave Kenny Pretlow the substitute teacher treatment and horsed around in the girls' gym.

Danny Turner sat outside the gym and took issue with Renan Ebeid, who was quoted in the *Daily News* story saying, "We support the kids," when asked if the Lincoln administration supported Morton. "She's never been on our side," Turner said. "She's been consistent that way."

When Morton finally arrived at practice, 45 minutes late, he began putting the Railsplitters through two-on-two drills, coaching as if he didn't have a care in the world. Morton eventually moved his practice from the girls' gym to the main gym, once the girls were done there exercising their equal-opportunity rights. On the way down the hall, near the security guard station at the front doors, the Lincoln team passed a frayed posting titled "The No Bullying Promise."

"I will eliminate bullying from my own behavior," it read. "I will encourage others to do the same."

Morton could bully with the best of them, but he saw himself as a teacher, an educator, a role model for the young black men who lived in a place where role models were in short supply.

So he couldn't understand why the walls of his own school were closing in on him. A part of Morton felt glorified by the *Daily News* piece: It's not every day when a high school coach gets two pages in a Sunday edition of one of America's biggest newspapers.

Morton would keep the article in his handbag. He would inquire about getting it framed. He would pull it out and point to the small photo of Michael Jordan atop one of the pages, a photo alerting the reader to a story on another page. "They played me bigger than Jordan," Morton said through his glow.

When I told him that the piece had elevated his profile, Morton smiled and put his finger to his lips and said, "Shhhhhh. Don't tell anyone."

Later, I asked Heslin about having her basketball coach as the subject of yet another investigation. "Dwayne knows my feelings that this is an educational institution," she said, "and that when you're having an ice cream sundae, the ice cream is the education and the cherry and whipped cream are sports and other activities. . . . If I had proof Dwayne was mistreating the kids or doing something that was hurting the kids or was criminal, then I would really have to just step in. He's under investigation now. There's allegations of recruiting. . . . We'll wait to hear from the Department of Education."

Ebeid put public distance between her office and Morton's in the story. She had been quoted in the piece saying, "I do not think a high school coach should be involved in AAU basketball. The coaches get dirty with each other."

I asked Ebeid if she was considering the option of firing Morton. "He hasn't done anything bad enough to fire him from my observation," she said. "If the investigators feel they find stuff on him, that's their call. I hope it doesn't come down to that. He's done nothing but positives for the school. He's won championships, and it's going to be hard to fill his shoes. . . . But I won't be surprised if (the investigators) tell us in the summer that we need to do something."

Kenny Pretlow, normally the quiet assistant coach, was enraged at the mere suggestion. "Tiny gets blamed for every fucking thing that's wrong with high school basketball, and it's not right," Pretlow said. "He doesn't do any illegal recruiting, but he's won and kids know who he is. They come up to him and say they want to play for Lincoln. What's he supposed to do?"

Clearly Morton wasn't cornering the market on high school recruiting in New York. One high-ranking Lincoln official said that the school administration assumed Morton was doing some recruiting, "but we also know everybody else is doing some recruiting, too."

Morton was the one in the crosshairs, so I asked him if he thought he was in trouble.

"No," he said. "For what?"

"Because you're being investigated by the NCAA and Department of Education."

"That's rumors. . . . I don't have any meeting set up with the Department of Education, but I'm not messing around with the NCAA."

"Would you consider giving up the Juice All-Stars?"

"No way. . . . It's not that I want power. I'm not that type of person. I want to have a chance to help kids out. Other coaches want power."

"Sonny Vaccaro's telling everyone you're receiving $80,000 a year from Adidas for 5 years. Can you confirm exactly what Adidas is paying you?"

"Nah, can't do that. It might not be true. (Sebastian) might go with Adidas and I might get more money."

Tiny laughed at the thought.

"How concerned are you about going through another investigation?"

"I've got my lawyer ready, so I don't have to go through all that. Charge me or do something."

Morton laughed again. He would remain in a jovial, talkative mood all day. Same went for Telfair.

But there was a form of denial in the glee. The night before, Coney Island reality came crashing through everyone's charmed basketball existence.

Three young men were shot 25 feet outside the Telfair family door.

o   o   o   o   o

"When I saw the cops," Sebastian Telfair said outside the gym, "I went like this." Telfair made off down the hallway like an Olympic sprinter exploding out of the blocks. More laughter, more denial. This was the easiest way for Telfair to deal with the fact that he could have been on that elevator where three acquaintances had taken bullets, two at the price of their lives.

Ethan, Telfair's 9-year-old brother, often played within that elevator and hallway. Erica Telfair had just come down from her mother's apartment on the 11th floor before the shootings took place. Danny Turner and his brother, Deon, walked through the building's front doors minutes after the shootings, and arbitrarily chose to take the stairs over the elevators.

"It could've been any one of my kids," Erica said.

Including the golden child whose name was all over the TV, the radio, and the papers because he happened to grow up right where those bullets tore into three young men.

Robert Vaughn, 23, and his 18-year-old stepbrother, Isaiah Holmes, were murdered. Aaron Granton, 29, survived his critical wounds. Police believed the shootings were drug-related and/or gang-related, but the stepbrothers' family and friends swore in the papers that the memories of Vaughn and Holmes shouldn't be sullied in any such way.

The shootings took place around 7:05 the night of February 8th. Erica was in a back room watching TV when Ethan called out to her. "Mom, did you hear that? Four shots."

Ethan's mother actually went to open the front door before her child advised against it. She listened to Ethan, for a moment, anyway.

"I heard a boy crying out, 'Please, someone help me. Help me,'" Erica said. "I finally opened the door and saw one of them lying there, and then I called the cops. I've got six sons. Danny and Deon were coming up the staircase. If they saw those kids on the elevator a few minutes earlier, kids they knew, they probably would've gotten on with them."

Sebastian wasn't in the building at the time; he was said to be with his girlfriend, Samantha. Sebastian's father was away, visiting family in South Carolina.

As the cops were putting Surfside Gardens in lockdown, Rasheem (Bubba) Barker, Sebastian's best friend, heard an urgent knock on his door four blocks away.

"I was in my house when somebody called and said something stupid, something like, 'Sebastian just got shot,'" Barker said. He ran out of the house and toward 31st Street before these sudden thoughts stopped him cold: "I just talked to Sebastian. I know he's not home. It can't be him."

Barker returned home. Ten minutes later, a cop was at his door.

"Rob and Isaiah were like my brothers," Barker said. Before the shootings, Rob had stopped by Barker's to borrow his jacket. Barker called Rob's cell phone a number of times that night; he'd left his keys in the jacket pocket. The cop wanted to know about the calls and the keys.

"Me and my aunt didn't know what was going on," Barker said. "The cop said, 'Do you know Robert? He just got shot.' He didn't say he was dead, just that he got shot. I said, 'What hospital?' and the cop said,

'Kings County.' I started getting dressed to go to the hospital and my aunt said, 'Bubba, Rob's dead.' She knew that when they say Kings County, that's where the morgue is. The cop started asking me questions, like, 'Why was I calling him?' but I started going crazy. I was in the house for 4 days. Bassy left school one of those days to see me because he knew I was going crazy."

Jack Ringel, the coach at Grady High during Vaughn's time there, remembered a good player who "started to drift" during his junior and senior years, becoming academically ineligible to play in either season. Ringel recalled that Holmes had more talent than his older stepbrother but also failed to remain eligible.

"I knew their father for 25 years," Ringel said, "and he was close with both kids, and not one of those fathers who didn't care. He was always trying to get them to focus on their studies."

Ziggy Sicignano, the Brooklyn USA coach who had Telfair and Holmes on his team, recalled Isaiah as "one of the five nicest kids I've ever come across." Ziggy cited Holmes's death as another reason why Erica Telfair's stated preference to remain in Surfside Gardens, even if Sebastian became a multimillionaire, did not jibe with reality.

"They think you can live in the Coney Island projects when your son has millions," Ziggy said, "and they have no clue."

In the days after the shootings, the bullet-scarred elevator was shut down. A sign posted by cops from the 60th precinct told residents there was a $2,000 reward for any information leading to an arrest and conviction.

"A lot of times street justice settles these cases," said Telfair's father, Otis. "Guys don't want people put in jail. They want them out on the streets, where they can take care of it on their own."

On the streets outside the building with the sign that read, "Surfside Gardens. Home of People Who Care." Sebastian Telfair passed that sign on his way to his apartment the night of February 8th, 2 hours after the shootings. He made his way through the heavily armed cops and walked up the narrow urine-scented stairway, the one that welcomed visitors with profound graffiti-artist greetings such as "suck my dick."

"Those were two friends I grew up playing ball with," Sebastian said. "One of those kids, Isaiah, reminded me of Ethan because he was so small. I mean, it's so terrible."

In the wake of this double murder, Sebastian Telfair didn't want to say more than that. He was 18, and Coney Island reality could interfere only so much with his NBA fantasy.

The city tournament was about to begin. Lincoln desperately wanted that historic three-peat, and its point guard had to keep his eye on the prize.

The power of the sneaker man to make an NBA franchise, and break another, was never more evident than the day Sonny Vaccaro decided Kobe Bryant needed to become a Los Angeles Laker.

On the eve of the 1996 draft, the New Jersey Nets were set to make Bryant the eighth overall pick. John Nash, the Nets' GM, and the new coach and VP, John Calipari, dined with Bryant's parents that night, and they agreed on far more than the choice of appetizers.

"Joe and Pam were begging us to take Kobe," Nash recalled. And why not? The senior from Lower Merion High in suburban Philly lived a reasonable drive away from the Nets' home in the Jersey marshes, and no other team sitting in the top 10 appeared willing to gamble on the reed-thin 6-foot-6 teenager.

But Adidas, in general, and Vaccaro, in particular, experienced an 11th-hour epiphany involving the future of the client they'd signed for $10 million. They concluded that East Rutherford, New Jersey, just wouldn't cut it. So Vaccaro and the good friend who was serving as Bryant's agent, Arn Tellem, came up with a plan.

Vaccaro and Tellem knew Jerry West and the Lakers had fallen head over heels for Bryant. So they found a willing business partner in the Charlotte Hornets, holding the 13th pick, and then bluffed their way through a high-stakes hand of fool's poker.

Tellem called Nash on draft day. "If you take Kobe," the agent told the GM, "he'll stand up and say he'll never play for the New Jersey Nets."

After so many years of so much dysfunction, the Nets were terrified of being embarrassed by a high school kid. This was Calipari's first draft.

The former University of Massachusetts coach was selling a new day, a new order, a promise to rid the organization of what he called a "culture of losing." Calipari couldn't bear the thought of his first big NBA day blowing up in his face. His fears were heightened by the fact that the draft was taking place at the Meadowlands, his home court.

The Jersey fans would welcome a safe pick from a comfortable Big East school—like Kerry Kittles of Villanova.

"And John fell for the bluff," Nash said. "We knew if we passed on Kobe, he'd slip to Charlotte, and we knew Sonny Vaccaro was involved. Joe got a job with Adidas, and that was all part of the package.

"David Falk was representing Kerry Kittles. He was telling us, 'If you don't take Kerry, I'll never help you guys sign a free agent again.' It was a typical Falk move."

As a Philly guy himself, Nash suspected Kobe was a once-in-a-generation talent. Tellem had called at 2:00 P.M., and by 6:00 P.M. Nash knew what was going down. He knew Vaccaro and Tellem had a trade in place, and he wanted to draft Kobe anyway. "Kobe would've played for us," Nash said. "He would've had no choice. Where was he going to go?"

Vaccaro and Tellem came up with a place for Bryant to go: Italy. Kobe spent his formative years there while his father finished off his journeyman basketball career. That was the backup plan. Plan A called for the sneaker man and the agent to deliver their client to the big-market, prime-time Lakers.

To help convince the Bryants that this was the way to go, Vaccaro gave Kobe's father, Joe, something better than a free predraft dinner. "I hired him for $100,000 a year," Vaccaro said.

"And I get sick every time I think about it," Nash said. "Cal could still be coaching the Nets, and I could still be their GM. Those decisions alter an organization and the people who work for it. Kobe has since admitted publicly that he would've played for us."

In fact, Bryant told me, "Jersey would've been fine with me. Close to home, family and friends coming to the game. No problem."

No problem? Calipari and Nash took Kittles and were fired long before Jason Kidd's Nets made appearances in two straight Finals. Nash ultimately landed in Portland as GM, and Calipari resurfaced as a 76ers assistant and then as head coach at the University of Memphis.

In Los Angeles, Bryant won three championships with Shaquille O'Neal and Phil Jackson and became a worthy heir to Michael Jordan as the greatest perimeter player in the game. To Vaccaro, that end more than justified his means.

"I think the results speak for themselves," he said.

o   o   o   o   o

One way or another, Sonny Vaccaro would determine Sebastian Telfair's destination just like he had determined Kobe Bryant's destination. Vaccaro said he had a deep personal affection for Telfair. He said he would either pay Telfair millions, or he would make sure someone else did.

This was the same man who signed a North Carolina Tar Heel named Michael Jordan for Nike—"It changed my life, it changed Nike's life, and it changed Michael's life," he said. This was the same man who signed Kobe, Kevin Garnett, and Tracy McGrady out of high school for Adidas.

This was the same man who needed to make a big score at Reebok, if only to pay back his former employers.

Nike terminated his 13-year run in 1991, Vaccaro said, "because they got corporate over the years, and I didn't meet that image." His bosses at Adidas embarrassed him into leaving, at least in Vaccaro's mind. In 2003, Vaccaro said he was told he had the $100 million and change it would take to win the sneaker war's defining battle. He was told he'd get everything he needed to sign LeBron James.

"Only on the day of the presentation (to LeBron) did my bosses tell me I had a lot less to offer," Vaccaro said. The minute he left that presentation, Vaccaro knew he was done at Adidas.

On October 7, 2003, Reebok released a statement confirming it had hired "sports marketing legend" Sonny Vaccaro to be the company's senior director of grassroots basketball. This was Reebok's way of upping the ante in the wild and crazy game of summer ball, a game getting bigger by the hour.

The three major shoe companies—Nike, Adidas, and Reebok—kept pouring cash into the hundreds of high school and summer teams they sponsored, this while more and more NBA players were "giving back" by donating five-figure sums to their former summer programs. With so much currency flowing through the system, the temptations to cheat multiplied. Summer basketball took on the feel of the wild, wild West.

This lawless place was universally known as AAU basketball, even though the Amateur Athletic Union—an organization governing 32 sports and 500,000 members—didn't govern it. Everyone from college presidents to 14-year-old point guards described the summer leagues, camps, and teams as AAU ball, a fact that amused the AAU president and CEO, Bobby Dodd, more than it angered him.

"We're to summer basketball what Xerox is to copiers and Kleenex is to tissues," Dodd said. "But it's a total misnomer. We don't run any teams. We don't select coaches. We don't pay the bills of teams. All we are is an event organizer, and we only run a handful of events."

Dodd said that the players and coaches who compete in those events have to be members of the AAU, "and we've eliminated people who haven't met our requirements." Asked if the AAU had any role in an event such as Vaccaro's Big Time Tournament in Vegas, Dodd said, "Absolutely not. Hell no. Is that strong enough for you? We have absolutely nothing to do with (sneaker) tournaments and camps like those."

Dodd railed against the widely held belief that summer basketball's ills—everything from illegal recruiting to excessive travel to coaches with drug records—carry the AAU label. Dodd said the AAU has cracked down on coaches convicted of felonies and on teams that recruit players from all over the country. "Basically, we try to do it the right way," Dodd said. "You see things out there like people ranking the number one 12-year-old in the country and you say, 'My God, what are we doing to our kids?' And the scouting service gurus that keep popping up are an absolute travesty to the game.

"It's not the AAU, and yet writers and college coaches and administrators call it AAU. It does give us a lot of publicity."

And enough name recognition to earn the corporate backing of Nike, an AAU sponsor.

The sneaker guys wielded influence all across the summer ball map. Vaccaro was the most recognizable of those sneaker guys, the face most likely to show up on a magazine show. His strategy at Reebok was as simple as his early strategy at Adidas, where he signed a procession of summer teams to answer Nike's choke hold on major college programs. With Nike and Adidas entrenched in the Division I and summer markets, Vaccaro figured he would attack on the junior-high front.

"I'm going younger and younger because I have no choice," he said.

Vaccaro started something he called Camp Next for players finishing up the seventh, eighth, and ninth grades. He created one to be held at UC-Irvine for the West Coast kids and another to be held on his ABCD stomping grounds, Fairleigh Dickinson in New Jersey, for the East Coast kids.

Vaccaro also signed up the summer teams that starred O.J. Mayo, the Ohio freshman sensation often compared to LeBron James, Greg Oden, the 6-foot-11 Indianapolis sophomore already expected to be the number one pick in the 2006 draft, and Derrick Caracter, the New Jersey phenom. He committed $100,000 a year over 5 years to each of their teams. "The senior class (of 2005) is the worst senior class in the last 10 years; not one kid in it is ready to go to the NBA," Vaccaro said. "So this was the perfect time for me to get the younger kids."

But none of this meant that Sebastian Telfair had dropped off his radar. Far from it. Telfair was his baby, the first 4-year prodigy he'd raised through the ABCD system. When he was with Adidas, Vaccaro had given Tiny Morton the Juice All-Stars in the hope that Telfair would always remember which company had first bankrolled his dream.

Now that he was with Reebok, Vaccaro hoped his personal relationship with Telfair would trump company loyalty and shape the point guard's decision.

"Sebastian's the most charismatic kid I've ever met in my life," Vaccaro said. "He's got everything going for him except 3 more inches. . . . I swear to Jesus I told the kid this: 'Take the best business deal you can. I'll help you. LeBron wouldn't have gotten $100 million from Nike if not for me.' . . . I drove up the price for LeBron, and I want to do the same for Sebastian.

"But I want Sebastian. We're starting with an empty plate at Reebok. We have room to create Sebastian on a bigger scale."

Vaccaro was known as a serial gobbler, a recruiter who handed out too many scholarships. Sometimes his philosophy paid huge dividends, and sometimes it didn't. No, Vaccaro's shopping sprees weren't always ahead of the curve. Adidas wasn't all that sad to see him go, according to one company official, because it felt Vaccaro's major signings were neutralized by the cash he burned on the likes of Kwame Brown, Travis Outlaw, and Kendrick Perkins.

Vaccaro countered that claim by saying he gave $25,000 deals to Outlaw and Perkins only as a reward for being good ABCD campers ("I plead guilty to that"), and that the $400,000-a-year Brown signing was the brainchild of his Adidas bosses.

Conflicting accounts and blood feuds were as common to the shoe business as laces and soles. The dispute best known to the casual sneaker-war observer was the oft-documented one between Vaccaro and Nike's George Raveling, the best man at Vaccaro's wedding. The breakup occurred over the recruitment of Ed O'Bannon. As the head coach at Southern California, Raveling said he needed to sign O'Bannon. As the grassroots chief at Nike, Vaccaro said he couldn't deliver him. O'Bannon enrolled at Southern Cal's main rival, UCLA, and, just like that, best friends became as neighborly as India and Pakistan.

Vaccaro would say he'd never again speak to his Nike competitor. He called Raveling a hypocrite for using his head coach's pulpit to preach against the evils of summer circuit ball, only to dive headfirst into that circuit. On his end, Raveling downplayed the notion of mutual hostility, if only to marginalize the significance of Vaccaro in his life.

Vaccaro versus Raveling was hardly the lone fight on the sneaker-war card. In fact, Nike wasn't even the opponent Vaccaro and Reebok saw on the other side of the ring. Nike was deep in the distance, an opponent to be dealt with in a different time and place. Vaccaro wanted to take on his most recent former employer first.

"I think it will be interesting from the standpoint that a two-man fight is different from a three-man fight," said Adidas executive Daren Kalish. "And to be honest with you, my feeling all along was to coexist with Reebok and Sonny, and I've seen that is not their intention. They might tell me that, but their intention is to fucking cut my nuts off, as soon as they can, and then worry about Nike."

The grassroots board of directors Adidas formed to combat Vaccaro included Kalish and Kevin Wulff, the Adidas director of sports marketing, and major summer players such as twin brothers David and Dana Pump (Double Pump), Wallace Prather (Atlanta Celtics), Jimmy Salmon (the Playaz), Darren Matsubara (EBO), Curtis Malone (D.C. Assault), Karl McCray (Atlanta Celtics), and Criss Beyers (Indiana Elite). Tiny Morton was among the six summer coaches promoted to the grassroots advisory board.

Vaccaro said Adidas gave Salmon a new deal worth $170,000 a year, Prather a new deal worth $140,000 a year, and Morton a new deal worth $80,000 a year; Adidas claimed his figures were exaggerated. "We've extended agreements and given some coaches more responsibility and more money," Kalish allowed. On his way out the Adidas door, Kalish claimed, Vaccaro advised his former colleagues that they should stop giving money to summer coaches. "In my opinion," Kalish said, "he wanted to deal with them. I said to Sonny, 'I don't understand. Why shouldn't I pay them? You taught me that.' So he couldn't really say anything."

Vaccaro could say plenty.

"The fact that I supposedly said, 'Don't pay the AAU guys,' is the biggest contradiction in the world, since we paid 40 AAU guys when I was there," Vaccaro said. "I'm going to pay guys at Reebok, too. . . . Adidas gave obscene amounts of money for people to stay with them, but in 18 months Reebok will be where everyone wants to be."

Adidas and Reebok would fight an elimination bout for the right to take on the heavyweight champ, Nike. Everyone knew Phil Knight's Nike as the elephant in the room that would not be wished away. Knight wanted his minions involved with every high school superstar who promised to alter the way consumers looked at their athletic shoe options, and Raveling was already on record saying that Nike was "very interested in Sebastian."

Raveling also said Nike's $103 million commitment to LeBron James wouldn't inspire the company to retreat from any future bidding wars. "I think 10 years from now, that LeBron deal will look like a bargain," Raveling said.

So if Nike truly wanted Telfair, there was a strong chance it would swoosh in and get Telfair.

"Sebastian would be a great addition to our family," said Nike executive Lynn Merritt. "Kids like to emulate who they can be like, and there's a better chance of most kids being Sebastian's size and doing the things he does than what you'll see LeBron James do."

When reminded that Telfair played for an Adidas-sponsored high school team and an Adidas-sponsored AAU team, and spent 4 years in the Adidas ABCD camp, Merritt said, "I kind of like kids who have been in other programs, because it gives me an opportunity to show them the other side of the tracks. And anytime I can show them Nike against whomever else, I feel I'm going to win that battle every time. It's something I always tell the kids. 'If you're going to be really, really, really good, the only place you want to be is at Nike, because there's more opportunity for you to have the resources around your ability to help make you bigger than the game of basketball.'

"That was one of the reasons I think LeBron, being an Adidas kid for a lot of years, decided to sign with Nike."

To be bigger than the game itself.

But Nike did make its mistakes, too. After Kobe Bryant left Adidas, Nike signed him for $45 million, an investment that went up in smoke when Bryant was accused of raping a young Colorado woman. But even before Bryant, the bilingual boy next door, became the improbable face of reckless athlete conduct, he had already proven to be a personality lacking that certain something it took to sell a shoe.

"I signed Kobe," Vaccaro said, "and everything was right. Kobe was right. The Italian thing was right. Except, it wasn't right. . . . The biggest problem Kobe had was Tracy (McGrady). They're the same people, same time, both great players. One resonated with the public, and the other didn't. Kobe didn't resonate. It had nothing to do with his ability, but you can't equate McGrady's shoe sales to Kobe's.

"McGrady had never won a championship, plays on a team that may never get out of the first round of the play-offs, and yet he's the third-highest-selling guy. We went the limit with him and gave him a lifetime contract with Adidas. The very fact that Kobe didn't get what LeBron got is an interesting psychological profile on the whole industry. He got half. Kobe won three world championships, he's everything you want, and he's playing in Los Angeles. LeBron's playing in Cleveland and Tracy's playing in Orlando. It's just something you can't define."

Nike, Adidas, and Reebok would do their damnedest to define it, anyway, sinking millions into a grassroots movement that was shaping where basketball's prodigies went to school, or if they went to school at all. Despite denials from all concerned, Nike, Adidas, and Reebok officials encouraged kids who attended their camps and played for the high schools and summer teams they sponsored to sign with their college coaching clients.

So nobody was surprised when Telfair signed with Louisville—an Adidas school—and its coach, Rick Pitino, among Vaccaro's closest friends. Telfair had been an Adidas billboard on the various magazine covers he graced, wearing its headbands, sweat suits, and shoes.

These images troubled those who believed in the findings of an NCAA committee that declared shoe companies as contributors to a "corrupting influence" on young players. While college coaches were forbidden from supplying recruits with extra benefits, the shoe companies were free to keep plying their high school-age summer players with shoes, gear, and all-expenses-paid trips to places such as Las Vegas.

Nike, Adidas, and Reebok enjoyed unlimited and unregulated access to America's top high school prospects. The shoe companies created summer league teams. They funded those teams. They approved the teams' coaches. They paid those coaches. They paid for the players' airfare, lodging, and meals on their junkets across the land.

The shoe companies did everything but pay the players a salary; such compensation would make the players ineligible under NCAA rules. At a time when the Mike Krzyzewskis of the world were landing huge sneaker contracts, and when major universities were cutting exclusive and excessive campuswide deals with shoe companies, NCAA critics argued that the governing body was feigning sincerity.

"It's the biggest hypocrisy in amateur sports," Vaccaro said.

One high-profile NBA agent echoed Vaccaro's sentiment. "The NCAA took the Judas bag of gold," he said. "They say the shoe companies are behind the evil empire of AAU, but who are they kidding? They've got themselves to blame. Right now, everyone's at the mercy of the shoe companies. If the NCAA stops taking their money and rules that taking shoe money violates your amateur status, that would be the death of AAU and everyone would move on.

"But why even control these benefits? In every other industry in the world, if you're a talented musician, writer, or rap star, or if you're a soccer player in Europe, you get compensated. Why can't Sebastian Telfair capitalize on his talents without jeopardizing his eligibility? Amateurism is only for the players who generate the money. . . . It's a total joke."

Only the NCAA never laughed when accused of embracing a double standard.

"Nobody ever said that people who administrate have to be amateurs," said Bill Saum, the NCAA's director of agent, gambling and amateurism activities. "This is about the participants being amateurs. To run amateur athletics at the level of expertise we run it, you have to have revenue streams.

"If some of (the players) want sneaker contracts, they can go to the NBA."

When reminded that Krzyzewski didn't have to leave Duke for the Lakers to land a Nike deal, Saum said, "Last time I checked, we live in the United States. It's a capitalist society."

But that's exactly the point made by amateur athletes and the NCAA critics who believe those athletes should be paid for their services. It's a capitalist society. Why do only the adults get to be capitalists?

o   o   o   o   o

The intensity of the shoe companies' search had turned the summer circuit into a saloon without inhibition. Agents paying off summer coaches, and using runners as bag men. Coaches taking cuts of their players' sneaker deals. Unregulated money managers cutting shadow deals with agents, coaches, and players. Sneaker reps steering prospects to this agent and that school. Coaches stealing players from other coaches with promises of better gear, better shoes, and better road trips.

The most visible embodiment of this anything-goes culture was found on past and present payrolls at Nike and Adidas. Nike came under intense scrutiny for once funding a Kansas City summer coach named Myron Piggie, who had been convicted of dealing crack cocaine and indicted on a charge of shooting at a cop before being jailed for paying players and defrauding universities. In the spring of 2004, Adidas promoted Curtis Malone of the D.C. Assault summer team to its grassroots board of directors. *The Washington Post* first reported that Malone had been convicted in 1991 of selling crack before pleading guilty to charges of reckless driving and eluding police.

In New York, the wealthy founders of the city's sneaker-backed powerhouses, Lou d'Almeida of the Bronx Gauchos and Ernie Lorch of the Riverside Hawks, retreated from the summer stage after being hit with allegations of sexual abuse that they vehemently denied.

These tales only hardened the perception of summer circuit ball as an enterprise lacking in redeeming social value, and inspired college coaches to point hypocritical fingers at their summertime counterparts.

The Division I landscape was so littered with scandal, so overrun by crooked coaches, that the notion of summer coaches being solely responsible for the amateur basketball mess was absurd.

"At the college level," said Paul Brown, head of the Nike-sponsored Gauchos, "there's 10 times more wrongdoing than you'll find in AAU."

"The AAU coaches have the supply and the college coaches have the demand," said Gary Charles, head of the Reebok-sponsored Panthers. "If you didn't have the demand, then AAU coaches couldn't cheat. So when they do cheat, they're cheating with college coaches."

And with agents, of course.

"With all these high school players turning pro," Charles said, "agents feel now that they have to get involved with the kids at an earlier stage."

In an attempt to clean this septic tank, the NCAA started naming overzealous non-scholastic coaches as representatives of universities' athletic interests and holding them to the same standards as boosters. The NCAA stopped non-scholastic coaches from recruiting summer players from all over the country, outlawed summer camp contact between college and summer coaches, and began threatening to deny uncooperative non-scholastic coaches entry into its sanctioned tournaments and camps.

The NCAA also killed the practice of exhibition games with summer clubs, games that landed those clubs appearance fees between $10,000 and $25,000 and left the schools to face suspicions that they were trying to buy recruits. Jim Calhoun and the defending national champion University of Connecticut Huskies faced those suspicions when ESPN.com reported they paid $22,000 to the Beltway Ballers, a club affiliated with the summer team that featured Rudy Gay, UConn's number one recruit (Calhoun denied that the Ballers' exhibition game played a role in the signing of Gay).

"I don't know that we ever proved that a college team bought a player through an exhibition game," said the NCAA's Bill Saum, "but this reduces the possibility of that accusation being made."

The biggest losers in the demise of the exhibition tour were Adidas's David and Dana Pump, identical twin brothers who lorded over their own California summer ball empire and routinely sent out six teams of former college stars to play major college programs. Sonny Vaccaro said the Pumps grossed more than $800,000 by playing as many as 92 games in one year.

"We only played 50 to 60 games," David Pump countered, "and we didn't even come close to that figure. But we were doing well."

Asked if he was disappointed in the NCAA's decision, David Pump said, "Of course. We were doing it for the right reasons. . . . We were giving jobs to a lot of kids, and schools could play them instead of the Indonesia national team. . . . We were playing North Carolina, Duke, Kansas, and Kentucky, but it got to a point where too many people were holding schools hostage over recruits."

If nothing else, the Pumps had another source of income the NCAA hadn't attacked, and another avenue to advance Adidas's influence across the major college market. The Pumps were in the business of buying Final Four tickets from coaches and athletic directors and selling them to corporate clients. Never mind that the profiting coaches and athletic directors were among those preaching reform; the practice was in violation of National Association of Basketball Coaches (NABC) policy.

"The Pumps basically have ingratiated themselves with enough coaches and ADs to do this," said one major college coach who sold his tickets to the brothers. "They put together this massive retreat every August, where coaches and ADs get together and everything is done first class. That's where they developed their network of people to buy from.

"At one Final Four, the Pumps called me and asked if I wanted to get rid of my tickets. I had two seats behind the basket that were 50 rows up, and two seats at midcourt that were 30 rows up. They wanted to give me three grand for them, and I said, 'I don't think so. I want to go to the game.' Then they call back and say they'll give me two grand plus two seats right behind the basket, 20 rows up. That was a deal. They're marketing whizzes."

This former major college coach estimated that one-third to 40 percent of Division I coaches and ADs sell their tickets for profit. When I asked Saum if he had information that coaches were selling their Final Four tickets, he declined comment. But if coaches were indeed cashing in, Saum said, "that would be inappropriate and against our policy of no ticket scalping."

Asked if he bought tickets from coaches and ADs, David Pump said, "I don't want to comment on that." Asked if he was concerned that the NABC might move to eliminate that practice if it were made public, Pump said, "No comment."

Vaccaro was not as quiet on the subject of his former friends and protégés. "They shouldn't be allowed to do what they're doing," he said.

Some on the summer circuit felt the same way about Vaccaro, who also moved his fair share of Final Four tickets to and from college coaching friends.

"Sonny destroyed college, high school, and AAU ball as much as he built it," said Ziggy Sicignano, coach of Brooklyn USA. "He's Dr. Frankenstein, and he created 1,000 monsters."

Vaccaro conceded that he was to blame for some of the problems that plague the summer programs. "But I'm the only one in my industry calling for reform," he said.

Reform? Nobody figured the summer circuit would see true reform any time soon, not with Nike, Adidas, and Reebok frantically chasing the Sebastian Telfairs of the world in order to find the next Michael Jordan.

Not with the shoe companies leaving the sport of youth basketball in one big knot.

14

Andy Miller had just flown in from Spain when Sebastian Telfair greeted him at the Lincoln gym like he would a long-lost friend. Telfair initiated one of those high handshake, forearm, and shoulder bump welcomes that suburban white guys were forever screwing up, and yet Miller nailed his attempt so cleanly, the Russian judge would have awarded him a perfect 10.

Miller had arrived from JFK after meetings with a Spanish company interested in an intercontinental partnership with the young American agent. Some of the company's officials had done a background check on Miller and told him they'd heard he liked to insulate himself from other agents.

"That's absolutely right," Miller told them. "Why would I want to talk to people who are saying behind my back that I'm a pedophile?"

Tough business, this agent racket, and it was about to get tougher. With Telfair having played himself into lottery-pick contention, Miller was ready to talk serious business. He would take Telfair and Tiny Morton to the famous Sheepshead Bay restaurant, Lundy's, in an attempt to convince the point guard that no agent was more qualified to land him the highest draft position and best endorsement deals.

But Miller maintained he was taking a cautious approach. Telfair hadn't yet officially named him his agent, and the draft was still months away. "Everybody's talking a good game now about where Sebastian's getting drafted," Miller said, "but is anyone making a guarantee? When it gets down to crunch time on draft night, will they be there?"

It was February 26th, 2 days after Lincoln had beaten Wadleigh to reach the quarterfinals of the city's championship tournament. Telfair appeared to be hotter than ever, and he told me he was confident he had moved into the top 10 of the draft.

It was a fine time to be young, fast, and gifted with the ball. The previous Sunday, Telfair had joined Jay-Z for LeBron James's debut at Madison Square Garden, and listened from his front-row seat as LeBron teased him about his future NBA plans. "He said, 'How would you like to play with me in Cleveland?'" Telfair said. "He's always talking about me playing with him next year, but I don't know if he's talking to his GM about that."

Telfair had too much fun in the Garden for his day to be ruined by an awkward pregame scene. When Knicks officials saw Telfair sitting in one of the two comped seats they'd provided Jay-Z, they knew they had a problem. An NBA team, much like a major university, cannot give money or gifts to high school athletes considering a jump to the pros. So Dan Schoenberg, the Knicks' director of public relations, approached Jay-Z and asked him to pay for Telfair's seat. Right then and there, the rapper ripped off a check for $1,700, saying, "I don't want to cause Sebastian any problems."

Problems. Telfair would have enough of those before the night of February 26th was over. With the season playing out so perfectly, with *Sports Illustrated* even talking about putting him on its cover, Telfair would feel his world rocked by the news that his brother, Sylvester, was back in police custody in the wake of yet another Coney Island shooting.

And if that wasn't enough to handle for one night, a dizzying blitz of business meetings with agents and shoe reps would begin, according to Telfair, with interference coming from a most unwelcome source.

o   o   o   o   o

Sylvester Telfair was out of jail only 9 weeks when Detective Darryl Haynes of the 60th Precinct arrested him February 26th, after the 8:55

A.M. shooting of Ahmad Rennick at 2930 West 30th Street, across the street from the Telfairs' Surfside Gardens home.

According to the District Attorney's Office, Rennick said Sylvester entered his building, pointed his handgun at him, and shot him in the face. Rennick said Sylvester did this from close range, after the victim looked through a stairway window. Rennick escaped with flesh wounds and was treated at a local hospital and released.

This apparently wasn't the first time Sylvester had run afoul of the law since being paroled in December after serving 3 years on weapons charges. Father Robert Lacombe, the Telfair family friend who had mentored Jamel Thomas at Providence College, said Sylvester was apprehended by housing authority cops in January for violating a provision banning him from Surfside Gardens.

Only this was a far more serious allegation. This was attempted murder. This was a case that could have put Sylvester behind bars for 25 years.

The Telfair family moved to keep the arrest quiet, in the hope Sebastian would get through the play-offs before it became public. Sylvester's indictment would be sealed until early April, and the District Attorney's Office wouldn't release any information until then. But inside the family, Sylvester's arrest was a constant source of conversation. Most family members were incredulous that Sebastian's older brother couldn't stay out of trouble until the NBA draft had come and gone.

"I did everything for Sylvester, just like I did for Sebastian," Danny Turner said. "But he was just one of those kids you couldn't save. I think there was a little jealousy over the attention Sebastian got, but I blame myself for Sylvester. I was supposed to be his protector, and I failed. I know this time, Sebastian was real mad at Sylvester for getting in trouble, and so was my stepdad. But then they found out Sylvester didn't really do it."

Sylvester told investigators that he wasn't the triggerman. His credibility wasn't helped by a criminal record that dated back to 1996, when he was a high school student who had completely lost his way.

Renan Ebeid, Lincoln AD, remembered Sylvester making frequent trips to the dean's office before he got arrested and kicked out of school. Bobby Hartstein, former Lincoln coach, spoke often with Sylvester in his role as special ed dean. "It was a constant fight for him to stay out of trouble," Hartstein said. "He was a street kid, and he was like that long before Sebastian got the attention he did."

Sylvester was a role player for Tiny Morton. He was never considered a star, a basketball prodigy, like Sebastian or Stephon Marbury. He was a promising shortstop in the Gil Hodges Little League, but didn't play baseball at Lincoln.

"Sylvester and Sebastian were like night and day," Turner said. He mentioned that 2-inch scar over Sebastian's left eyelid. "They used to fight all the time," Turner continued. "We were teasing Sylvester once when Sebastian was killing him on the court, and Sylvester threw a mad elbow. I took Bassy to the hospital, and we were there for 6 hours. He got stitches and a scar for life."

Sylvester was the one who could never piece himself back together. In this latest brush with the law, Sebastian also paid a price.

"After (Sylvester's) latest arrest, I said something to Sebastian like, 'Try not to let it get to you,'" said Corinne Heslin, the Lincoln principal. "Of course, how can you not let it get to you? . . . All I know is this has put a lot of pressure on Sebastian at a time when he's in the middle of all this frenzy."

The frenzy that was the courtship of a high school point guard. A frenzy of agent and sneaker company meetings that kicked into high gear during that Lundy's sit-down with Miller on February 26th, when Telfair had an unexpected audience with someone who wanted to help guide his career.

Father Robert Lacombe.

o   o   o   o   o

So many people in and around the Telfair family did not want Andy Miller representing Sebastian. Miller was on the Eric Fleisher team that signed Stephon Marbury out of Georgia Tech, and that was strike one.

Miller's approach represented strike two: He didn't court Sebastian's parents or siblings when establishing a relationship with the point guard, whom he met through Marbury when Sebastian was the ripe old age of 9. Sebastian more or less grew up "on the periphery of my circle of guys," Miller said, meaning that the boy wonder would have phone and face-to-face contact with the likes of John Wallace, Al Harrington, and Kevin Garnett.

Strike three? Miller forged an alliance with Tiny Morton to gain greater access to Sebastian, hardening the Telfair family members' suspicions that the agent was trying to cut them out of the process.

Otis and Erica and Jamel Thomas were on the anti-Miller side. Morton and Danny Turner were on the pro-Miller side. Such was the hostile environment the night of February 26th, when Miller arrived at Lundy's with Sebastian and Morton in the expectation, he said, of brokering a peace with Erica.

"We didn't want to go with Andy Miller," Erica confirmed. "You have a tendency to run with things you hear, and I'd heard bad things about Andy Miller, that he did this and that. He had a little something to do with Stephon, and we had a tendency to shy away from that."

Miller did carry some baggage into this meeting. At 34, he'd already been waist-deep in high-profile controversies.

Fleisher sued his former protégé after their bitter divorce, claiming Miller had stolen Garnett and 15 other clients from him, and a jury granted Fleisher a $4.6 million award (some $2 million of that figure was assigned to Miller). Fleisher also claimed that Miller used a modeling agency and the lure of "romantic liaisons" with its talent to entice players to sign with him.

Miller had been linked to the NCAA investigation of St. John's guard Erick Barkley, who became a client, and was himself the target of an investigation in Florida after making at least 45 phone calls to Gators star Mike Miller while not registered to act as an agent in that state.

Despite the judgment against him, Andy Miller maintained that he didn't steal clients from Fleisher and that the lawsuit was "a shakedown of me . . . when I was young and naive." On the Barkley front, Miller claimed he never provided any improper benefits to the St. John's guard and that "nobody found me doing anything as far as giving kids money or doing things morally and ethically wrong."

The case of Mike Miller (no relation), the agent said, was a case of wasted time and newsprint. "I had a previous relationship with him when he was in high school; he was a big fan of Garnett's," Andy Miller said. "I wasn't registered in Florida, but I had no idea I was supposed to register. . . . I made phone calls. I never made any promises to Mike Miller. I went down to Florida and met with the DA down there and the head of agent and registration policies and explained the situation, and that was the end of it, other than I wasn't able to represent Mike Miller. Sonny Vaccaro swooped in and delivered him to Arn Tellem."

And on the most salacious charge—that Andy Miller was acting as a de facto pimp—the agent delivered his stock answer. "The only model I've ever introduced my clients to was my wife. It's a sad day when good-looking millionaires with good bodies are going to need help getting laid by a fat Jewish guy."

Miller wasn't fat, but he was living large despite his troubles. A former unpaid intern for Fleisher, Miller still represented 15 NBA players, including Garnett, a megastar working on his second nine-figure contract with the Timberwolves.

Despite the turmoil that had, at times, engulfed Miller's career, Telfair was impressed by the agent's roster of clients. He began talking seriously to Miller about skipping college sometime around the 2003 draft. Telfair asked the agent if he thought it was possible then for a guard to make the jump, and Miller told him he didn't believe so.

Only in December, after Telfair returned from his ankle injury to beat Darius Washington on ESPN2, did Miller begin to change his mind. Telfair's game at UCLA and his dramatic conquest of

Dwight Howard in Trenton had brought the point guard, the agent, and Morton to Lundy's in the middle of the city's championship tournament.

When Miller walked through the door, he found Erica eating with a man the agent wasn't expecting to see: Father Lacombe.

The 40-year-old priest had become a family friend after meeting Jamel Thomas while Thomas was playing ball at Providence. Lacombe was teaching theology at the school when he said the Friars' coach, Pete Gillen, asked him for tutoring help during the latter part of Thomas's sophomore season. The player had a learning disability and was in dire academic straits.

"Pete Gillen had asked me, 'Can you take Jamel under your wing? We think we're going to lose him,'" Lacombe said. "I met with Jamel, and for several weeks he was sullen and uncommunicative."

Thomas attended the rectory sessions every Sunday through Thursday night for 2 years, and grew more and more enthusiastic as the tutorials helped him in the classroom. "It clicked right away for Jamel," Gillen recalled. "Western Civilization was brutal, with a ton of reading, and Father Lacombe really helped Jamel get through that. Father did great. He was a real big plus."

During his senior year, Thomas told the *Providence Journal* that Lacombe "tutors me every night. He's an unbelievable guy. He takes his time out to help me with my studies. I've never really had a person like him in my life. It's an honor for me to have him in my life." Thomas later told me in a brief interview, "(Lacombe) helped me at Providence my junior and senior years. He helped me a lot." Asked if he considered Lacombe an advisor of his, Thomas said, "He's not really an advisor. He's a friend."

But some members of the Providence athletic department weren't quite sure what to make of Lacombe's presence around Thomas and the basketball team. They would see the priest at the Capital Grille bar after games, attempting to hold court. "He was always talking to alumni and trying to impress people with a story," said one regular at the postgame hangout. "He was kind of like the guy who crashes a party."

One member of the basketball staff during Lacombe's time at Providence wondered why the priest needed to drive a BMW. "He was a mystery to a lot of people," the staff member said. "He would talk about meeting someone at the Ritz in New York, or having a drink with Bibi Netanyahu or someone like that. It seemed like he had two audiences with the Pope every month."

Another member of the basketball staff said the Providence coaches were under the impression Lacombe was a man of independent wealth. Lacombe confirmed he drove a BMW but said he was not a wealthy man and that, as a secular priest, he didn't take a vow of poverty. The staff member recalled that Lacombe had twice grilled him on Thomas's NBA prospects. "(Lacombe) was talking about Jamel's plan, how he was going to this camp and signing with that agent and that he was going to get a tryout," the staff member said. "He was hitting me with all this stuff, telling me about Jamel's situation and how upset he was that Jamel wasn't drafted. . . . I thought it was a little much."

A Lincoln High official close to Lenore Braverman, the English teacher who had taken in Thomas, said Braverman was concerned that Lacombe was gaining too much influence in her former student's life. "She thought it was a little over the top," the official said. "He was at Jamel's graduation party at the Braverman house, and they thought that would be the end of it. Then we saw (Lacombe) at a couple of Sebastian's functions, and we were wondering what he was still doing around."

Braverman declined to be interviewed. But Lacombe insisted he was merely interested in doing what Gillen had asked him to do: help a young student-athlete in need.

Lacombe said his lessons were spiritual as well as educational. When their Providence tutoring sessions were complete, the priest said he would ask Thomas to stop at the church on the way back to his room and simply spend 10 or 15 minutes there. After graduating, Thomas asked Lacombe if he would baptize him a Catholic.

The priest performed the baptism. Lacombe said he was working part-time for the Archdiocese of New York when he'd meet Thomas in Manhattan, at least until the player was comfortable inviting him to Coney Island. "He didn't want me to see where he came from," Lacombe said. "Now I count (the Telfairs) among my most trusted friends. (Erica) calls me every day and tells me what's going on and what Otis is doing and how her mother's doing and what's going on with Sebastian."

Otis Telfair would say this of Lacombe: "He's like family. Whatever we do, he's involved in. He'll do anything for us. Any kind of problem or anything, he's involved. He's there for us. Father is always there for us. Always."

In the winter of 2004, with Lacombe stationed at St. Timothy's Church in Warwick, Rhode Island, Erica informed the priest that Miller was the leading candidate to represent her son, and that she was concerned Miller's hiring would amount to a poor career choice. So there was no surprise at Lundy's when the priest and the agent didn't hit it off on introduction.

"I think I know who you are," Lacombe said. "You're Eric Fleisher." This was the wrong thing to say to Miller. "No, I'm not Eric Fleisher," the agent said, "and you don't know anything about me."

Miller, Telfair, and Morton sat at a separate table in an otherwise empty restaurant and began talking basketball and business. Lacombe eventually approached their table and asked Telfair if he could have a minute with him. Telfair reluctantly complied, rising from his chair and walking with the priest to a spot some 50 to 60 feet from the table he'd just left.

Miller said nobody was within earshot of the conversation held between Lacombe and Telfair.

"It was a very animated conversation between (Sebastian) and Father Lacombe," Miller said. "Sebastian had his back to the table. Father Lacombe was facing me, looking at Sebastian."

Miller said Telfair's body language suggested that he was "very uncomfortable and embarrassed." The agent estimated the conversation lasted 25 minutes.

"Sebastian came back to the table," Miller recalled, "and he said, 'Let's get the fuck out of here.'" Morton had returned to the table after visiting with Erica. Danny Turner, a late arrival at the restaurant, would eventually make his way over.

"Sebastian was very upset, very hurt by the conversation (with Lacombe)," Miller said. Sebastian was offended by the priest's meddling.

After Sebastian returned to his seat, Miller said Lacombe made three more trips to the table to invite everyone to join him and Erica for coffee and dessert. "(Lacombe) said something to Sebastian like, 'Your mother would like that,'" Miller said, "and Sebastian said, 'I know what my mother would like and I don't need you to tell me.' (Sebastian) was despondent, distressed. He was like, 'Do you believe this shit?' He was almost disgusted."

Disgusted? I asked Sebastian if he was mad at the priest. "I was mad with him talking to me," he said. "But I was like, he's a priest, so I sit there and listened to everything he has to say, and after that I was like, all right, peace.

"So many people are out there trying to be a part of you. They give you money, but what they don't realize is that money is like fucking peanuts to the money that you're going to be making over here."

Lacombe contradicted Miller's claim that the agent was scheduled to meet with Erica that night; the priest said his trip with Erica to Lundy's was unscheduled. Lacombe did confirm that he had a conversation with Telfair in the restaurant, that Miller's name came up in the conversation, and that Telfair wasn't happy with the priest during the conversation. Lacombe said he merely wanted to express his concern to a young man who was removing loved ones from an important decision in his life.

At the time, Telfair had told me he was spending some of his days in Turner's apartment and in his girlfriend's apartment in the Bronx. Lacombe said he'd been told Telfair might have been living in his own apartment.

"The gist of that conversation was that I was perturbed with (Sebastian's) behavior," Lacombe said. "I only heard it from one side of the coin, from Erica and Otis. I was disappointed he moved out of the house, and also disappointed he limited contact at that time with Jamel on that matter. I said, 'If Andy Miller's trying to pull you away from your family in a critical process, I don't think that's a class act. What he should do is make them part of the process.'"

Lacombe said his conversation with Telfair took place "in the midst of family tension" because family members didn't want the point guard to hire Miller. "There were other offers," Lacombe said, "including SFX, Arn Tellem."

Lacombe said he regularly offered support and counsel to the family. He confirmed that he'd offered some financial assistance to the Telfairs in the past. "I've helped them in terms of practical things and so forth," the priest said.

Lacombe mentioned to me in one phone call that Erica had wanted him to go to the garment district to buy her a dress for Sebastian's June graduation. He mentioned in a different phone call that he'd never given the Telfairs any financial assistance exceeding $300. Lacombe maintained he was "one of the few people around Sebastian at that time with no financial interest in him whatsoever."

When I first asked Telfair about Lacombe, 3 weeks before the Lundy's meeting, he grew agitated as he stood outside the Lincoln gym. "The priest has nothing to do with me," he said. "I'm calling my mother. Everybody keeps bringing this guy up, and that's my mother's friend. He's talking too much. He's saying . . . it's like, he's got nothing to do with me. That's Jamel's friend."

Lacombe later said he got involved in the tug-of-war between Miller and Telfair's parents and Jamel when Otis called him and asked if he'd investigate the agent. Lacombe, who said he was an attorney, had a private investigator look into Miller's background, an investigator the priest said had worked sex abuse cases in the church. Lacombe said the investigator came up with Internet stories on the Eric Fleisher lawsuit and the Mike Miller case. Lacombe confirmed that when he greeted Andy Miller at Lundy's and mistook him for Fleisher, "(Miller) got all bent out of shape."

The information on Miller that Lacombe provided Otis somehow ended up in the hands of Morton's brother, Jeff, according to the priest. Lacombe said Jeff Morton, who went by the nickname Slice, told Miller "that I had provided information against him." Miller said he never received any such information from Slice.

"I didn't know anything about (Miller) before," Lacombe said. "I didn't know about Fleisher and the investigation in Florida. That was my only involvement. . . . I told Sebastian, 'If these people are pulling you away from your family, that is not a good thing.' My primary concern was why he was living away from the house. He explained it had something to do with his father, and I fully understood where he was coming from.

"I had arrived that afternoon, had a meeting with Cardinal Egan that evening, and took Sebastian's mother out to dinner, and it was completely unplanned that we went to Lundy's. They came in after us. (Erica) said, 'Please don't mention this to Otis. It will look like we were making plans that didn't involve him.' That was the extent of that."

Lacombe said he helped the Telfair family deal with one of Sylvester's legal problems. But when Otis once handed him the business card of an agent and asked him to contact the man, Lacombe said he refused and told Otis he would not get involved with agents.

"I don't know enough about (Miller) to make a personal judgment about him," Lacombe said. "What I've been told by everyone in regard to Andy Miller was unfavorable. I'm the type of person who suspends judgment until I know it as fact. One of the things I intentionally did was to withdraw altogether from Sebastian's signing of this and that. I don't want to give the perception that the Catholic Church has an interest in the situation. That was advertent on my part.

"But I was led to believe (Miller) was trying to distance Sebastian from the family to try to sign him. There was an accusation from people in Coney Island that Tiny Morton was hand in hand with Andy and Adidas on this."

Lacombe wasn't the only one who had heard the allegation that Miller had made a deal with Morton. Gary Charles, the longtime coach of the Panthers, a summer powerhouse in New York, accused the agent of being in business with the Lincoln coach.

"We knew over 2 years ago that it was going to be Andy Miller," Charles said. "We knew he was already dealing with Tiny. I take everything case by case, and I don't think most people are happy with the way Tiny handled the situation with Sebastian. Even if you talk to people with Sebastian's family, they don't like the way Tiny handled the situation. . . . Tiny was taking care of Tiny and not necessarily taking care of Sebastian's family."

Miller denied Charles's claim that he had funneled money to Morton or anyone else. "I never gave any inducements to Sebastian or his family or to Tiny," the agent said. "In defense of Tiny, he's an aboveboard kind of guy. I never gave him anything. I know he's taken a bad rap on a number of levels, and I think a lot of it is based more on jealousy than anything else. But as crazy as Tiny is and as unorganized as he is, he's a decent and genuine human being through and through. . . . I don't think Tiny's ever taken any money from anyone. At one point Sonny Vaccaro said I bought him his Escalade, which is really a slap to Tiny. I mean, Tiny's a working man. He's capable of financing or leasing his own car. It's really a derogatory comment."

Morton also denied Charles's accusation, which came after the two were involved in a scuffle during the annual tournament at I.S. 8. A player's desire to compete for the Juice All-Stars despite his commitment to the Panthers inspired Morton to throw a water bottle at Charles, who responded with a leaping kick to Morton's chest.

"The rumor out there is that I got $50,000 from Andy," Morton said. "That's what a lot of people think, and it's bullshit. I haven't taken anything. . . . I've had stuff thrown at me for Sebastian from (college) coaches, too, and turned it down. You wouldn't believe how much some guys would do to keep their jobs."

Charles wasn't the only one who believed Morton had some misguided problem with him. Father Lacombe said Morton harbored "an aversion to me." Only on the night of February 26, Morton wasn't the one angry with the priest.

"Sebastian was perturbed with me on that particular night," Lacombe said. "I was very high-handed. . . . There was a tremendous misunderstanding over what transpired when Sebastian went back to the table. At that point, he was really putty in Andy Miller's hands. . . . It was more about, 'What are you doing not living at home? What are you doing not listening to Jamel's advice? You're now listening to all kinds of other people. What are these other people looking for in you? You have to understand that the people who should advise you are people who will not profit on your success financially speaking.'

"I reminded him of Jamel's draft situation, and how sad that was that Jamel did not involve the family in his decision-making when hiring an agent. I said, 'Now you seem to be repeating his mistakes.' It had nothing to do personally with Andy Miller."

I asked Lacombe if he believed it possible that Telfair somehow left their conversation confused over what was said, and whether that possible confusion might have been caused by Lacombe's alleging that Miller had offered money to Telfair. "That might've been the case," the priest said. "I did say something to that effect. Like, 'Who's offering you money to pay for an apartment? You haven't graduated from high school and you haven't even signed with an agent or declared for the NBA draft.' My suspicion was someone was offering money at the time."

Erica said that she didn't hear Lacombe's conversation with her son, and that if the priest was concerned about Miller's relationship with Sebastian, "maybe he got that idea from me because I was concerned about Miller, too. . . . But Father never did anything with Sebastian. He was Jamel's friend. . . . He's been a really nice friend to us. He was good to Jamel in school, and always there to help Jamel out. He doesn't have too many dealings with Sebastian."

Lacombe didn't care to have too many dealings with me either. When I asked Lacombe for names of peers or parishioners who could speak on his behalf, he declined to provide them, saying he wanted to limit his presence in this book. Phone calls seeking comment on Lacombe were not returned by the head of Providence's theology department and the pastor of St. Timothy's.

Lacombe blamed the meeting-gone-sour with Telfair on a misunderstanding. He maintained he was simply trying to guide a family friend through a seminal moment in his young life. "I think he's a wonderful young man," Lacombe said of Sebastian. "A very generous kid. A nice kid, enthusiastic. He's naive in many ways, but growing in sophistication. I've nothing negative to say about him."

Sebastian appeared to feel differently. The matter ended as a jump ball between the point guard and the priest.

The world was moving too fast for the quickest point guard in New York. While Sebastian Telfair was chasing history in the city play-offs, trying to lead Lincoln High to a three-peat, the agents and sneaker men had suddenly applied their full-court press.

This wasn't just any press. This was Nolan Richardson's old 40 minutes of hell at the University of Arkansas. Behind the meetings at Lundy's with Andy Miller and Father Lacombe came a torrent of pitches from some of the biggest pitchmen in sports.

All while *Sports Illustrated* was preparing to put Telfair on its cover.

Sonny Vaccaro, at different times the face of Nike, Adidas, and Reebok. Super-agents Arn Tellem, Bill Duffy, and Aaron Goodwin.

One by one they all came after Telfair, trying to unseat Miller and, by extension, Adidas. "A frenzy," Miller called it. Miller was told that someone had offered Sebastian hundreds of thousands of dollars to gain influence over his choice of agents and to steer him toward a different representative.

Sebastian said he rejected the offer.

"It wasn't enough money for me to get in trouble, for one," Sebastian said. "My family can't live off (of that). . . . The position I was in, it was like, four years ago, if somebody offered me (that kind of money), I would've took it. Just take it and just to do something, you know what I'm saying? . . . I could've took the money but I was like, no."

So the fun began. Jamel Thomas had traveled all the way from Greece to lend his voice. Vaccaro worked through the agents he had long granted favored nations status, Duffy and Tellem, who were part of a weeklong blitz of Manhattan hotel and restaurant meetings designed to win Telfair's affection, or sway the right confidant or family member with the influence to shape a deal.

By most accounts, Duffy was a disaster. "Terrible, bad, awful," said Miller, who wasn't present for Duffy's presentation.

"He wasn't that awful," said Tiny Morton, who was present and among Telfair family members. "But he made it clear he wasn't going to be doing Bassy."

Duffy was going to let his assistant, Calvin Andrews, run the Bassy show, and there wasn't any imaginable way Team Telfair was going for that.

So Vaccaro rushed in a replacement. "Arn Tellem flew across the country," Miller said. "He's not a dynamic presence. It's likely he didn't give a great presentation."

Actually, Tellem scored major points with the Telfairs when he talked of splashing Sebastian's face across subways and trains. "My mom liked that," Danny Turner said. But Morton was among the skeptical.

"Tellem was good if you're blinded by the lights," the Lincoln coach said. "He said he'd put Bassy's face on trains, TV, billboards. . . . How are you going to tell a kid you're going to put his face on trains when you don't even know where he's going to be drafted?"

Good question, but Tellem was convincing enough to put himself in the game.

Like Duffy, Goodwin failed to make the cut. He told Team Telfair he could do for Sebastian what he did for his number one client, LeBron James, but nobody was buying that. The Telfairs all knew that LeBron would always be Goodwin's priority.

Meaning the Telfairs all knew that Goodwin wasn't going to be Sebastian's agent.

The race came down to two horses. "Andy and Tellem are in the lead," Sebastian said.

It was March 4th, a couple of days before the city quarterfinal game against Boys and Girls High, and Telfair was in a good mood. The new edition of *Sports Illustrated*—his edition of *Sports Illustrated*—was finding its way into homes all across America, elevating the celebrity of the Lincoln star to a place even he couldn't fathom.

The *SI* cover, in high school. Telfair had entered that rare LeBron

James air. He now belonged to the general marketplace, well beyond the confined borders of basketball-only fame.

"Watch Me Now" read the cover, graced by a picture of a wide-smiling Telfair in his Lincoln uniform, dribbling a ball while he soared above a pier. Telfair hung suspended in a blue sky against a typical Coney Island backdrop of water, sand, and project buildings. "Sebastian Telfair," read the name below the player's right elbow. The question and answer were stated below his left hand: "Can a 6-foot high school point guard from Brooklyn make the leap to the NBA? Yes he can."

SI had used a trampoline for the cover shot. During the photo shoot, Telfair was savvy enough to wear Adidas sneakers for some shots, Nikes for others. He was trying to play one shoe company against the other.

When I found him inside the Lincoln gym, Telfair said he was thrilled with the story despite the fact that *SI's* Chris Ballard wrote that there was distance between Telfair and his cousin, Stephon Marbury.

"It is what it is, you know what I'm saying?" Telfair said while sitting in the gym bleachers. "Me and (Stephon) can try to hide it as much as possible, but people know."

A half-hour earlier, after Telfair was done helping Nyan Boateng work on his jab steps, the point guard said of his teammate, "If I could jump like him, I'd be the best player ever. I'd be Jordan."

To which Tiny Morton replied, "You'd be Stephon Marbury."

A very good line.

Back in the bleachers, sitting next to Telfair, I wondered aloud what Stephon thought of the *SI* cover.

"I've got something good for you," Telfair said. "Me and him were supposed to do the cover together, and he didn't want to do it. The (*SI*) guy called me and said Stephon wants to do it alone, and he said, 'What do you want to do?' We were about to say, 'Forget it,' but then the guy was like, 'We're going to put you on the cover alone.' They called Stephon and canceled."

An *SI* source confirmed that Marbury "emphatically shot down" the idea of sharing the cover with his little cousin, and that Marbury was interested in appearing by himself.

"I guess you should've let him win those playground games," I told Telfair.

"Maybe I should have," he said. "It would've been better. I think he'd have been a lot of help right now for me. . . . But I tried to hide this for so long. This *Sports Illustrated* thing doesn't make me look bad, it makes him look bad. I can't tell you how many NBA people, that's the first thing they ask. 'Is he anything like Stephon?' When they find out I'm not, they're relieved."

We talked about the Trail Blazers and their apparently strong interest in drafting Telfair. "I'm not coming out," the point guard said through a laugh. "No, I ain't coming out. Me and my man Rick Pitino are going to get our national championship, then I'm going to come out. Sound good?"

Telfair laughed again. In preparation for the draft, he'd already been working out with the IMG Academies trainer, Joe Abunassar, who'd worked with Miller clients such as Joe Smith, Al Harrington, and Chauncey Billups. "When's this book coming out again?" he asked me.

"Next season," I answered.

"I might be in Louisville then," Telfair said. "This will mess me up. . . . But (Abunassar) can't come in here, in this gym. We go to other gyms. . . . He comes in every other weekend."

If Telfair ultimately paid Abunassar's fees (the trainer bills on an end-of-the-year basis), he would have likely retained his college eligibility. But if Telfair wasn't a professional in the early evening of March 4th, he was only hours away from unwittingly becoming one.

"I'm going to a meeting right now," Telfair told me, "to get my first offer for a sneaker contract."

I asked if Adidas, Nike, and Reebok were still in the ball game. "Yes," he said, "and a lot more than before. It's crazy."

"Who are you meeting tonight?" I asked. "(Adidas's) Daren Kalish?"

"I'm going to meet with the people who sign the checks," he said. "We're going to meet at their Manhattan hotel right now."

Telfair surveyed his post-practice gear and wondered if it represented appropriate attire for a big business meeting. "I look like a bum," he said, "but I'm poor."

Not for long.

Kalish was part of the Adidas meeting after all. He was joined by fellow executives Kevin Wulff, Jim Gatto, and David Bond. Miller was present, as was Telfair, his parents, Danny Turner, Morton, and Morton's brother, Slice. They ended up inside an Italian restaurant in midtown, and urgency was the order of the night.

The *SI* cover only intensified the fight over Telfair. Miller needed to regain control after Tellem created some momentum going the other way. Tellem was the agent of choice for Erica and Otis and Jamel Thomas, the cabinet members swayed by Vaccaro's lobbying.

Over dinner, Miller had his chance to strike a lethal blow to the opposition. He had brought Adidas executives to the table to let all members of the fractious Team Telfair know that they were prepared to make Sebastian a rich young man.

"There was a lot of hostility in the room," Miller said. So the agent took a backseat and let the Adidas men do his bidding.

No contract was presented between appetizers and dessert. "But numbers did come up in the meeting," Miller said. According to two people at the table, Adidas passed around outlines of an offer as if they were dinner menus. One person said the proposal guaranteed Sebastian $15 million over 6 years, with incentives that could have made the deal worth $32 million. "They gave each one of us a copy," the person said. "(Erica and Otis) were practically ready to sign."

The second person confirmed that Adidas executives handed out an outline, and that the guaranteed portion of the proposal had Sebastian taking in $15 million over 6 years. But the second person claimed the deal maxed out at $42 million "if Sebastian hits the jackpot with all of his incentives. He'd get $2 million up front. . . . Adidas wants him badly. They told us Sebastian is the most marketable guy in the draft."

Miller's point, exactly. He said he didn't see the "presentation packet" that was handed out to the guests of honor—"I was negotiating a contract with (Adidas), so I didn't need to see everything," he said—but conceded it was possible the outline of an offer was included in the packet. "Maybe it was a worksheet," the agent said.

Maybe it was the piece of paper that would bridge the gap between the pro-Miller and anti-Miller camps.

One person at the table said Adidas executives showed off the design they had in mind for Telfair's sneaker. That person would later produce a tall, thin book with a black cover that detailed the shoe company's presentation. The marketing slogan "Impossible is Nothing" was written in white letters across black pages, before photographs of Muhammad Ali and Jesse Owens. A section titled "We are the Past" included shots of Oscar Robertson, "Pistol" Pete Maravich, and Kareem Abdul-Jabbar, this before a "We are the Present" section showed portraits of Tim Duncan, Tracy McGrady, and Kevin Garnett.

The word "YOU" was printed over the next two pages, followed by two more pages carrying the message "Are the Future." The presentation included a picture of Telfair in his black and gold Adidas ABCD camp uniform, and a picture of a black sneaker with three gold stripes meant to be Telfair's sneaker. Finally, across from the image of a smiling Telfair was the picture of a low-cut white leisure sneaker and the words, "Invention is a two-way street. We provide the tools. You light them up. Without you, it's just a shoe in a box. With you, it's a shoe with a soul—making history."

When the Adidas meeting broke up, it was clear no consensus had been reached within the Telfair household. Thomas phoned Vaccaro and told him he'd better call Erica and come in with an offer before it was too late. Vaccaro told Thomas and Telfair he would give it some thought.

Truth be told, Reebok's grassroots chief figured the Adidas deal was all but done. If nothing else, Vaccaro might have faked an offer to force Adidas to increase its bid. Vaccaro figured that once his former employer had told Telfair he was its number one priority, and the marketing prize of the Class of 2004, it would have no choice but to keep throwing money at Team Telfair.

By his own admission, Vaccaro had "an ulterior motive" beyond his curiosity in the Telfair-Adidas talks. Vaccaro wanted to see Adidas pay the price for what he characterized as premature negotiations with a high school star.

"It's illegal," Vaccaro said. "I'm not letting this go. . . . The bad guy here is Adidas."

Vaccaro claimed Telfair had forfeited his amateur status by negotiating with a shoe company in the presence of an agent. Asked if he had informed Telfair of this, Vaccaro said, "I didn't. I didn't want him to have a heart attack. He still had to play play-off games. Tiny was running around all excited and telling everyone, and Jamel got in there right away. I called Bobby Hartstein and told him to shut it down. If I'd told Sebastian (he'd forfeited his eligibility), he would've known and then he couldn't have lied. I just don't think you can blame Sebastian. You can't blame a kid."

Vaccaro claimed Bill Saum of the NCAA had told him that a prospect wouldn't be eligible to play college ball if he had engaged in financial negotiations with a sneaker company. I asked Saum, the NCAA's director of agent, gambling, and amateurism activities, if an amateur could speak with an agent about the terms of a marketing deal. "If (the agent) says, 'I have for you X amount of dollars for a shoe contract with X company,'" Saum said, "now you may have crossed the line."

I asked Saum if a player could have an agent present when contract terms were being discussed with a shoe company. "You can't do that," he said. "(The player) would certainly put his eligibility at risk. You would try to determine how far that crosses the line. If there's an agent sitting in a meeting helping negotiate a marketing contract, whether you have an official agreement or not, you can't do that."

Public Schools Athletic League (PSAL) rules said a student would forfeit his or her amateur status by signing a professional contract (Sebastian hadn't signed), or by "capitalizing on athletic fame by receiving gifts of monetary value." Sebastian was negotiating to receive millions of dollars in gifts, but hadn't yet received them. Would the PSAL interpret its rules any differently than NCAA officials interpreted theirs?

Better question: Why did Adidas rush into negotiations with Telfair and risk his eligibility? In the weeks after the meeting, Kalish and Travis Gonzolez, the Adidas PR man, declined to return several calls seeking comment on the talks. After receiving word of my inquiries, Morton angrily confronted me and claimed I was "looking around too much." Kevin Wulff ultimately denied that Adidas presented any financial terms to Telfair until after his high school season was complete.

Vaccaro didn't buy any of that. "Adidas was bidding against a ghost," he said. "Everyone knows they were so afraid of me, and that's why they went after Sebastian the way they did."

o   o   o   o   o

Fresh from a film session in Room 105, the Hygiene classroom cluttered with chipped, markered-up school desks, Sebastian Telfair walked me to his Nissan with the silver Z—his mark of Zorro—glistening in the sunlight sneaking through the hatchback glass.

The Railsplitters had taken their city quarterfinal game with Boys and Girls High by a 66–54 count, avenging an earlier defeat. It was Telfair's first game since the *SI* cover, and the *SI* jinx applied—sort of. Lincoln won, but Telfair shot 3 for 14 and scored a sleepy 13 points, inspiring Boys and Girls guard Tyrell Cruz to say, "He's a lot overrated, not a little."

Telfair generally dismissed these assessments as the laments of frustrated opponents with dim basketball futures. So on this warm March day, his disposition was sunny—at least until he encountered a couple of heavy-set Lincoln students throwing toilet paper in the trees outside the school's front doors. One of them called out to Telfair, smiled, and pointed toward his handiwork.

"What are you doing?" Telfair said with disgust. "I don't go to the same school as you."

Telfair turned to me. "You see these derelicts? I can't stand that, just ruining property. Then they try to act like my friend."

Telfair was carrying five big cardboard blowups of his *SI* cover; a Lincoln security guard had just finished pestering him for one, acting like the worst kind of groupie. This was after a student in a black skullcap approached Telfair and said that he'd just had a dream, and in it the Lincoln star was buying him a brand-new Bentley.

"I know this is going to happen more in the NBA," Telfair said. "Maybe I need to get my own guard."

We walked up to his Z, parked, as always, in a prime spot in front of the school. Telfair stopped and fixed his gaze on the seven-story brick buildings on the other side of Ocean Parkway. "I'm going to buy my mom one of these," he said. "But she doesn't want to leave our apartment."

He opened the passenger-side door and pulled out a Chrysler brochure. Telfair flipped through five or six pages before stopping to show me a picture of a new Crossfire. "This is what I'm going to get Bubba," he said of his best friend.

Telfair talked of paying back Thomas for the Z and the bling. He said he would give his Z to his younger sister, Octavia, when he was ready to buy his fresh wheels. The money would start rolling in, Telfair said, when he made his NBA and shoe endorsement announcements. He was planning to do both on April 2nd, but said the big date could be pushed into May.

"How much do you think I'll get in a sneaker deal?" he asked me.

This was sort of like a woman asking you to guess her age.

But I had a little inside information, so I played along. "If you asked me at the beginning of the year," I said, "I would've guessed $400,000 a year for 3 years. Now, I don't know. After the *SI* cover and all, I'll say $15 million total."

"Man," Telfair said, "you've been talking to a lot of people, too many people. That's a good guess."

Telfair again started talking about everything he was planning to buy for family and friends.

"You better save some for yourself," I told him.

"Don't worry," Telfair answered. "When you see my sneaker deal, you'll know I'll have plenty left over for me."

16

The public relations man at Madison Square Garden was caught between reality and responsibility, between business and morality. Could he put a high school player's name on the Seventh Avenue marquee? Could he put an 18-year-old ballplayer in the same lights that told the naked city Elvis, Sinatra, and Ali were about to play the world's most famous arena?

Or should he just announce that Lincoln High School of Brooklyn would face Cardozo High School of Queens for the heavyweight championship of New York City ball?

"We decided it wasn't right to promote a high school player," Eric Gelfand said. "We'll let the *Daily News* and *Post* do that."

Good move. Sebastian Telfair didn't need any introduction, anyway. He was about the most publicized scholastic player in the history of the city game, and anyone remotely interested in buying a ticket for the March 17th night game would have already known that Telfair was the main attraction. If Lincoln was the longest-running high school show on Broadway, Telfair was Nathan Lane and Matthew Broderick rolled into one.

"We know we have a chance to make history," Telfair said at a Garden news conference 2 days before the game. When it was mentioned that DeWitt Clinton had won three straight in 4 years from 1916 to 1919— the war inspired the postponement of the city tournament in 1917— Telfair declared he wasn't interested.

He wanted only to talk about seizing this moment in the lights. "You want to win so bad in the Garden," he said.

So, apparently, did Tiny Morton. Before Telfair walked out of the press conference and onto the big Manhattan streets, joking that I should write about the oversize watch Jay-Z had given him, the point guard talked up Morton the way a Big East senior might talk up his college coach.

"I think Coach did a great job of surrounding me with great players every year," Telfair said.

In fact, Tiny had done such a great job surrounding Telfair with talent that he inspired an interested observer to land in Brooklyn 3 days earlier. Only Rachel Newman-Baker, NCAA investigator, didn't come to town to present Morton with a Coach of the Year award. She came only with a playbook full of questions.

o   o   o   o   o

Ziggy Sicignano was presiding over his 10:00 A.M. Brooklyn USA tryouts at the I.S. 271 gym when the NCAA walked through the door. Rachel Newman-Baker didn't exactly blend in, not with her young, blonde, and Jodie Foster-as-Clarice Starling country girl kind of way.

No, Newman-Baker wasn't what anyone around the border of Brownsville and Bed-Stuy would consider a familiar face. She wore jeans and a dark blue fleece pullover with gold lining that proudly carried the NCAA logo. As high school and junior high players raced up and down the floor and responded to the orders Ziggy barked into his microphone, Newman-Baker sat on the luggage she'd wheeled into the gym and placed a 20-ounce bottle of soda between her feet.

The pages of notes she placed on the nearby scorer's table suggested it wasn't too early for a hard caffeine blast. I approached Newman-Baker understanding that there was no shot she would grant an interview. NCAA investigators are not to be seen, never mind heard. She rejected my request and advised me to call Bill Saum.

Saum, the NCAA's director of agent, gambling, and amateurism activities, wouldn't say any more than this: "The division I head up routinely tracks elite athletes and their relationships with nonscholastic coaches."

Tiny Morton was Sebastian Telfair's nonscholastic coach for the Juice

All-Stars. Though the NCAA had no jurisdiction over high school coaches, it had the power to ban summer circuit teams from the camps stamped with the NCAA seal of approval. It was Ziggy's hope that Newman-Baker would dig up enough on Morton to deny the Juice entry into big-ticket events.

As an assistant director under Saum, Newman-Baker had investigated University of Washington football coach Rick Neuheisel in the infamous March Madness gambling pool case that got him good and fired. (Neuheisel was later cleared of wrongdoing by the NCAA.)

"Bill Saum ain't sending no idiot to hang with Ziggy," Ziggy said.

Before she began her interviews, Newman-Baker made small talk with a Ziggy aide and helped the kid work the clock. Ziggy had told her she couldn't just parachute into Brooklyn for 48 hours and expect to secure the trust of young men who weren't inclined to give it, but the NCAA was a busy place. With a scandal a day breaking out across American campuses, Morton wasn't likely to command the NCAA's attention for very long. The Juice All-Stars weren't Baylor, Georgia, or Fresno State.

"But she's very interested in this," Ziggy maintained of Newman-Baker. "She's interested in (Morton's) Escalade." The night before, Ziggy took Newman-Baker to some high school games at St. Francis College, much to the chagrin of the college's head coach, Ron Ganulin. Division I coaches want NCAA investigators on their campuses as much as they want reporters in their locker rooms.

"This sounds like a vendetta against (Morton)," Ganulin told Ziggy.

Ganulin was right. This was a vendetta. Ziggy was out to ruin Tiny Morton, the coach who took Sebastian from Brooklyn USA.

Ziggy had Newman-Baker meet with his assistant, Jermaine Brown, also an assistant at Lincoln's archrival, Grady High. Brown was at the I.S. 271 tryouts with Newman-Baker just hours before Grady and Lincoln were to meet in the city semifinals at St. John's.

Brown said the Railsplitters had made the semis only because their coach was playing by his own set of rules. "Tiny's trying to turn the

PSAL into AAU," Brown said. "You're coaching one of the top players in the nation, so why would you recruit players away from other schools and risk all that?"

Brown claimed Morton had tried to pilfer Ramel Bradley from Park West; Bradley would play for the Juice All-Stars, but never for Lincoln. Brown claimed Morton had chased after stars all over the city, including two who attended Ziggy's tryout, Chris Lowery of Xaverian and Derrick Echols of Grady.

I asked Lowery if Morton had tried to convince him to transfer from Xaverian to Lincoln. "Well, my mother wouldn't let me go," he said. "She wanted me to stay in a Catholic school. Basically, Tiny talked to me about academics and how he could get tutors for me."

Brown responded, "Yeah, Tiny talked about academics. Xaverian is one of the best schools in the city."

Echols said Morton recruited him out of eighth grade, just like other high school coaches had. "Tiny was trying to get me to go (to Lincoln), saying I'd have a chance to play with the best point guard in the nation," Echols said. "He said I'd get good looks as far as going to college. But the reason I didn't go was I was already accepted into Grady."

I asked Echols if Morton had recruited him during his Grady career. "No, not really," he said. "(Morton) would say smart comments like, 'I've got two rings. You could've had two rings if you came.' But I didn't want to get it with Sebastian. I wanted to get it on my own."

Newman-Baker asked Lowery and Echols if Morton had tried to secure their ballplaying services and, if so, by what means. They weren't likely to give her much to work with, but Brown said he would provide a list of players Morton had chased with a free-agent fervor.

Newman-Baker had a plane to catch, so she wheeled her luggage out of the gym and back toward the heartland. "She's got to keep coming back," Ziggy said. "That's the only way to get kids comfortable."

Ziggy swore he would do his part. He said he would keep feeding information to Newman-Baker and Dennis Boyles, the Department of Education investigator. Ziggy said he'd keep calling the FBI contacts he'd made during the Gold Club case to pique their interest in the role of professional agents in youth basketball.

"I'm not going to let this die," Ziggy promised.

o   o   o   o   o

With Jermaine Brown on the sideline, overmatched again by the team Tiny Morton had assembled, Lincoln beat Grady later that day, avenging the bitter loss suffered in the Falcons' home gym.

Telfair jumped into Antonio Pena's arms and then embraced his father, Otis, on the St. John's court, this after the Lincoln fans inside St. John's Alumni Hall chanted "M-S-G." Telfair had picked up his fourth foul late in the third quarter, and he had shot 4 of 11 from the floor, felled again by the *Sports Illustrated* jinx. But he had made a great pass to Jamel Jackson on Jackson's critical 3-pointer in the final minutes, giving Lincoln a 4-point lead.

Morton had defiantly punched the air with his left fist at the buzzer, showing more endgame emotion than he had all year. He had no clue then that the NCAA had been in Brooklyn hours earlier. Morton knew only that anything short of a trip to the Garden would have marked the season a spectacular bust.

Telfair? Of course he wanted to win that third title, but he also needed to get back to playing the way he had against Dwight Howard in February. He looked like a surefire top 10 pick back then. Suddenly, his chances of landing in the lottery were beginning to dim.

o   o   o   o   o

Sebastian Telfair was standing in the Garden, the building that would house the 2004 draft, telling reporters that economics was his favorite course. He told the writers to run with that one, to have fun with it, because he was certain to do both.

Adidas and Telfair's agent-to-be, Andy Miller, were inching closer to a monster deal that would turn the sneaker business on its ear, and Nike and Reebok seemed oblivious to it all.

"I think we're in great shape with Sebastian," said Chris Rivers, Sonny Vaccaro's lieutenant at Reebok.

Of course, Vaccaro knew all about the Adidas meeting and the numbers being discussed. But he was the one who raised Telfair through the Adidas/ABCD system. He was the one who created the Juice All-Stars for the purpose of advancing his relationship with Telfair. He was the one who believed there was a small chance that once Telfair arrived in Chicago the following week for his Roundball Classic, everything could change.

In the wake of his big Adidas meeting, Sebastian had called Vaccaro to tell him of the offer and to assure him he would still play in the Roundball. "It made me feel our friendship will be there no matter what he does," Vaccaro said. "(Adidas) went in there and, it's illegal what they did, you know that don't you? They did talk money. It's the stupidest thing they ever did. But I don't want anyone to take away (Telfair's) high school trophies."

Vaccaro bought plane tickets for Sebastian's family, even bought one for Jamel Thomas to fly in from Greece. But first things first. Telfair hadn't lost a city play-off game since the semifinal round of his freshman year. His Railsplitters were the Lakers of the Public Schools Athletic League, a 100-year-old league of some 183 schools across New York's five boroughs that capped its season with a March Madness–style, single-elimination tournament.

League officials consulted with coaches, referees, and media members in selecting and seeding the field (a .500 record or better in PSAL play automatically qualified a team). The Railsplitters might have been the third seed this time around, and Cardozo the first, but there wasn't a single player, coach, official, or fan in New York who thought of Telfair and Lincoln as anything but overwhelming favorites.

Antonio Pena was "the team's main presence down low," read the 16-page scouting report prepared by Cardozo coach Ron Naclerio.

The report continued: "(Pena) has a long reach. They will lob it to him. Not fast. Can definitely be beaten down the court. . . . Very strong. . . . Must deny him the ball."

The report on Eugene Lawrence: "Can hit the 3-point shot, but inconsistent. Physically very strong. Looks to go to the basket. . . . If Telfair is out of the game, Lawrence becomes the main ball-handler."

On Boateng: "Great athlete. All-American in football as a wide receiver, so you know he likes physical contact. Lean, but surprisingly strong. Good speed. So-so dribbling the basketball."

On Yuriy Matsakov: "White Russian kid. Don't sleep on him. Many games gets 0, 2, or 4 points, but the ESPN game versus Edgewater had a big 10 points and 6 rebounds. . . . Physically not that strong."

Finally, on Telfair: "Good speed. Great acceleration, 0-60 in a flash. . . . Will push off (Be ready!) and even get dirty—kick, push, or punch. Too good a player to have to resort to that, but on several occasions does. Doesn't like when an opponent gets physical with him or gets in his space. . . . A tremendous passer. . . . Never relax on him as he can go from cold to hot very quickly."

Telfair would enter the Cardozo game as cold as ice. If he could deliver a hot shooting night in the Garden, for the championship of the city, he would erase from memory every single brick he tossed at St. John's.

o   o   o   o   o

The slate-gray, snowy day had given way to an electric night, and Tiny Morton let loose a nervous laugh in a Madison Square Garden hallway when I reminded him that a victory would give him more rings than all the Knicks coaches combined (Red Holzman had won the franchise's only two titles).

The Lincoln coach made the sign of the cross. Morton's typical knock-on-wood gesture wouldn't do on this night, not with so much at stake. He zipped in and out of the locker room and barked out ticket requests.

Morton was beyond superstitious; he was a complete wreck. "Don't act like you're in Madison Square Garden," he told his team in the locker room, sounding, of course, like he was trying to convince himself. "I mean, don't come in here with some scared shit."

Soon enough, Telfair shouted, "They're here to watch us. Yeaaaah. Fourteen thousand have come to watch us." Actually, 12,021 fans made it inside.

It felt like a big event all the same. On St. Patrick's Day, the parade of celebrities marched into the Lincoln locker room. Hot Sauce, star of the streetball craze, came in to share ballhandling tricks with Telfair. Spike Lee came in for a round of good-luck handshakes and hugs, and Jay-Z did the same.

Danny Turner tried to push an us-against-the-world platform. "That crowd is not here to cheer you'all motherfuckers on," he said. "They're here to see you'all motherfuckers go down."

With Telfair out in December, Cardozo had beaten Lincoln. With Telfair back for the rematch, the Railsplitters had evened the score. Morton would coach the rubber game dressed in a powder blue shirt and a checkered olive suit he pulled out of a Banana Republic travel bag. Naclerio would face him in his faded Cardozo short-sleeved golf shirt, khaki pants, sneakers, and a beige jacket that had no shot of making it to the fourth quarter.

Hector Roman, one of the team managers, was sporting the best pregame look because he was wearing all of Telfair's bling. Roman was the designated jewelry box for the night. Telfair wore his white Adidas sneakers with the S31T insignia stitched to the sides, this while the rest of the Railsplitters wore their new blue suede Adidas shoes.

Lincoln came out in its navy blue uniforms with a white and gray border; Cardozo came out in its white uniforms with blue and orange stripes. Jay-Z and Spike Lee held the same front-row view they had for Knicks games. They were joined by enough cops to fill 10 presidential motorcades.

The teams felt each other out in the first quarter, like cautious fighters exchanging jabs. Too cautious, in Morton's opinion, as he ripped into his favorite target, Boateng, after the small forward barreled into Cardozo's 6-foot-10 center, Theo Davis, and lost the ball out of bounds. "If you're going to go to the fucking basket," Morton shouted during the end-of-the-quarter huddle, "dunk the shit. Stop looking for a foul."

Telfair looked for a foul and got it early in the second, making the kind of smart play point guards are supposed to make. With Davis already saddled with two fouls, Telfair cut toward the baseline, took a pass from Lawrence, and threw his body into the Cardozo big man to draw a whistle. "Three," Telfair said, holding up the same amount of fingers as Davis headed for the bench.

Only Telfair found his own seat a minute later after picking up his second foul. Lincoln would have been in deep trouble then, if not for Lawrence's daring, ankle-busting drives and no-look passes. "He's balling," Morton said to his bench. Telfair had to answer his own teammate's challenge. With 1.2 seconds left in the half, he followed up his own miss in the lane to give Lincoln a 38–35 lead at the half.

Inside the locker room, Morton diagrammed a set on the grease board before grabbing a stat sheet and launching into Boateng one more time. "Nyan, you got zero, you got one rebound," he shouted. "You don't rebound, you're not playing, plain and simple. . . . I need rebounds. I don't need no fucking dunks or jump shots."

Boateng grabbed an early third-quarter rebound in traffic, and Morton actually complimented him. "That's what we need," he said. "Good job, Ny." If Boateng had heard it, he might have fainted on the spot.

Lawrence continued his brilliant play in the third quarter as his more celebrated backcourt partner began to come alive. Telfair made a wild and crazy left-handed layup off a Lawrence steal, and drilled a 3-pointer with 3:24 left in the third, inspiring a fan in the expensive seats to shout, "About time." Play was soon stopped for the following announcement: Telfair's 3-pointer gave him 3,002 points for his career, making him the first player in New York State history to crack the 3,000-point mark.

"Ladies and gentlemen," the PA man said, "let's have a big round of applause for Sebastian Telfair." Twelve thousand fans stood and cheered in defiance of this cold, hard fact:

Sebastian Telfair had "only" scored 2,760 points.

Mike Quick, the MSG Network's reliable high school man, had fallen for somebody's idea of a practical joke. That explained why Morton was shooting everyone confused looks from the bench, and why Telfair was stomping his foot on the court and calling his team together rather than bask in his hometown's love.

"This is it. This is it," Telfair said in the huddle before the fourth quarter began.

He made a pull-up jumper, two free throws, and a layup while getting fouled on the break to help Lincoln to a 63–54 lead midway through the final quarter. Naclerio was a manic mess in his faded golf shirt, his jacket discarded somewhere on the Cardozo sideline. He was powerless to stop the inevitable.

Otis and Erica Telfair were smiling in their front-row seats as the fans chanted, "three-peat . . . three-peat." With 25.1 seconds to play, the Lincoln starters came out as Telfair held up three fingers, this time for a different reason. Lawrence's father came down from the stands to hug his son. Yuriy Matsakov, the stoic Russian, pawed at the tears in his eyes. Corinne Heslin, the Lincoln principal, hugged her most famous student with 13 seconds to play. Morton, about to pass Red Holzman, kept skipping toward midcourt.

At the buzzer, Lincoln players, coaches, administrators, fans, and hangers-on formed a bouncing group hug. Several players lifted Morton onto their shoulders. Renan Ebeid, AD, hugged and kissed the coach she often clashed with. Antonio Pena embraced Telfair, who scored 10 of his 25 in the fourth quarter. Telfair embraced Lawrence, who finished with 14 points, 10 rebounds, 4 steals, 3 assists, and 1 MVP trophy. "You made a good move," Telfair said of Lawrence's transfer from Canarsie.

Naclerio couldn't have disagreed more. The Cardozo coach, who had called Lawrence's transfer to Lincoln "bullshit" earlier in the season, didn't appreciate the irony in Lawrence's MVP play.

"Unfortunately, Eugene didn't have the year people thought he was going to have," Naclerio said. "But of the five or six really good games he had, three were against me."

This was life in Tiny Morton's PSAL.

"I feel great," Morton said. "I feel loose. I'm going to talk some shit now."

On the court, Telfair thanked God and the teammates he said had "played like they were all Michael Jordans." Telfair credited his coach for challenging him at halftime. "He said, 'Everyone's stepping up except you. So you've got to go out there and show them and play like Sebastian.'"

Because Sebastian played like Sebastian in the end, Matsakov kissed the city championship trophy, Pena held up four fingers in advance of his senior season to come, and the Railsplitters wore gold medallions around their necks and white city championship caps on their heads.

Meanwhile, Telfair's father was gleefully accepting congratulations. I told him we should get together for lunch. "With the way things are going," Otis said, "I think it should be on me."

Business was looking as good as the bling Sebastian retrieved from Roman. Andy Miller was moving Adidas north of a $15 million guarantee, this while his client was prepared to play the sneaker-war game for all it was worth.

Telfair wasn't going to celebrate his historic feat by going to Disney World, but to Sonny Vaccaro's Roundball Classic. At least until big business crashed against amateur ideals, and the shoe industry came unlaced in the court of old-fashioned high school tournament ball.

o   o   o   o   o

Sebastian Telfair was at the airport when his cell phone rang. Pam Vaccaro, Sonny's wife, was calling to tell Sebastian that he'd be declared ineligible for the state championship game if he played in Sonny's Round-ball Classic.

New York State rules prohibited players from competing in all-star games before their high school seasons ended. The Roundball was scheduled for Wednesday, March 24th, in Chicago. The state final was scheduled for Saturday, March 27th, in Glens Falls. Sonny Vaccaro was prepared to fly Sebastian into upstate New York so he could meet his team a day or two before the big game.

But even if the state allowed Telfair to play in Vaccaro's game, he would have missed Monday, Tuesday, and Wednesday practices at Lincoln (never mind classes). "He was going to get killed in the press if he did that," Turner said. Reebok's Vaccaro and Chris Rivers kept calling Turner's cell so much that he had to turn it off. "They kept saying they had my tickets ready," Turner said.

His allegiance to Adidas aside, Morton was against any Telfair sabbatical in Chicago, and who could blame him? What coach in his right mind would allow his best player to separate himself from the team in the days before it would attempt to repeat as state champs?

"I would've preferred him to stay," Morton said, "but he helped me get three city championships, so if the rules allowed and he asked me to do him a favor, I think I would've allowed him to go. But the rules don't allow it. Right now, he's gone AWOL on me."

Right now was Monday, March 22nd, when Telfair skipped practice for about the 10th time that year. He skipped those practices for business meetings with family members, agents, sneaker reps, and money managers. This time around, Telfair had a sit-down with his father, Turner, and Jamel Thomas.

"It got heated," Turner said. Otis and Jamel maintained their position that Sebastian shouldn't sign with Andy Miller. "I think if Sebastian wants Andy," Turner said, "that's all that should matter."

Vaccaro wanted one of his friends, Tellem or Bill Duffy, to knock Miller out of the Bassy box. It was clear that wasn't going to happen, not with Miller enjoying the support of Telfair, Turner, and Morton. So when Vaccaro learned that he wouldn't even land Telfair for his Round-ball Classic, he took out his wrath on the Lincoln coach.

"Tiny could've found this out and told me 3 months ago, but he got me," Vaccaro said. "That's okay. No one is going to play for Juice. He's going to be persona non grata. And in the end, it didn't matter that Sebastian didn't come. We had a great game. We had 15,000 people show up in the United Center, and nobody remembered that Sebastian wasn't there."

A few hours before Shaun Livingston and Dwight Howard showed their lottery-pick stuff before 15,421 fans and a legion of NBA scouts, Rick Pitino called me to say he'd heard Telfair's draft stock was falling. He wanted to know if I'd heard the same thing. More than a month after sending Telfair into the draft with his Cardinals blessing, Pitino's voice was filled with renewed hope.

"I told Sebastian, 'Don't count on the Clippers,'" Pitino said. "I told him, 'They're the worst possible team to rely on with Donald Sterling as their owner. They can tell you that you're their guy, then make a trade or do something else entirely.'

"Sebastian actually wanted me to come to his press conference to announce that he's going to the NBA, and I can't do that. I mean, I support him 100 percent . . ."

Pitino laughed. "But he'd be going the wrong way there."

°　　°　　°　　°　　°

Sebastian Telfair buried his face in his hands and sobbed loudly in the corner of the locker room, sounding like a 9-year-old child whose bicycle was stolen. His Lincoln career had just ended in the Glens Falls Civic Center.

The scene of Telfair's last game was all wrong. It should have ended in the Garden, not in some old minor-league hockey arena with the likes of Duffy's Tavern holding signage rights, an arena surrounded by factories blowing depressing white clouds into a colorless sky.

Mount Vernon of New York City's Westchester burbs put a defensive choke hold on Telfair, holding him to 14 points and forcing him to commit 10 turnovers in a 66–52 triumph in the state final. Bob Cimmino, the highly regarded Mount Vernon coach, had used a strategy he borrowed from Villanova coach Jay Wright.

"We X'd out the player," Cimmino said. "Crossed him out. When Sebastian had the ball, all defenders had to help on penetration. And most importantly, when he passes off, deny it back to him. And when it did get back to him, the defensive adrenaline was up because he got the ball when he shouldn't have.

"But I've never seen anyone dribble in close quarters like Sebastian. He's amazingly fast with the ball close to his body, and he has such a high basketball IQ. I've seen great guards, and he's at the top of the list. You can't go wrong with Coach Pitino, but if he were my son, I'd tell him to take the guaranteed money."

Before Telfair could take the guaranteed money, he had to take off his Lincoln jersey for the last time. That wouldn't be easy.

"(The crying) shows you how much that Lincoln has done for me in my life, in my career," he said.

The Railsplitters finished at 26-6, and Tiny Morton told his players that losing was "a part of life." The coach thanked his seniors, and their teammates applauded. "We'll cry for a minute," Morton said, "but we had fun, man. As long as you had fun."

Apparently the hangers-on didn't find much fun in defeat. Morton held up his cell phone and said, "When we win, I get 13 messages. (Today) not . . . a . . . phone call."

Telfair was having a trainer look at his throbbing left hand, which was swollen beneath the base of his thumb. Eugene Lawrence was taking out his frustration on the Pittsburgh-bound Mount Vernon guard, Keith Benjamin, one of the few Knights who was held in check. "He ain't shit," Lawrence said.

Morton was accused of his own brand of trash talking when he told reporters that city people remember only the identity of the city champ, not the state champ. But he was only speaking the truth.

At one point, Morton said something about an ending. "My shit's just starting," Telfair responded. He'd just gone down as one of the greatest schoolboy guards the city had ever produced, right there with Bob Cousy, Tiny Archibald, Pearl Washington, Kenny Anderson, and Stephon Marbury, and it was already time to think like a businessman.

Telfair had to get ready for the McDonald's All-American Game in Oklahoma City, the Nike Hoop Summit in San Antonio, and all the workouts, negotiations, and news conferences that would follow. An end had inspired a beginning. Sebastian Telfair was about to start a journey that would prove the road to the NBA is as perilous as it is long.

This is it, Otis Telfair said. Our time. Our hour to shine.

This was not the city championship in Madison Square Garden, or the state championship in Glens Falls, or the NBA draft in the Garden Theater.

This was the McDonald's All-American Game in Oklahoma City, and Otis was home with family as he prepared to watch it live. He was acting as if this were the Super Bowl, and for good reason: In his corner of Coney Island, it *was* the Super Bowl.

Otis's son, Sebastian, had come too far to screw it up now. The way Otis saw it, his kid deserved to be a top five pick. Otis said all the way back in preseason that a record third straight city title in America's foremost city would prove that Sebastian was worthy of LeBron-like respect.

"Bassy's better than LeBron," Otis had said then. "All LeBron has on him is the dunk. Bassy has better skills than LeBron. He's better than Dwight Howard, too; Howard's only taller. I'm not looking past the top five in the draft, not if he keeps proving he's a championship-getter. If Bassy has the year I think he'll have, he'll even top LeBron's sneaker deal."

Sebastian had a great senior season at Lincoln, but there was no chance of him approaching LeBron's $103 million deal with Nike, just like there was no chance of him becoming the number one pick in the draft. No general manager with the first pick was about to risk his career on a 5-foot-11 high school player. The shortest high school player ever taken in the lottery was 6-foot-6 Kobe Bryant, and he went 13th in 1996.

But Telfair still had a shot at the top 10 despite his spotty play in the city and state play-offs. He needed to perform in Oklahoma City the way he had at UCLA and the Prime Time Shootout, and then he needed to do the same at the Nike Hoop Summit in San Antonio.

In the wake of the Roundball Classic debacle, Telfair decided to keep things simple. He would play only the McDonald's game and the Hoop Summit even though he could have signed up for a third all-star event without surrendering his college eligibility. High school players hoping to keep their college options open were allowed to play in two all-star games, but the Hoop Summit—a competition between the top American high schoolers and their international counterparts—was granted exempt status because it involved USA Basketball and the honor of playing for Uncle Sam.

For the moment, Telfair was done worrying about sneaker-war skirmishes. He was worried about outplaying Shaun Livingston, the 6-foot-7 beanpole from Peoria who was expected to be a top five pick. The same people who were calling Telfair the next Isiah Thomas were calling Livingston the next Magic Johnson. The point guards would go head-to-head in Oklahoma City with the entire NBA examining their every step.

But first came the practices. Many executives and scouts saw the McDonald's practices as more important than the actual game, which often deteriorated into an exercise in basket hanging and windmill dunking. In fact, Kevin McHale spent a first-round pick on Houston high school star Ndudi Ebi in the 2003 draft because of the way Ebi fearlessly defended LeBron James in McDonald's practices.

Only Telfair didn't get to go after Livingston in practice. The East and West teams worked out on adjacent courts at Oklahoma City University, courts separated by a white partition. Telfair spent his time matched up with his old friend, Darius Washington, and with Rajon Rondo, the Kentucky signee whom Rick Pitino wanted at Louisville in the event Telfair turned pro.

Telfair, Washington, and Rondo all had their moments while Darius Washington Sr. worked the perimeter and told anyone willing to listen that the NBA stands for No Boys Allowed, and that Telfair's game didn't measure up to the hype. Larry Bird, Danny Ainge, Mitch Kupchak, B. J.

Armstrong, and Kiki Vandeweghe were among the NBA executives on hand to find out for themselves. There wasn't a major college coach in sight.

A closed-door scrimmage in the Ford Center didn't offer much in the way of insight, and nothing there matched the excitement of 6-foot-3 Candace Parker, the new It Girl from Naperville, Illinois, winning the bigender dunk contest.

Telfair was favoring that left knee again, the one that had bothered him all year and the one he was trying to keep secret from inquiring NBA minds. Tiny Morton and Bubba Barker watched from behind one of the baskets. At the close of the scrimmage, Telfair walked over to Morton and heard his coach say he wanted two passes for every shot Sebastian took in the following night's game.

The head coach of the East team, Bob Flynn of Baltimore's Cardinal Gibbons High, made a similar request of his starting point guard. "He'll be our quarterback," Flynn said. "He's a great leader. He wants to win every drill, and he's great with his teammates. But he's got tendinitis in both knees now, and I think he's tired. . . . I still expect Sebastian to carry the team."

Telfair expected to break the McDonald's assist record—13, set by Jacque Vaughn in 1993. "I can close my eyes and throw it to Dwight Howard and these other big guys," Sebastian said. He figured the record was an easy mark. "Thirteen?" he said. "That's first quarter."

The master plan was for Telfair to turn the McDonald's game into a showcase for his team-first instinct. While everyone else was running and gunning, dunking and preening, Telfair figured he'd impress the NBA people with his selflessness and poise.

So much was at stake on so many levels. Adidas was continuing to negotiate with Andy Miller, and the numbers on a multi-year deal could go north or south depending on this game of East versus West.

Then there was Morton. "If the game goes the way I hope it goes, then they can all kiss my ass," the Lincoln coach said as he picked through a steak-and-fries lunch, careful not to stain his white Adidas sweat suit. "If Bassy gets drafted high, think of what that will mean to me on the streets. I'll be king of the streets. If he goes in the lottery, Ziggy is dead. Sonny is dead."

Sonny. The conversation never veered far from Sonny. Soon enough, the tale of how Vaccaro gave $900,000 each to Tracy McGrady's high school and summer coaches as part of his 6-year Adidas deal with T-Mac was served up like a tall glass of iced tea.

Joel Hopkins, McGrady's coach at North Carolina's Mount Zion Christian Academy, and Alvis Smith, McGrady's summer coach, earned a combined $1.8 million thank-you present from Adidas for steering T-Mac its way. Despite the fact Adidas was offering four times what Nike had, McGrady had wanted to sign with Nike because he idolized one of its endorsers, Penny Hardaway.

"I told Tracy I'd knock him upside his head if he didn't sign (the Adidas contract)," Hopkins said. "I told him, 'Are you out of your freakin' mind? This is it.' He said, 'Man, I want to go with Nike.' I said, 'Man, you ain't going with Nike.' It was the difference between $12 million guaranteed and like $3 million guaranteed."

And the difference between Hopkins and Smith getting their money and not getting it. Sonny Vaccaro would say this was the first such deal he'd worked for high school or AAU coaches, with others to come.

"I worked for that contract," Hopkins said. "Me and Alvis worked for that money. That's peanuts compared to what we got Tracy. He got $12 million and we got $900,000 each. . . . Everybody thinks Sonny Vaccaro was responsible for Tracy, and Sonny didn't do a damn thing."

"We made the kid a multimillionaire," Smith said. "Tracy just got another Adidas deal worth more than $100 million, bigger than LeBron's. So we deserved the money we got."

Vaccaro related this story to Morton, and the Lincoln coach had his suspicions over why he did. "I think Sonny told me that so maybe I'd think, 'If Sebastian goes to Reebok, I can get a cut of his action,'" Morton said. "But I'm not working that way. . . . Some people think I'm leaving Lincoln after this, and I'm definitely coming back next year. Unless someone gives me $2 million, I'm coming back. People think Sebastian might give me $100,000 from his shoe contract. Even if he did, I'm not retiring on $100,000."

Adidas had just announced that Morton was promoted to its grassroots advisory board, making him the company's number one man in New York. It was yet another signal that Telfair would sign with Adidas, which wasn't fond of throwing guaranteed contracts at 5-foot-11 high school kids who looked ordinary on ESPN.

And Telfair had the strangest bedfellow counseling him before this momentous night—Darius Washington. As fate would have it, the Memphis signee and Telfair antagonist was Sebastian's assigned roommate in Oklahoma City. Oscar Madison and Felix Unger had nothing on them.

Washington said people had "overexaggerated" his differences with Telfair, a player Washington had mercilessly ripped to me and others. Washington said he merely offered agenda-free advice to Telfair as the two lay in bed at night.

"I hope that Sebastian sits down and really goes through the pros and cons," Washington said. "I hope he prays over the decision. I hope he doesn't rush into anything. . . . I told him, 'Block everybody out. Block the media out. Block out all the (magazine) covers. . . . The common Joe is going to tell you to go, go, go, go, go, but when you fail, he's not going to be around.'"

Failure wasn't an option for Telfair. He was hell-bent on skipping college, no matter what his roommate or anyone else said.

o   o   o   o   o

"Shoot the fucking ball," Otis Telfair yelled at the televised image of his son.

It was all coming back to Otis now. All the bullshit the family went through with Jamel Thomas. Someone played a cruel draft night hoax on them back then, and that someone was behind the shit going down in this McDonald's game on ESPN.

Everybody's all-Americans were shooting and scoring except Bassy, and it was driving Otis mad.

He was furious that his son kept passing to the East's big men, Dwight Howard and Al Jefferson, and to the high-leaping, long-range-shooting star out of St. Benedict's in Jersey, J.R. Smith. Telfair was trying to show executives and scouts that he wasn't a shot-happy point guard, that he was a far more complete player than his scoring average (33.2 points per game) suggested.

His father didn't want to hear it. "Show everyone that you're the best scorer that ever came out of a New York high school," Otis said. His son would later explain that the NBA scouts already knew he could score, and that he needed to shoot for the assist record instead.

Telfair fell two short of that record, finishing with 11 assists in the East's 126–96 victory over the West. He attempted a mere two shots— a jumper and a driving layup—and made the driving layup. If Telfair thought he had satisfied the executives and scouts who wondered if he could quarterback a winning team, he knew he had no shot of satisfying his father.

Otis thought his son could have moved into the top five of the draft if he lit up the scoreboard. "He should've never held back," Otis said. "He gave other guys a chance to shine over him. I wanted him to go for broke. I mean, I was yelling at the TV, yelling at everything. I kept saying, 'Take over. Take over,' but he never did. I said, 'Somebody had to tell him not to shoot, and I'm going to find out who.' Ethan was watching me hollering, and he started going crazy, too. He was like, 'Oh, Bassy's scared to shoot the ball.' Ethan was so mad he started crying."

At least Ethan had company. Sebastian reported that Livingston was crying after he finished with 1 point and 3 assists, making a happy man of the college coach who had signed him, Mike Krzyzewski.

Telfair figured he showed scouts that he could shut down a bigger guard on defense, only he didn't move up or down in most draft projections. Teams appreciated Telfair's poise and passing, but some figured his reluctance to shoot was a sign that he didn't believe in his jumper.

"Sebastian was average," said one Eastern Conference general manager. "But I don't think teams are that down on him. It only takes one team, anyway, and you know the Clippers love him. If Sebastian knows he's going in the first round, why not come out? Look at (Duke's) Chris Duhon. If he comes out of high school, he's a top 15 pick. Now he's lucky if he's early second round. There's a lot of cases like that, where a kid goes to school and loses a ton of money."

This GM asked me if Arn Tellem had a shot at representing Telfair. I told him Andy Miller was the guy. The GM thought Miller was a good agent, but not necessarily one who could serve Telfair quite like Tellem. "Arn's got a way of moving guys up in the draft," the GM said. "And let me tell you something: If you guarantee Arn Tellem you're taking his client, you better fucking take his client."

Telfair wasn't about to turn away from Miller. And in the wake of Sebastian's middling McDonald's performance, Miller was still sounding hopeful on all fronts.

"I think that McDonald's game put Livingston in college," Miller said. "It's not about what Sebastian did in that game, but what he did to Livingston. And I think Josh Smith cost himself a good $5 million to $10 million with his body language."

That would be a good $5 million to $10 million that might be available to Miller's client. Adidas was talking to Telfair and Smith, and Miller was trying to push the shoe company closer to a $3-million-per-year commitment for Telfair.

Now Miller needed Telfair to go to San Antonio and provide him with a little extra negotiating leverage. Telfair was still considered a top 15 pick. He was still considered the favorite to land the richest shoe endorsement deal in his class. He was still a young, famous, good-looking kid with a beautiful girlfriend and a shiny 350Z.

Telfair was still a lucky soul, too, for 5 weeks had passed since his older brother had been arrested, and not a single reporter in New York's relentlessly competitive market had uncovered it. Telfair was hoping Sylvester's case would either go away or somehow remain quiet until the

NBA draft was complete. But when he landed in San Antonio, Telfair's luck turned sour.

Sylvester's troubles wouldn't just go public at a time when Telfair desperately needed a singular focus; they would imperil everything—the lottery pick, the shoe money, the life a kid from the projects wasn't supposed to imagine when his ex-con brother was locked inside a Rikers Island cell.

○   ○   ○   ○   ○

I was interviewing Telfair after a Team USA practice at the University of Texas at San Antonio when Tiny Morton called me out of my chair.

"Have you read the New York papers on the Internet today?" he asked.

"Not yet," I answered.

"Well, there's something in there about his brother today," he said. "Do me a favor and don't ask him about it until after this game."

Morton wasn't aware that a Telfair family member had tipped me off weeks earlier about Sylvester's latest arrest, on the condition that I wait until all games were played before I attempted to interview Telfair about his older brother. But now there were no more secrets to be guarded like a playmaker's dribble. The city tabloids had the scoop that Sylvester had been arrested February 26th for allegedly shooting a man across the street from the Telfair family's home.

"Hoop Star's Bro Held in Murder Bid," was the *Post's* headline. "Slay-Try Rap for Brother of Top HS Hoops Player," read the headline in the *Daily News*, which mentioned Otis Telfair's manslaughter conviction.

Sylvester was being held at Rikers Island on $150,000 bail; he was on probation at the time of the shooting. But it was Sebastian's photo and name that made the story, a truth that enraged the Telfair family.

"Sylvester has nothing to do with Sebastian," Otis said. "Everything was looking wonderful, and now we have to deal with this bad press. I told Sebastian, 'Don't be ashamed or embarrassed. If I caused you any embarrassment, or if your brother did, I'm sorry. Don't put it on yourself. You've never done no harm to anybody.'

"I know it's embarrassing to him to a certain degree. His own record is so perfect, so they've got to go pick something out of his family. . . . I honestly feel in my heart my family and kids are good people, or God would not have blessed us like this with Bassy. We must have good hearts. I don't care what I read in the paper; I'm not a bad person. I'm not an evil person. I don't sit around thinking up evil things to do. They took me out of my mother's house and put me in the middle of the jungle when I was 19 years old. I came back and they dumped me on the city streets. I was Bassy's age then. All these years later, people should leave Bassy out of what happened to me and Sylvester."

With NBA and shoe executives considering whether to invest millions in Sebastian, that was easier said than done. Telfair knew the disclosure of Sylvester's arrest wouldn't do him any favors on Madison Avenue, but he also knew he couldn't let the news shatter his concentration.

The Hoop Summit offered the perfect faraway refuge from troubled Coney Island waters. USA Basketball, which organized the event, credentialed 107 NBA reps for the one practice those reps were permitted to watch. So Telfair had the desired audience, and a leading role on the stage, too. Dwight Howard and Shaun Livingston were among the invited Americans who wouldn't play because of other commitments.

Telfair would be given the ball, the playing time, and the scoring opportunities to make the kind of indelible mark he didn't make in Oklahoma City. "My mission in the McDonald's game was to get everybody involved and shut Shaun Livingston down, and I did both," Telfair said. "I think Shaun was getting a lot of good things said about him because he's tall. I was trying to prove that being tall is a good thing, but it's not going to help you that much. I mean, Shaun was crying after the game, very frustrated."

Sebastian couldn't afford to feel frustrated after the Hoop Summit. The world team featured five players between 6-foot-10 and 7-foot-1; the tallest American was Al Jefferson at 6-foot-10. The visitors were expected to own a significant advantage on the boards, but they were also expected to have major trouble with Telfair's quickness. At 5-foot-11, Sebastian was 4 inches shorter than the world team's smallest player, Spain's Sergio Rodriguez.

Telfair was all set to make up for lost time. He planned on dribbling circles around the lumbering foreigners, Globetrotter style.

What could possibly make this event any better? Nothing but the look on Bubba's face when he lifted his opened cell phone with his left hand and motioned toward his best friend with his right.

"Who is it?" Bassy asked.

Bubba smiled wide, and let a few silent seconds pass for the sake of dramatic effect.

"Steph," he said.

o   o   o   o   o

Something had pulled at Stephon Marbury. Perhaps it was guilt. Perhaps it was the *Sports Illustrated* cover story on Telfair that mentioned the fracture in their relationship. Perhaps it was the realization that life was too short and the draft lottery odds were too long for an NBA star to withhold invaluable wisdom from his own blood.

Whatever it was, it inspired Marbury to pick up that phone and begin a thawing-out process that would likely move at a glacial pace. "I just called him because that's my little cousin and I love him," Marbury said. "I don't want him to make any bad decisions, and I didn't want that to be on my conscience if something bad was to happen out of the whole thing."

Marbury had been reading the papers and checking the mock drafts on the Internet. "And now I'm hearing my cousin might go like 20, or in the twenties," he said. "He needs to be careful."

Telfair was stunned that Marbury had called. They talked for 45 minutes. Marbury advised Sebastian to go to school, but also gave him tips on preparing for the draft.

This phone call, one of several Marbury would make to Telfair and Danny Turner, clearly had a profound impact on the heir to the Coney Island throne. "Sebastian was so happy," Turner said. "Deep down, he loves Stephon. That's his idol. Stephon told me, 'I was hurt because Sebastian disrespected me on the street.' I think Stephon's trying to get past it. He told Sebastian he should've shot more in the McDonald's game, and said that he shouldn't sign with an agent, that he should keep his options open."

Telfair didn't agree with everything Marbury said, but appreciated the call all the same.

"I told him what he was getting himself into," Marbury said. "I told him that it's different when you play in the NBA as a point guard instead of as a big man or a three man. There's so much stuff that you've got to learn.

"I want to help my little cousin. I know when he says things like, 'Jason Kidd is my favorite player,' it's because we've had our differences. I know how my little cousin really looks at me. I grew, and he's growing. Right now, he has to get his circle tight. He has to know who's around to help him, and who's not going to do what's in his best interests."

Was Marbury serving Telfair's best interests by nudging him away from the draft and toward the kind of one-and-done career he had at Georgia Tech? Or was Marbury merely hoping that the little cousin who outdid him at Lincoln wouldn't trump him again by going straight into the draft lottery out of high school, with a richer sneaker deal than any Marbury had signed?

"I love Stephon so much," Telfair said. "I've been mad that me and him have had differences. Indirectly, Stephon's a role model to me like nobody else could be. Conflict in the family messed that up. . . . But I still love Stephon, and I still believe he wants me to do well."

° ° ° ° °

Telfair looked great in a USA uniform that was as white as his perfectly straight teeth. The Grizzlies' Jerry West led the contingent of NBA reps who paid to sit in their Texas-San Antonio seats—USA Basketball wouldn't credential the pros, according to spokesman Craig Miller, "because that would send a conflicting message. We're associated with the NCAA."

Telfair promised to be worth the price of admission this time around. Tiny Morton and Bubba Barker sat side by side in the front row, Bubba wearing a Red Sox cap and Morton going with his reliable Yankee cap. Morton had ordered his point guard to shoot more, as if Telfair hadn't fielded that piece of post-McDonald's advice a thousand times.

But everyone's expectations and enthusiasm were tempered on the very first possession, when Telfair took a knee to the right thigh. The injury put the brakes on his grand plan. Instead of beating bigger opponents off the dribble, a hobbled Telfair would have to shoot over the top and put his questionable range to the test.

He had his moments, just like in Oklahoma City. Some brilliant passes. Some sweet ballhandling. Some selfless cheering from the bench. All in all, his efficient quarterbacking helped the Junior National Select Team score a 99–79 victory over the World Select Team, this while high-scoring teammates again dominated the stage.

Josh Smith finished with 27 points, perhaps making up all that money Andy Miller said he'd lost during McDonald's week. J.R. Smith added 17 to the 25 he scored in Oklahoma City. Just weeks after sounding certain that he'd attend North Carolina, J.R. had vaulted into the top 20 of the draft.

Telfair again made only one basket, albeit a dramatic one—a 3-pointer to beat the half-time buzzer. But he needed 10 shots to make that one basket. Though Telfair did finish with 7 assists, giving him 18 in two postseason games, the NBA reps had come to see something else.

"Sebastian's a great leader," said Joe Kleine, the longtime NBA veteran and assistant coach for the U.S. team. "He's a great kid who looks at you when you're talking to him, and he really knows how to get somebody else a shot. But he's got to get a better jumper."

This critique didn't temper Telfair's mass appeal. Outside the young Americans' locker room, there were far more autograph seekers around the 1-for-10 point guard than there were around Josh or J.R. Smith.

Into his postgame news conference, Telfair wore one of those March Madness T-shirts that read, "Welcome to Bracketville. Stay as long as you can." Telfair didn't want to spend even one day in Bracketville. He wanted to get to the NBA as quickly as possible, and the Hoop Summit didn't help him toward that end.

Telfair put a happy face on his postseason experience. Point guards were judged on wins and losses, he reminded, and Telfair's teams were 2–0.

"If we didn't come in and share the ball like we did," the point guard said, "maybe we would've lost."

One reporter asked Telfair if the disclosure of Sylvester's arrest was a distraction ("No, it's not a distraction"), then asked if the two had spoken since the story broke ("Next question, please").

The most telling give-and-take came when Sebastian was asked about being the most publicized member of the Class of 2004. "I think being on magazines and things like that, that's cool, that's cute," he said. "But my mother's still in the projects."

No, Louisville's scholarship wasn't getting Erica Telfair out of Surf-side Gardens.

o   o   o   o   o

Rick Pitino was back on the phone. Before the postseason games, he said he'd heard his number one recruit, Sebastian Telfair, had slipped in the draft. Now Pitino was talking possible free fall.

"I just hope Sebastian doesn't become another Omar Cook," the Louisville coach said of the New York point guard who played one season at St. John's, entered the draft, and crash-landed in the second round.

Omar Cook had been given a 10-day contract by Portland in February and was kept on for the season's balance. He told me that draft night, 2001, a night he spent in a midtown hotel suite, was the worst night of his life. But despite his own experiences riding minor-league buses and staying in economy hotels, Cook said Telfair should still turn pro.

"You do have your LeBron Jameses and your Omar Cooks in the draft," Cook said. "But I think Sebastian's ready. He plays better when he's playing against better players. He's just got to hope the draft turns out the way it should, because one pick can change everything and leave you waiting for that call."

Would Telfair take that gamble, or make the safe play and go with one year of college ball? I told Pitino I thought he had no shot of seeing Telfair in Louisville. I told him I thought the *Sports Illustrated* cover was the final dagger, and that, most unfortunately, Sebastian probably feels he'd look like a chump if he goes to school.

"He'll look like a bigger chump at the draft if he's stuck in that green room all night," Pitino replied. "Andy Miller has some job ahead of him, and he's got to be careful. Andy doesn't want to ruin his own career with this kid."

No, Andy didn't want to do that. "I don't need Kevin Garnett saying, 'You fucked this up,'" Miller said. "I don't need Kevin saying, 'You had a great point guard and you turned him into the next Omar Cook.' It's not worth me losing my business on a 6-foot point guard who's not ready."

But there was Miller with Telfair, Tiny Morton, and Jamel Thomas in a New Jersey restaurant two nights after the point guard returned from the Hoop Summit. For 3½ hours, Miller mapped out the 2½-month commitment it would take to become a high draft choice.

He explained just how demanding the NBA's predraft workouts could be, and just how critical they were to a team's final evaluation. The agent wanted to send Telfair to IMG Academies in Bradenton, Florida, and put him back in the hands of Joe Abunassar, the trainer who spent time with Telfair during the Lincoln season. Miller asked Morton and Thomas to work out an arrangement with Lincoln officials that would allow Telfair as much time as possible in Florida without jeopardizing the kid's plans to graduate.

"I wanted Sebastian to know he was facing a daunting task," Miller said. "He listened carefully and said, 'This is what I wanted to do my whole life. This is a dream come true for me. I'll do whatever I have to do to make it work and come out on top.'"

Miller was still confident he could find his client a place in the lottery. He talked to 10 teams within 48 hours of the Hoop Summit's completion, and figured Sebastian should still go somewhere between the 6th and 14th pick of the draft.

At least one GM contacted by Miller shared the agent's rose-colored perspective. "I didn't think it was possible for Sebastian to be as sensational in the all-star games as he was at UCLA and in Trenton," said John Nash of the Blazers. "There is a perception in our organization that Sebastian brings with him a lot of baggage, that he has a posse, a brother with problems, all the trouble with being a New York phenom. But I think it's too early to get caught up in that, and I draft on talent anyway.

"If we're picking 13th or 14th, I don't think he'll get to us. Andy told us he'd like to see him in Portland and I said, 'I'd like to see him here, too.'"

Of the teams with serious interest in Telfair, the Clippers were expected to hold the highest pick. Elgin Baylor, GM, had been noncommittal in conversations with Miller, but Evan Pickman, assistant director of player personnel Gary Sacks, and Sacks's boss, Barry Hecker, were big Telfair fans.

One Clippers official said his team had tempered its public enthusiasm for Sebastian by design, hoping to fool other suitors. "When you compare Sebastian to Livingston, it's night and day," the official said. "Livingston doesn't have the competitive nature that Sebastian has. Livingston doesn't have Sebastian's I'm-going-to-kick-your-ass attitude."

When told Pitino had expressed a fear that Telfair might become another Omar Cook, another tale of second-round woe, the Clippers official said, "That's a joke. Rick's just trying to find a silver lining. To mention Sebastian Telfair in the same breath with Omar Cook is ridiculous."

To mention Sebastian Telfair in the same breath with Sylvester Telfair was not. Two interested teams had already peppered Miller with questions about Sylvester's arrest on attempted murder, and within 48 hours, the case was back in the public eye.

Sylvester pleaded not guilty in Brooklyn Supreme Court to shooting a Coney Island man named Ahmad Rennick, whose rap sheet included a prison term for attempted criminal sale of a controlled substance. Sylvester couldn't post the $150,000 bail, and he rejected the prosecution's plea offer that would have meant 15 years in prison; he faced a maximum sentence of 25 years.

Telfair didn't attend the arraignment, but his picture appeared in the *Post* and his name was all over the proceedings. Now the question begged to be asked: Had Sylvester's arrest affected his brother on the court?

"Sebastian said it didn't bother him," Morton said, "but he's 18, how can it not? He's not going to say he struggled in some of those games because his brother was back in jail. That's going to sound like an excuse, and he doesn't make excuses."

Corinne Heslin put it more directly. "I think part of Sebastian's stinky basketball playing over some games is because of Sylvester," she said.

This much was indisputable: Telfair needed an escape. Two so-so games in Oklahoma and Texas had turned up the heat in Coney Island, where flighty draft projections, family paranoia, and Sylvester's jailing conspired to send Telfair fleeing from his life as a playmaking prodigy.

The point guard was seeking a sanctuary from those all-American pressures, and so he left his 'hood, left his family, left his school, and boarded a plane that would take him and his NBA ambitions to an unlikely faraway place.

Sebastian Telfair had never been overseas when he asked his parents if he could spend some time with Jamel Thomas in Greece. Thomas had seen his own draft dreams go up in flames 5 years earlier, and he wasn't about to stand by and watch the same thing happen to the kid who saw him as a second father.

Greece was Thomas's idea and Thomas's idea alone. He was putting up big numbers for the Apollon team in Patras, but he wasn't interested in showing Telfair the finer points of his game. Thomas was interested in shielding Telfair from the madness engulfing him in New York.

Only Thomas didn't take into account the classwork Telfair would miss from Glens Falls to Oklahoma City to San Antonio. Telfair had fallen behind in his schoolwork. He was taking only four courses, and yet there were many days when his accounting teacher, Jeff Nash, excused him from his elective class so the point guard could leave Lincoln before 11:00 A.M. and speed off to his afternoon workout.

Heslin didn't want to cut Telfair any more academic slack, and she wasn't alone in hoping this trip never got off the ground. Andy Miller was beyond upset. He wanted Telfair to train with his guy in Florida. Miller didn't have a good relationship with Thomas to begin with, and he didn't see the logic behind a 2-week sabbatical in Greece.

Morton and Turner agreed with Miller but met with Heslin, anyway, in an attempt to convince the principal that Telfair needed to be excused from school. Heslin relented on Greece, and Turner pledged to fax all of Telfair's homework across the sea. "There were family issues and Sebastian's going to be out of school," Heslin said. "I got a letter from his parent. I cannot tell a parent that you can't take your kid out of school, even if I disagree with it."

Telfair joined Thomas on a 2-week journey that would return him to New York on May 2nd. Andrew Amigo, trainer and friend and member of Lincoln's 1991 city championship team, flew to Greece to put Telfair and Thomas through a series of rigorous drills. Telfair watched Thomas play in one of his league games. Alastair Christopher of Jonathan Hock's documentary crew wired Thomas for sound like he'd wired Telfair during Lincoln games, and listened as Thomas cursed out an overzealous Greek defender who was powerless to stop the very spin moves and jumpers that didn't interest NBA scouts.

"We just focused on school and ball (in Greece)," said Thomas. "It's school, ball, and Hollywood in New York, so I thought taking (Sebastian) out of Hollywood for a couple of weeks would be good for him."

Apparently not everyone agreed. Stephon Marbury would call Miller and say, "You take care of my little cousin, and just make sure you keep him as far away from Jamel as possible. Jamel has no fucking idea how to make it in this league."

Back home, even those who had worked over Heslin on Thomas's behalf didn't understand the point of this road trip. When Dan Martin of the *Post* broke the story that Telfair had been excused from Lincoln to work out in Greece, laughter broke out across the PSAL.

"How do you possibly pass this kid and let him graduate?" asked one head coach of a Lincoln rival. "He missed all those days for the all-star trips, and then he goes to Greece for 2 weeks? Sebastian might as well be the principal over there."

This was the kind of reaction that kicked Danny Turner straight into I-told-you-so gear.

"You can't go to Greece for 2 weeks and have nobody find out," he said. "I knew it would get out. You know, this whole thing is pulling the family apart, and I'm upset about that. It's my job to hold this family together. I argued with Jamel about this. I didn't want him to go to Greece, despite what I said to Mrs. Heslin. I just did that because Sebastian asked me to.

"The problem is, everyone in this family is trying to be a chief now. Jamel wants to be the chief. My stepdad wants to be the chief. Tiny wants to be the chief. Jamel said that I was trying to turn Sebastian against him, and I told him I'm not. I just want Sebastian to be happy.

I'm the one who put in the most work with him, and now I feel like I'm being disrespected. I gave up my life for this, and . . . it hurts to be pushed aside."

It hurt Turner even more when Telfair and Thomas returned to New York and took less than 24 hours to flaunt their new and improved intercontinental bond.

On May 3rd, a day before he was to step up to a Times Square mike and announce his future plans, Telfair returned an old favor. He bought Thomas a new BMW worth 80 grand.

18

The document sat in the middle of a round sports bar table, as if it were an order of cheese fries. The cover sheet read "Agreement between Adidas International Marketing BV and S31T, Inc.," and behind it were two dozen 8½-by-11 pages that were about to make Sebastian Telfair a multimillionaire before he turned 19.

This was in a dimly lit corner of the ESPN Zone on May 4, 2004, after the notebooks and cameras and most of the party's guests had already packed up and headed out into the Times Square bustle. I sat at the table with Telfair, Andy Miller, and Kevin Wulff, the director of sports marketing at Adidas. Just four guys talking sports under a dizzying web of monitors showing Telfair highlights and, then, Mike Wilbon and Tony Kornheiser doing their *Pardon the Interruption* (PTI) show.

"You're big, Sebastian," I told Telfair, pointing at the monitor above his left shoulder. "You're the first item on PTI."

He swiveled his head to see his name highlighted above the ESPN show's lineup of subjects. Again, at 5-foot-11, Telfair had become the largest figure in the prom-to-the-pros debate. He watched Wilbon and Kornheiser do their routine for a bit before fixing his gaze back on that waiting document.

Telfair nodded at Miller, sitting directly across from him. Above Miller's head hung a stained-glass portrait of a sliding Jackie Robinson. Telfair had entered his big day wearing a white Brooklyn Dodgers cap. By the time he nodded for the pen that would earn him a guaranteed payday of more than $18 million over 6 years, Telfair had already made a trade. He was wearing a red, white, and blue Adidas cap that inspired him to see nothing but green.

What a moment. Telfair had arrived at his news conference in a black stretch limo, and walked into a celebration of himself arranged by Ron Berkowitz, Jay-Z's PR guy. He was wearing the white Brooklyn Dodgers cap, a white sports jacket, a pink dress shirt, baggy blue jeans, and white Adidas sneakers. Berkowitz introduced him as "Sebastian Telfair, New York City high school legend."

The press release had said there would be two announcements, and, priorities being priorities, the sneaker deal was announced first. Telfair's parents and most of his siblings hadn't yet arrived when Berkowitz called for lights, cameras, and action.

Before rows of reporters and photographers flanked by Telfair relatives, friends, teammates, interested observers, and Omar Cook, the cautionary tale himself, Telfair thanked God, his family, his chroniclers, and Adidas. He took off Jackie Robinson's cap while declaring himself "the newest member of the Adidas team."

The Adidas cap was two sizes too big for his head, but this was, after all, a larger-than-life affair.

"And now," Telfair said, "what everyone in here really came to hear. What every reporter asked me, what my decision was going to be. And sorry to hold you all off on the decision; it's been a long process for me and my family. I think we came together and made a great decision.

"I will be entering the 2004 NBA draft."

Applause broke out across the room. Telfair would be one of 13 high school players to declare for the draft, and he wasn't done yet. He had a third announcement to make, an unscheduled confirmation of another poorly kept secret.

"Andy Miller will be my agent," he said.

As Telfair beamed under his oversize cap, he looked about 12 years old. He said his cousin, Stephon Marbury, and LeBron James had given him support, before he stepped away from the podium to do more interviews and share more hugs.

Jamel Thomas was in the house and wearing a pin in the form of Telfair's number, 31, on the right lapel of his blue blazer, the pin as shiny as that new BMW Telfair had bought him. Bubba Barker was on hand, too, and he'd remind me that the guest of honor was still a child. In the hours before the press conference, Bubba said, they were watching cartoons in the room Adidas provided them at the W hotel.

"Daffy Duck," Bubba said, "stuff like that."

The entire Lincoln team, with the exception of Nyan Boateng, was in attendance, along with Chris Taft, the Pittsburgh big man and member of Tiny Morton's Juice All-Stars. Father Lacombe made an appearance as well. He spent most of his time with Erica and Otis Telfair, who blamed the traffic for arriving at 4:28 Lincoln Standard Time, long after the announcements were made.

Wulff, the Adidas executive in the blue blazer and yellow power tie, drew a big media crowd. He wore the look of someone who commuted from Greenwich to Madison Avenue, and yet he couldn't stop talking about the "street cred" Telfair brought to Adidas.

"We feel Sebastian has that extra heartbeat," Wulff said. "He also brings something only a few can do, such as Kevin Garnett, who we also have. He brings that instant street credibility, street cred, with the real urban ballers, and we're pretty excited about that, too."

Wulff said Dwight Howard and Shaun Livingston were not "street cred" guys, and therefore not a good fit at Adidas. Miller joked that Howard's stated hope of having Jesus Christ's cross as part of the NBA logo "was a real good way of getting an endorsement deal."

Now that it had Telfair in the fold, Adidas was hot and heavy for Howard's summer ball teammate, Josh Smith, the Oak Hill forward. But there was no doubt that Telfair was Adidas's number one target. At 5-foot-11, he fit neatly inside Adidas's impossible-is-nothing campaign. "Impossible is a little guy making the big jump," read the black T-shirts being handed out at the ESPN Zone.

"Everyone wants to emulate the small guy," Wulff said.

The Adidas executive revealed that Telfair would be used to promote performance and lifestyle products, and that there were opportunities for a signature shoe. Wulff confirmed there were no provisions in the

6-year deal based on draft position, meaning Adidas was gambling, and gambling big, that Telfair wouldn't fall into the back end of the first round or, worse yet, into the early part of the second.

"We know he's going to be a great point guard," Wulff said. "We've had great success with Tracy McGrady and Kobe Bryant, and they weren't in the top five or seven of the draft, either."

Wulff claimed the Telfair contract figures reported in the media—generally in the $12 million to $15 million range—were "all rumors and innuendo and . . . exaggerated." Wulff wouldn't disclose the terms of the contract, other than to say it was incentive-driven and that the incentives were based on the standard fare—assist totals, point totals, making the All-Rookie team, making the All-Defensive and All-Star teams as a veteran.

Contrary to Sonny Vaccaro's claim that his former employer was talking dollars with the Lincoln star during the Railsplitters' season, a claim confirmed by Miller, Telfair, and other Team Telfair members, Wulff said Adidas didn't begin negotiating terms until "after (Sebastian) signed with an agent and indicated he was turning pro." When I pressed him on his timetable, on when Adidas first floated numbers Telfair's way, Wulff maintained, "After he really signed with his agent. Then we had conversations with Andy."

Problem was, Telfair hadn't yet signed with Miller. The agent was still waiting for his new client to return the unsigned contract he had just given him a day earlier.

"Do you mean you've just started negotiating with Sebastian in the last couple of weeks?" I asked.

"Yes," Wulff said. "In fact, we're going to sign the deal in about 5 minutes. Right here. Let's find a table."

Wulff was carrying a small satchel that contained Telfair's life-altering deal. Adidas had invested plenty of time and resources into this transaction. It started with Vaccaro's decision to create the Juice All-Stars and, in extension, to provide sneakers and gear to the Lincoln team. Adidas made Morton a powerful force in the New York basketball market, and then widened his influence (and solidified its position with his point guard) by promoting Morton to its grassroots advisory board and giving him a 5-year, $400,000 deal with the Juice.

"We're very proud to be associated with Tiny's teams," Wulff said. "He's a presence in New York, and I think really good basketball players gravitate toward him."

Adidas also agreed to give Danny Turner a deal to run a community event. Miller said he "carved out" the arrangement, one he described as "small." Turner said it was part of a "package deal" worth $20,000 per year.

Across from the Adidas side of the table, Miller had invested more time and effort into Telfair's deal than he had for any he scored for Kevin Garnett, who had just been named league MVP and who had landed a lifetime contract with Adidas. Miller started talking to Adidas about his prospective client, Telfair, on a visit to the company's U.S. headquarters in the summer of 2003.

Miller knew Adidas needed a young endorser it could develop, someone who had enough flair to carry a signature shoe. "I knew I could go into attack mode then," the agent said. "They wanted a linkage between the modern player and the throwback player, and Sebastian is that."

With Garnett as his lead client, Miller had a strong working relationship with Adidas. He didn't trust Sonny Vaccaro, but did call Reebok senior VP Tom Shine to gauge his interest. Shine told Miller he saw Sebastian as a bigger version of T.J. Ford, whom Reebok was paying in the mid-six figures.

"You've got to have an understanding of the trend in this business," Miller said. "For instance, when Tiny (Morton) re-signed with Adidas, Reebok was talking that big stink about how they were going to overpay him. And Reebok came in at 30 cents on the dollar to what Adidas offered. They're full of shit. . . . So Nike was the only other real player that I believe would've stepped up and done something significant. If I put my faith in Sonny, we'd be sitting here today and Sebastian would be without a sneaker deal, and maybe with a different agent, which was obviously the only agenda Sonny truly had."

Miller's work brought Telfair to this defining hour. The point guard hadn't slept a wink the previous night, not with so many thoughts running wind sprints through his head. He rose before dawn for his preschool workout, attended class, crashed at the W hotel, and then stepped into the ESPN Zone and out of a life of abject poverty.

"I dreamt about this day," Telfair said. He said he'd buy his mother "something nice" with his first Adidas check, and that, eventually, he wanted to move her out of Surfside Gardens. Telfair didn't mention that he'd already moved himself into a large Jersey City apartment on the waterfront, with floor-to-ceiling windows and a view of the Manhattan skyline. He didn't mention that a car dealer had already let him borrow against his future earnings to buy Jamel his fresh $80,000 set of wheels.

"I'm not worried about money," Telfair said.

Citing a mutual confidentiality agreement, Adidas and Miller declined to give an exact measurement on Telfair's deal. Telfair said the contract was worth more than $15 million; an Adidas rep whispered to inquiring minds that the deal guaranteed the Lincoln star only about $6 million, or $1 million per year.

Telfair was the most candid party; Adidas was the party terrified of the actual figures being leaked. The shoe company was concerned that Telfair's deal could cost it money in other negotiations. Burned by harsh critiques of its extravagant investment in a 5-foot-11 teenager, Adidas also feared being embarrassed in the event Telfair fell in the draft.

Neither Miller nor Telfair would confirm the true value of the contract, but a source close to the negotiations said Telfair was guaranteed between $18 million and $19 million, including a $2 million signing bonus. The reachable incentives made the likely payout between $20 million and $25 million. If Sebastian somehow hit the incentives he wasn't likely to hit, he would earn between $30 million and $40 million. Miller's take would be 15 percent.

This was the second largest contract ever granted a high school player, smaller than LeBron's but bigger than Kobe's and T-Mac's. This was a deal so staggering that it put Telfair among the top 10 paid shoe endorsers in the NBA before he'd even been drafted. Without the certainty of being a lottery pick, or even a top 20 pick, Telfair was in possession of a better shoe deal than any owned by Shaquille O'Neal, Tim Duncan, Jason Kidd, and a legion of fellow All-Stars that included Telfair's cousin, Stephon Marbury. Duncan, maybe the best player in the world, was getting a lousy $350,000 per year from Adidas.

Only LeBron, McGrady, Kobe, Garnett, Allen Iverson, Yao Ming, and Carmelo Anthony were believed to have richer deals than Telfair. Anthony's contract was believed to be worth just a nickel or three more than Telfair's.

Longtime sneaker-war observers were most stunned by the fact Miller made this deal without formal offers from Nike or Reebok. Neither company wanted to compete with Adidas like it had for LeBron; Nike was weighing Telfair against Shaun Livingston when Adidas made it clear it was taking negotiations to a level no competitor would touch.

Nike did have LeBron's best friend, Maverick Carter, and other reps track Telfair across the Lincoln season. "They wouldn't have had LeBron's guy at games if they weren't interested in signing Sebastian," said one Adidas official. "And don't tell me Sonny didn't want the kid for Reebok when he ran his guys (Arn Tellem and Bill Duffy) through there. Everybody was interested in Sebastian."

Including the most powerful sneaker man of all.

"I met Phil Knight three times," Telfair said. "Eventually, I think Nike would've come up to $13 million or $14 million. But I knew from the start Reebok wasn't going to make a big offer. How much more money can you give Sebastian Telfair when you're only paying Baron Davis $350,000? You're talking All-Stars. The most they would've given me was a million a year.

"Me and Sonny, we're the best of friends. And Sonny was the first guy who taught me to be a businessman. But at that time, I knew Reebok wasn't going to be players. I just wish Sonny would've stayed with Adidas, because he did so much to help me in my career."

If Sonny was nowhere to be found at the ESPN Zone, he was surely there in spirit. Sebastian had played Vaccaro (or the specter of Vaccaro) against Adidas and won. With the help of his strong Adidas ties, Miller beat Vaccaro in the battle for Sebastian's sole. Sonny didn't believe in Telfair's talent enough to match Adidas's offer, and, in the end, he wouldn't have had the juice to push Reebok toward the $3 million per year mark, anyway.

But Sonny would have made a formal offer to Sebastian if he felt his company had a fair-and-square chance of signing him. Reebok would have offered Telfair $1 million per year, confirmed Vaccaro, who railed against Adidas's choice to spend so large on a player so small. Vaccaro was still angry at Adidas executives who led him to believe they would provide all the resources he needed in 2003 to sign LeBron.

He carried the blood feud into the spring of 2004, when Adidas's signing of Telfair served to pour gasoline on his raging fire. "With all the money they're throwing at Sebastian and Josh Smith and all the AAU coaches they overpaid," Vaccaro said, "they should've given that to me last year and I could've signed LeBron. That deal Nike made with LeBron will be the best deal ever made."

Vaccaro predicted that Telfair would pay Miller for landing the Adidas deal, and then fire him in favor of Tellem. When he wasn't openly rooting for that divorce, Vaccaro was shredding his former employer over the magnitude of its Telfair investment.

"Phil Knight is laughing now," he said. "Adidas just grossly overpaid this child, and he doesn't even have a high-powered agent to get him moved up. I'm not an Andy Miller fan, but I'll say this: What he did to Adidas is one of the best coups ever done. He really bamboozled my old friends. . . . But Andy doesn't have the power that Arn Tellem has. That really hurts Sebastian in the draft."

Rick Pitino wasn't worried about Miller; the Louisville coach was too busy feeling wronged by the very company he endorsed. Though he publicly rooted for Telfair to cash in, and privately told his top recruit that he should take the guaranteed money and run, Pitino felt Adidas was overzealous in its courtship of Sebastian.

"Pitino called up Wulff," said Vaccaro, one of Pitino's closest friends in basketball. "Rick told him, 'The kid's falling off the charts. The game plan was to have the kid go to school if he wasn't in the lottery. You and Adidas induced the kid to come out.'"

Pitino disputed his friend's account of that call and said he actually thought Adidas made a wise investment given Telfair's charisma. "I believe he'll pan out," Pitino said. "I only asked Sebastian for one favor: get a good business manager to watch over your money."

Telfair would disappoint Pitino on this front. He signed with Bret Bearup, the former Kentucky player who had become the most prominent and controversial money manager in sports. Bearup's detractors accused him of steering players to favored coaches and agents, claims Bearup denied. Pitino became one of those detractors when Bearup spoke publicly about bygone recruiting irregularities inside the Kentucky program.

"I think Andy's great," Pitino said of Telfair's agent, "but I don't care for Bearup at all. Bearup and I are mortal enemies and will stay that way until the day I die. I don't think he's good for the game. Here's a guy, reputation-wise, who doesn't do it by the book. He's one of the biggest hypocrites of all time."

To which Bearup replied: "Rick is a hothead. I do not care what Rick Pitino thinks. Rick Pitino is irrelevant to me. . . . I think Rick Pitino is a great basketball coach; I always have and always will. But I think as a human being, he's somewhat substandard."

Beyond a healthy respect for Pitino's sideline brilliance, Bearup and the Louisville coach had something else in common: "I liked Sebastian from the first time I saw him at ABCD," the money manager said.

Adidas agreed, and now it was time to express its full appreciation. In that corner of the ESPN Zone, under the TV monitors and the stained-glass portrait of a sliding Jackie Robinson, the one marked April 15, 1947, Miller handed his client his lucky silver pen as Wulff readied a second copy of the contract.

"Initial each page when you're ready," Miller said.

"Both of them," Telfair answered.

"Both of them," Wulff said. "That way we know we didn't switch, or whatever, in legal terms."

Sebastian began racing through the first copy of the 25-page contract, initialing each sheet as if he were checking off a grocery list.

"Sebastian," Miller said, "you're not signing trading cards. Enjoy the moment."

Just then, Renan Ebeid stopped by the table to embrace Telfair and to reintroduce herself to Miller.

"Take care of this kid," Ebeid said.

"We definitely will," Miller responded.

Sebastian handed back the original contract. "You didn't sign everywhere you're supposed to," Miller shot back, pointing to the final—and most important—page. "Thank God we're all here."

Miller flipped through some papers to find his client's new Tax ID number; athletes due a considerable income were better off taking the money as a corporation rather than as an individual.

"Did Devin Harris declare for the draft yet?" Miller asked.

"Not yet," I said.

"What's the deadline again?" Wulff asked.

"May 10th," I answered.

"When do your tryouts start?" Wulff asked Sebastian, showing a weak handle on the accepted predraft dialect.

"Tryouts?" Bassy said with a quizzical look. "Oh, workouts. Sometime between the 17th and 20th."

"I'll go to Portland," Wulff said, "and go to the workout with (Blazers president) Steve Patterson."

"Yeah," Miller said. "We've got to talk about that."

Finally, with Telfair's initials and signature on every relevant contract page, the new multimillionaire rose from his chair and offered hearty handshakes around the table.

"Congratulations," Wulff said.

"My man," Telfair said.

At the same table where so many faceless Joe Six-Packs had talked up fantasy deals over Bud Lights and nachos, Sebastian Telfair, Andy Miller, and Kevin Wulff had just made one of those fantasy deals come to life. A kid who still didn't shave had just become filthy rich.

As the last of the celebrants headed for the door, Otis Telfair chewed on a toothpick, peered out from behind his omnipresent dark shades, and declared that nobody in his family was satisfied by the day's events. "This is only half the dream," Otis said. "I know Bassy will do a lot for us, for his brothers and sisters and mother, everybody. But after what we went through with Jamel, we've got to get Bassy called in the draft. We've got to see him go in the first round."

That was the hard part. Telfair didn't only have to live up to the hype anymore. He had to live up to the contract, too.

He was officially a paid professional, so there was no turning back. No pulling out of the draft at the last second and scurrying back to Piti-noville.

Telfair would compete against other first-round candidates, and he would do so under the watchful eyes of the NBA executives, coaches, and scouts who would determine his draft-night fate. First out of the gate were the Los Angeles Clippers, a lottery team in dire need of a point guard.

The Clippers invited Telfair to a workout on the morning of Friday, May 21st, and told him they'd made a reservation for two. Joining the Lincoln High star would be Jameer Nelson, only the best college player in the land.

o   o   o   o   o

They entered the Spectrum Club in Manhattan Beach, side by side, passing row after row of tanned bodies working up a membership lather on their treadmills. Sebastian Telfair of Lincoln High and Jameer Nelson of St. Joseph's University parted this sweat-stained sea on their way to the fitness club's basketball court. In his right hand, Telfair was carrying his S31T Adidas specials, his weapons for the day.

They pushed through the glass doors and entered the no-frills, bleachers-free gym with beige padded walls. Telfair and Nelson stretched and jogged and then joined Pape Sow of Cal State Fullerton and T.J. Cummings of UCLA, the two big men hired by the Clippers to fill out the two-on-two games the NBA allows; league rules prohibited teams from putting more than four players on the court for a predraft workout.

Telfair and Nelson were complete opposites in more ways than one. Telfair represented the trend of high school stars making the jump; Nelson was a dinosaur, an actual 4-year college player who led tiny St. Joe's to the brink of the Final Four and who won the John Wooden Award as America's best player.

Telfair walked into the fitness center with unblemished skin, while Nelson appeared with a Marbury's stash of tattoos. They both wore blue shorts and white sleeveless shirts bearing the Clippers' name. If this were a boxing match, Nelson would have looked like Joe Frazier and Telfair Sugar Ray Leonard. Built like an icebox, the 5-foot-11 Nelson had more than 3 years and 20 pounds on Telfair, whose arms and torso looked leaner and meaner than they were a month earlier.

Telfair had been working out at 5:30 every morning in the Lincoln gym, launching hundreds of NBA threes and practicing the standard NBA drills Jamel Thomas had recalled from his own brief experiences in the league. Telfair had been attending morning classes and then driving through Manhattan, over the George Washington Bridge, and onto Route 4 to the Hoop Zone in Englewood, New Jersey, where he would race through another round of drills.

As Telfair and Nelson started their duel, shooting around-the-horn jumpers at a rapid-fire pace, the Clippers' brain trust looked on. Elgin Baylor, the GM and former Laker great. Mike Dunleavy, the head coach, former NBA point guard, and son of Brooklyn. Barry Hecker, the director of player personnel and grandson of a man who owned a Brooklyn moving company. Gary Sacks, the young Hecker aide and a rising star in the organization.

Evan Pickman, the New York–based scout who attended Lincoln games and championed Telfair at every turn, didn't make the cross-country trip, but had Hecker and Sacks promise to call him as soon as the Telfair-Nelson face-off was done.

A weekend warrior occasionally pressed his face against the gym's doors for a quick survey of the goings-on, only to be waved away. Pre-draft workouts were off-limits to the media and often guarded as if peace in the Middle East were at stake. Team officials lived in fear of information leaking into enemy hands, information that could ruin their draft-night hopes. But the Clippers had agreed to let me watch this workout on the condition that I kept my observations in confidence until the postdraft publishing of this book.

The draft lottery was yet to be held, so the Clippers weren't sure where they would pick. If they ended up in the top 5, Telfair was likely out. If they ended up between 8 and 10, Telfair would have a shot. In either scenario, the Clippers had little interest in drafting Nelson.

Telfair was scheduled to show his skills to the Clippers, then the Trail Blazers, and then the Jazz, before flying back to New York. He didn't appear nervous at the start of his first NBA workout, though he'd been on the phone with Miller at 6:00 A.M., asking his agent how to dress, how to act, how to exude the right body language. Whatever Miller told him had worked. Telfair's weakness—his jumper—was Nelson's strength, but the high school phenom matched the college all-American shot for shot, this while Hecker noticed a flaw in Nelson's release.

"Look at Jameer's eyes," he said. "He's looking up and following the arc of the ball when he shoots. That's bad."

Two Clippers aides were filming every move Nelson and Telfair made. Hecker suddenly noticed a flaw in Telfair's release, too. He watched the Lincoln point guard shoot from straight over his head and said he needed to move his hands to the side.

"Sebastian's a special kid," Hecker said, "but I want all these kids to go to college. Other than LeBron, who's a freak, they should all go to school. The system's all fucked up."

Hecker had taken an immediate liking to Telfair, in part because the personnel man used to buy 10-cent hot dogs at Nathan's when visiting his grandfather. Hecker and Sacks had taken Telfair to dinner the night before. "He's very mature," Sacks said, "but he's definitely still a kid."

Telfair had to play like a man on this morning, as the Clippers were pushing the two point guards at a frantic pace. One drill charged Telfair and Nelson to dribble from half-court to a chair positioned above the 3-point line, execute a crossover, spin back the other way, and shoot a contested pull-up jumper. Nelson remained silent through this exercise. Halfway through, Telfair sounded like Monica Seles at the end of a long rally.

Telfair wasn't tired as much as he was determined. When Dunleavy started the two-on-two half-court games, Telfair teamed up with Cummings, the son of former NBA star Terry Cummings, and Nelson drew Sow. Telfair christened the competition by nailing a jumper over Nelson for a 1–0 lead; the first team to five would win the game.

A series of misses led to a long Telfair jumper and a 2–0 lead. Nelson found he couldn't beat his younger opponent off the dribble, and Telfair found his older opponent was so in-your-face rugged, he needed to shoot over him. A Telfair pull-up jumper made it 3–1. With Dunleavy serving as the on-court supervisor, but not a referee, Nelson called a foul on Telfair and kept possession. After the players changed ends to play on a surface that wasn't glazed with their sweat, Telfair made one of his most profound plays of the session.

Nelson was running down a loose ball near half-court when Telfair came flying out of nowhere, diving head-first for the ball, cutting Nelson at his feet and dropping him on his ass. Dunleavy smiled and Baylor nodded. If ever there was a foul worth taking, this was it.

Telfair's team won that first game, 5–4, on a Cummings jumper. Dunleavy lost track of the score in the second game, a game of picks-and-rolls, and erroneously awarded the victory to Nelson and Cummings (the big men had switched sides), who were actually trailing by a 4–3 count. Telfair and Cummings won the third game, and the fourth game—a full-court run charging the point guards to beat the trap—went to Nelson and Cummings. Telfair made the play of that game, too, hitting the floor hard to steal the ball from Nelson when the St. Joe's star repeatedly dribbled between his legs.

"He definitely didn't hurt himself," Hecker said of Telfair. "If you put these two kids in a gym and didn't know their names, you'd say it was a draw."

"Sebastian did very well," Sacks said. "He's a very, very good player, and so is Jameer. You've got to remember upside, and Jameer's older than Sebastian. But the hardest thing for a guy his size to do in our league is finish around the basket. If Sebastian were 6-foot-2 or 6-foot-3, it would make such a difference."

Dunleavy refused to tip his hand. He acknowledged that the Clippers needed a point guard, but said he was more concerned about spending a lottery pick on a player who was sure to become a star.

Baylor, the man in charge of making the Clippers' pick, was willing to say a little more. "Sebastian is very competitive, a leader, a guy with a great upside," Baylor said. "He's got very good quickness and handles the ball well. They keep talking about his size, and I think if you have the talent, that sort of compensates for a lot of things."

Unlike Baylor, who was there for Telfair's 37-point game at UCLA, Nelson had never before seen the kid play. Even though public praise of Telfair could have hurt his own cause, Nelson was generous in his assessment.

"I believe Sebastian is ready," he said. "I think he made the right decision coming out. . . . Obviously, I weigh more than him and I'm stronger. But he's just as quick and just as good."

Telfair came off the Spectrum Club floor confused over why the workout lasted a little less than an hour. Jamel Thomas had tricked him into thinking the average NBA workout was a 2½-hour marathon, this in the hope that Telfair would be extra fresh for a 50-minute session.

"I think I can work out again right now," Sebastian said. "(Nelson) is strong, but I thought he was going to be a lot stronger."

Telfair and Nelson exited the gym together, walked back past the procession of treadmill warriors, and entered a locker room full of bald and pot-bellied businessmen. At his stall, Telfair showed Nelson a fresh inch-and-a-half-long scar running down his left index finger. "I had a knife," he told Nelson, "and I was opening a DVD. My girl said something and I got distracted, and the blood flew over the counter."

I asked Telfair if he'd brought his girlfriend on this West Coast workout swing.

"Girlfriend?" he said. "Why?"

"I don't know," I answered. "Company?"

"This is business, man," Nelson interrupted. "We're trying to eat."

Baylor and Dunleavy took Telfair to lunch, and the Clippers started finalizing plans to bring in Livingston, Wisconsin's Devin Harris, and the University of Connecticut's Ben Gordon for their own point guard auditions.

Hecker, meanwhile, left a prank message on Pickman's answering machine saying that Nelson had kicked Telfair's ass and that Pickman hadn't been right about a prospect in 18 years. When the scout reached Sacks, Pickman asked him, "Did the workout look like a real good high school player versus a real good college player?" Sacks answered, "Absolutely not."

Pickman was fired up. The kid he'd been selling to the Clippers all along hadn't let him down. "If we're at seven or eight," Pickman said, "it might come down to Telfair or Devin Harris."

An hour later, Telfair and Nelson were exchanging cell phone numbers in the lobby of the Sheraton Gateway near LAX. Telfair invited me up to his room to talk about his first playing experience in an NBA setting.

Telfair sat on his king-size bed, pulled a frayed Bible from a new gym bag ("I carry that Bible with me everywhere," he said), and started digging into a small bag of trail mix. His mind was going a mile a minute, and his mouth wanted to keep up. So Telfair started talking about life, about money, about cars, about everything.

About cars: "I got a Lexus truck on a trade-in deal, and I bought myself the same BMW I bought Jamel. The base was $74,000, but it's fully loaded. I gave the (Nissan 350) Z to Bubba, and he's going to trade it in for that Crossfire. . . . The Z that I gave Bubba, that was Jamel's money. So we're going to trade in Jamel's Denali and get my brother Danny a car. He's going to get that new Chrysler, the 300. It's a cheap car, but it looks like a Bentley. My mom? She'll get whatever she wants, but she still doesn't want to move."

About Sylvester: "I talk to him all the time now on the phone. He calls me (from Rikers Island). He should be home this week, or next week. It's already resolved. He didn't do it. My mother is holding him there right now, and we're trying to find him an apartment. He's going to be cleared of (the attempted murder charge). . . . We always fought as kids. I got a slash above my left eye, and a knot above my right eye from him. He gave me three black eyes. I was more talented than him in basketball, but he was good, too. He could punk me, so me and him fought every day on the court. . . . What happened to my brother was, he grew up with no father. It was hard times then. He grew up on the streets, really. I'm not putting my father down, but he wasn't there for Sylvester."

About Tiny Morton: "He was too perfect for me. People around me say bad things about Tiny because he was around me, and they were jealous. Tiny didn't have any problems at Lincoln before I got there; everyone loved him then. And Tiny didn't get shit in this deal. Tiny's getting fucked over. He should've gotten something; everybody else got something. Tiny didn't get nothing."

About Andy Miller: "People think Andy gave Tiny money, and Andy is the cheapest guy in the world. If Andy gave me money, I would tell you. What the hell is anyone going to do to me now? Nothing. Yo, Andy is the cheapest guy. . . . When I'd go with him sometimes and we'd put our cars in the lot, I'd say, 'Oh, I've got no money for the parking.' And he'd be like, 'Oh shit, you really don't have any money?' But Andy is the best. He navigates me through everything."

About the draft: "Man, I want to get picked high. People ask my why I chose the NBA over college, and it's simple: It's the opportunity I've dreamed about my whole life. I'm like, how can you turn it down? I still would've declared for the draft even if I didn't get the sneaker deal. . . . I really didn't want to go to school. I want to make my family happy and let them live a good life, but it's more than that.

"I want to play in the NBA so bad. I put so much into this. I mean, I really can't wait to get there."

19

It was draft night, June 24th, and Sebastian Telfair had sacrificed a piece of his vision to end up inside Trump International Hotel and Tower Suite 510. Telfair was supposed to be wearing Armani and shaking David Stern's hand in front of the hometown crowd. He wasn't supposed to be wearing a David Beckham T-shirt and staring out a window at the evening traffic snaking around Central Park.

Beckham. What an unfortunate choice of attire. That very day, the English megahunk had missed a penalty kick in a shoot-out that helped Portugal advance in the European Championships, a development that had some countrymen calling for his captaincy.

Telfair knew only that Beckham was an Adidas teammate and a man who charmed his own girlfriend, Samantha Rodriguez. "She loves him," Telfair said as Samantha nodded her head in confirmation. Besides, Telfair figured he had it all covered with the silver Jesus Christ medallion that was dangling from his neck, a piece that cost him about $4,000 earlier that day.

The draft had already started at the Theater inside Madison Square Garden, and Telfair and guests were picking through take-out steak in plastic containers and drinking from bottles of water that carried the image of Donald Trump's face. Telfair would take in the biggest night of his basketball life with Samantha, Bubba Barker, Tiny Morton, Andy Miller, and Miller's marketing rep, Chris Brantley, a former receiver for the Los Angeles Rams and Buffalo Bills. Miller had allowed me to document the occasion. He hadn't authorized the appearance of the eighth and final person in the room, a man in a gray suit Telfair jokingly introduced as his lawyer, Desmond.

Desmond was actually Telfair's driver for the night, and Miller didn't find any humor in his presence. The agent refused to make eye contact with the driver, and did a slow burn when the man began joining the conversation while Miller frantically worked his cell trying to get his client drafted.

This was dead-serious business, with millions of dollars at stake, and Miller couldn't believe he had to conduct it in the company of a complete stranger. The agent hadn't even invited Telfair's parents and siblings to their Trump station. He couldn't take a chance on Telfair's father, Otis, or Jamel Thomas erupting in the event the first round rumbled toward the second round with the Lincoln star still on the board.

The Telfairs fell apart that 1999 night when Jamel's name wasn't called, and Miller had no interest in living out a sequel. So he had Telfair instruct his family to meet him at Jay-Z's club, 40/40, on 25th and Broadway. Telfair was to let his family members believe he would join them for the draft. He was not to tell them where he was actually heading, whom he would be with, or when he would finally show at 40/40.

Telfair's secret draft-night hideout became a story all its own. It started when Miller and Stu Jackson, the NBA's senior VP of basketball operations, talked about the draft's green room and whether Sebastian should be in it. The NBA generally invited the 15 players who had the best chance of becoming lottery picks, and it was hardly an exact science. Rashard Lewis broke down in nationally televised tears at the 1998 draft before he was made the 32nd pick. The idea was to avoid these embarrassing episodes as much as possible.

Jackson knew the latest word on Telfair had him slip-sliding away from Lotteryville. So Jackson didn't extend an invitation to Telfair, but told Miller he would put one in the mail if the agent needed to save face.

Miller was caught between a desire to market a client with a great smile—a client Adidas didn't make a multimillionaire so he could hide in the shadows—and a need to protect that client from a humiliating experience in his own backyard. Miller knew there was a chance Telfair could take a plunge. He feared those ESPN cameras catching a family member in full rage. "Potentially," Miller said, "it could be the biggest nightmare of my career. I don't need Sebastian as the last person in the green room, and then have him crying on the back page of the *New York Post*."

The agent told Jackson he'd take a pass. As much as he wanted Telfair to light up the New York crowd, and as much as he wanted to honor that Adidas investment, Miller didn't believe the risk was worth the reward.

That's when David Stern got involved.

Knowing that the Knicks didn't have a first-round pick, and that there was no LeBron-like star in the field, and that analysts were calling this among the weakest drafts ever, Stern called Miller and told him he wanted Sebastian in the house. Telfair represented the sexiest story line of the draft. Would he fall? How far would he fall? Would Adidas look foolish? Who would have the stones to bank a first-round pick on a 5-foot-11 high school player with holes in his game?

Stern needed Telfair to pump life into an otherwise limp event. It was a curious stance, given that the commissioner had suddenly started talking tough again about pushing the union on an age requirement of 20. Stern didn't want a draft night dominated by high school prom kings—unless one served his marketing purposes, of course.

The NBA wasn't alone in applying this double standard. With the NFL celebrating its legal victory over Maurice Clarett, representatives of the Indianapolis Colts attended a spring football workout at Lincoln and observed its highly regarded receiver, Nyan Boateng. "They told me I reminded them of Marvin Harrison," Boateng said.

Beautiful.

Stern couldn't plow through Miller's resistance, and word was the commissioner let Stu Jackson have it for his failure to insist from the start that Telfair be on the premises. Miller didn't care that Stern was furious at him. His client wasn't guaranteed to go before number 20, and Miller wasn't about to have Telfair play the fool on the Garden's Theater stage. The agent and the league discussed a scenario where Miller and Telfair would watch the draft from a hotel room near the Garden, and then rush on down if the pick was to their liking. But in the end, Miller chose Trump and the Central Park view.

The confusion led ESPN and other news outlets to deliver conflicting reports on whether Telfair had been invited to the draft. A premature news release from JA Apparel said it was outfitting Telfair for the draft and putting him in a Joseph Abboud Black Label dark gray pin-striped suit, a lavender shirt, and silk tie—a release that infuriated Miller.

To complicate matters, Telfair told the *New York Times* that he would attend the draft, even though he had no intention of doing just that. The point guard was amused by the fuss over an issue that only enhanced the interest in the draft's biggest mystery.

In his white number seven Beckham T-shirt, silver Christ medallion, long gray shorts, and white Adidas headband and wristband and sneakers, Telfair watched the ESPN coverage from a chair in his suite's living room. Miller was sitting across the room and closest to the TV, his cell phone earpiece never leaving his left ear.

Stern called up Dwight Howard to the podium as the third high school player in 4 years to go number one in the draft, and suddenly the phone rang. Telfair was summoned to the call by Samantha. When he returned, he joked, "That was my father. He said, 'Why the heck didn't you go number one?'"

The University of Connecticut's Emeka Okafor went second to Charlotte, which had swapped lottery picks with the Clippers, and then Okafor's teammate, Ben Gordon, went third to Chicago. Gordon said something about being the most versatile guard in the draft. "If I said that, they'd be killing me," Telfair said. "I can't say anything about myself."

Miller had Isiah Thomas on the line, and he was updating the Knicks' president on the other teams interested in the Pacers' Al Harrington. "I appreciate the nice things you said about Sebastian in the paper," Miller told Thomas before hanging up. The next call on the cell wouldn't meet the same welcome.

"Jamel," Miller said. "What do you want? We're busy."

Miller disconnected his phone from his earpiece and flipped it to Telfair in disgust. Jamel Thomas wanted to know why Telfair wasn't with him and the rest of the family at 40/40. "We've got to take care of business here," Telfair told him before abruptly hanging up and flipping back the cell to Miller with an equal measure of disgust. "I'm not dealing with that now," Telfair said. "Five Thirty is buggin'."

Telfair shook his head, took a deep breath, and slowly exhaled. His boyish charm wasn't part of this Trump Tower scene. In fact, Telfair began looking like Dick Clark—the world's oldest teenager. He was, after all, a kid who couldn't even share his moment of truth with his family. Telfair could joke about his father and Thomas and their off-the-wall expectations and needs, but he wouldn't say anything about the family member who caused him the most angst in the weeks leading up to the draft.

Sylvester wasn't pacing among his parents and siblings at 40/40. He was in a jail cell at Rikers Island, waiting to hear if his kid brother, the good son, had hit the lottery.

Sylvester was in that cell because Sebastian had decided against posting his $150,000 bail.

o   o   o   o   o

Inside Brooklyn Supreme Court, 2 weeks before the NBA draft, the Honorable Patricia DiMango was screaming at a weeping defendant accused of selling marijuana and Viagra.

"That really infuriates me," DiMango shouted as she pointed toward the tracks of the young man's tears. "Stop selling drugs. Do something with your life. Do it. Do it. Like the commercial says."

A stony silence gripped DiMango's packed ninth-floor courtroom as the defendant and his lawyer departed and the batter on deck stepped to the plate. Glen Singer, assistant district attorney, introduced himself as the prosecutor in the case against Sylvester Telfair, seated and handcuffed behind his back in the first of four long wooden benches that stretched from one end of the room to the other, benches defaced with angry scribblings and chewed-up gum.

This was the same scene, more or less, that Sylvester had starred in 13 days earlier, when his father, Otis, had come to Room 941 with the false expectation that his son would be released into his arms. During that appearance, DiMango heard prosecutors offer Sylvester 15 years for a plea, an offer immediately rejected by Jeffrey Sugarman, his attorney from Legal Aid.

"The complaining witness has completely changed his story," said Sugarman, who asked that the case be dismissed.

Sugarman would later tell me that Ahmad Rennick, the man whom Sylvester allegedly shot in the face on February 26th, had told police "he didn't recognize the perpetrator, whose face was covered in a white bandana. He told the DA he had no direct knowledge of who shot him. I took that as recanting his story."

Otis Telfair had said he had conversations with Rennick after the shooting, a fact that clearly wouldn't sit well with the prosecution. "(Rennick) told me that he told the cops it was Sylvester because that was the name out on the street," Otis said. "He knows now that Sylvester didn't do it. He's going to say that in court, and Sylvester's going to give up the person who did it and then he's going to get out of there."

But as Otis sat next to me in the courtroom on May 28th, wearing a blue Adidas sweat suit and holding his black cane, he was about to discover that Sylvester wasn't going anywhere. DiMango called the lawyers to the bench and scheduled a June 10th court appearance loud enough for most in the courtroom to hear. His hands cuffed below his jeans jacket, Sylvester wheeled left from his standing front-row position, looked at his father, and rolled his eyes. Otis waved in disgust at Sugarman, who asked for a reduction in the $150,000 bail because the complaining witness had "recanted his allegations."

"The people move against any reduction in bail," said prosecutor Richard Boye. "We're investigating tampering with the witness and request that bail remain the same."

Citing Sylvester's criminal record and the investigation into alleged tampering, DiMango kept the bail at $150,000. Otis picked up his *Post* and stormed out of the courtroom to meet with Sugarman, this while court officers escorted Sylvester through a door to DiMango's left and back to Rikers Island.

"They were supposed to let him out today," Otis barked at Sugarman in the hallway. "He was supposed to be coming home with me. They're using stall tactics."

"Mr. Telfair, I understand," Sugarman said. "But Charles Hynes, the district attorney, is investigating whether there was tampering with the complaining witness."

"There was no tampering," Otis snapped. "They're just trying to keep him in there all summer. (Rennick) said Sylvester didn't do it."

Otis headed for the elevators while Sugarman headed for the stairs.

"I told Jamel this wouldn't work," Otis said. "Jamel wanted to go with Legal Aid. He didn't want to put up a $5,000 retainer, and I knew that was a mistake. If we had a lawyer with power, Sylvester would be home already. This case would've been thrown out. Sylvester was with his girl. He wasn't even at the scene, and now they're trying to tie him to the two killings in our building, and he had nothing to do with that. They've been trying to interview him at Rikers, and Sylvester won't see them. He doesn't know anything about that shooting, and he doesn't want to talk to them.

"We didn't tamper with (Rennick). That guy called me and said he was sorry. We've known the guy. They must think because now we have that (Adidas) money, we gave (Rennick) money. We didn't do anything. And I'm not going to involve Bassy or Adidas in bailing (Sylvester) out. . . . We're not going to mess (Sebastian) up before the draft."

Back in Patricia DiMango's courtroom 2 weeks before that draft, Sugarman asked again for the case to be thrown out. Sylvester was cuffed and standing to his right, wearing a casual long-sleeve shirt and jeans. He resembled Sebastian, but his face was longer and leaner and not so boyish.

"We're not dismissing this case," Singer said. "We're still investigating and the police are still investigating. . . . There are allegations our witness has been tampered with by people associated with the defendant."

Sitting to my left, Otis responded, "Bullshit." Sitting to my right, his stepdaughter, Terica, shook her head. Terica was Danny Turner's 30-year-old sister, but she had a special affinity for her stepbrother, Sylvester. "That's my baby," she said. Sylvester had blown her a kiss when he took his front-row seat.

In a courtroom overflowing with family members, lawyers, and young black and Hispanic men in cuffs, one after the other, tempers were painfully short. DiMango, an attractive woman with long dirty blonde hair, didn't suffer commotion easily. She was about to prove that in a most forceful way.

Sugarman asked for bail to be reduced from $150,000 to $50,000, saying "the prosecution has indicated my client is a prime suspect in another incident. He's never been charged, and that incident was many months ago." DiMango cited Sylvester's record. "One felony as a youth offender," she said. "A second felony, weapons, 3 years in jail. I see he's on probation until 2008. This is a violent felony, attempted murder. He's had a number of bench warrants, too. He's offered 15 years (in prison). Bail will remain the same."

"Bitch," Terica said under her breath.

As the trial date was set for July 29th, Terica took the occasion to rise from her third-row seat, exit the bench from the right, and then, remarkably enough, approach her handcuffed stepbrother to give him a hug and kiss. A stunned female court officer hesitated before shouting at her to get back, and as Terica retreated, a male officer grabbed Sylvester and admonished him as he led him out of the courtroom. "You know you can't do that," the officer told Sylvester.

Otis sat silently next to me as Terica was called back to the front row by the female officer, who reprimanded her for approaching a defendant. When Terica hesitated and muttered something in return, DiMango screamed at her to do what the officer had ordered.

"You did something completely inappropriate," DiMango shouted. "You talked back to her with an attitude. That's totally unacceptable." When Terica tried to interrupt the judge, DiMango shouted her down. "In about 5 seconds you will be appearing before me," she said. DiMango ordered Terica to apologize to the officer. When Terica offered a less-than-half-hearted "sorry" and turned away, DiMango demanded a second apology. This time Terica sounded a tad more sincere.

"I don't want that woman back in here again," DiMango said. Outside the courtroom, Terica promised to defy that order. She said she was once arrested for talking back to a judge, an offense that earned her a $400 fine.

"This whole thing is the one negative in my life," Otis said. "Everything else is going great, but we've got to get past this. My kids have basically stayed out of trouble, but Sylvester has made some mistakes. Just like I did, I guess."

Sugarman emerged with the grand jury minutes in his hand, and he offered them to his client's father. Otis flipped through the pages until he reached the point where Rennick apparently told the grand jury he did indeed see Sylvester shoot him. "That's not what he told us," Otis told Sugarman.

Sylvester declined my requests to talk to him about the case at Rikers or by phone, and Singer, the prosecutor, declined comment. Rennick couldn't be reached for comment. Sugarman wouldn't say where his client was at the time of the shooting, or whether the police had hard evidence that Sylvester was involved in the double homicide.

"My client is adamant that he is innocent," Sugarman said. "He's obviously distraught over being falsely accused, but he's a very intelligent person who's maintaining a positive outlook. Their case against him isn't a strong one. We're very confident in the outcome."

That outcome, according to Otis, would determine whether Sylvester ever again had a place in their family. "This is it for Sylvester," his father said. "If he comes out and messes up again, we're done with him as a family. He's on his own then.

"But when he gets out of jail, I think we've got to get him out of Coney Island. . . . I never wanted Bassy involved in this, but he said he was going to bail out Sylvester on June 20th. I think it's time. I think Sylvester should be home before the draft."

o   o   o   o   o

Sylvester wasn't home before the draft; he was phoning Sugarman from the Otis Bantum Correctional Center on Rikers Island and telling him he heard Portland would take his brother with one of their three first-round picks, perhaps at number 13. Sugarman was a Celtics fan who wondered if Danny Ainge might take his client's brother at 15.

Sebastian would have taken either one, and not out of any desire to stuff his already overstuffed wallet. In addition to the $18 million-plus already guaranteed by Adidas, Andy Miller had cut marketing deals with Lexus, Sprint, Armani, Joseph Abboud, David Yurman, five trading card companies, and an Internet company, deals expected to earn Sebastian more than $500,000 a year.

But as Sebastian sat and paced and waited inside his Trump Tower suite on draft night, money didn't mean a damn thing to him. He wanted respect and vindication. He wanted to prove that he was a ballplayer, the real article, and not some grossly overhyped and over-paid kid. To accomplish that, Telfair needed to get drafted before the twenties.

He needed to get in the teens. He needed to get in the lottery, this year defined as the top 14 because of the inclusion of the expansion Charlotte Bobcats.

Telfair shared that sentiment with his agent and shoe company. Adidas officials were sweating profusely as the draft approached and the reports on Telfair's position got gloomier by the hour. "They were afraid they were going to be the laughingstock of the draft," Miller said.

The same went for the agent. Professionally and personally, it was a stressful time for Miller. His wife, Ilene, was pregnant and due to give birth the week after the draft. And, like Rick Pitino had said, Miller couldn't afford to go down as the agent who made Telfair rich with sneaker money, but who sabotaged his career by rushing him into the NBA. Competing agents would have used that against Miller at every turn.

"There was so much negativity and so much scrutiny around Sebastian before the draft," Miller said, "that I had to try to make a run at the highest number possible. I had to turn a negative into a positive. I never let Sebastian work out for any team lower than number 20. I didn't want the words 'fell to 23' in every newspaper."

In the Trump suite, Miller worked his cell as the picks ticked off the board. Shaun Livingston went to the Clippers at number 4, formally ending Evan Pickman's hopes of seeing Telfair run his team. The Clippers' officials who worked out Telfair all liked him, but Mike Dunleavy—once a small point guard—didn't want to coach a small point guard. The Clippers nearly took Wisconsin's Devin Harris, who would have made a more immediate impact than Livingston, but decided in the end that the 6-foot-7 Livingston might someday be another Magic Johnson.

The Wizards scooped up Harris at number 5, this as Tiny Morton arrived in a huff on Lincoln Standard Time. Morton was wearing a white tank top and the look of a man possessed. "I'm going to take care of you if this kid isn't drafted," the coach told Miller through a smile. Morton immediately cranked open an Amstel Light and pumped up the volume, making everyone more nervous than they had any desire to be.

The Hawks took Stanford's Josh Childress at number 6, prompting Miller to turn to Telfair and Morton and say, "Your boy is dead now." Miller was referring to Oak Hill's Josh Smith, whose agent, Wallace Prather Jr., happened to be the son of Smith's summer coach. In negotiations with Adidas, Miller said, Prather had asked "for a dollar more than Sebastian got." Adidas didn't give it to him.

"My body's so numb," Sebastian said as he eyed his barely eaten dinner, "I can't even tell if this steak is cold."

The pace started to pick up in the room. Miller was working a backup plan at number 20, in the event Portland passed on Telfair at 13, and Boston and Miami did the same at 15 and 19. Miller knew Orlando wanted a point guard, so as soon as the Magic took Dwight Howard with the first pick, the agent began trying to convince John Weisbrod, Orlando GM, that he should make a deal with the Denver Nuggets, who were willing to surrender number 20 for a future first-rounder.

Plenty of teams were willing to give up their slots in a draft some felt was dreadfully weak. "If they could have," said one Western Conference official, "half the league would've passed on their picks rather than give three-year guarantees to whoever was available. David Stern would've called their number, and they would've said, 'Pass.'"

The Suns took Luol Deng at number 7, and the Raptors, in a shock, took BYU's Rafael Araujo at number 8, before Arizona's Andre Iguodala went to the Sixers at number 9. Suddenly there came the most pivotal moment of Telfair's draft. Cleveland was up next at number 10. LeBron James had said that he wanted his good friend, Telfair, on his team. Jim Paxson, GM, didn't share LeBron's enthusiasm for the Lincoln star.

But the Cavaliers were in position to give Telfair an assist by taking a pass on Jameer Nelson and plucking Oregon's Luke Jackson off the board. At 13, the Blazers had no interest in Nelson. They did have interest in the local boy, Jackson.

When Stern appeared on the TV screen and announced that the Cavaliers had chosen Jackson, Miller shouted, "Yes!"

Then his cell rang. John Nash, Portland GM, was on the line. "John," Miller said. "Okay. We'll be here. Thank you."

Miller turned to Telfair, sitting at the dining table and no longer even remotely interested in his take-out steak. "We're getting close," the agent said. "We're 75 percent there at 13."

Telfair buried his face in his quivering hands and whispered, "He just made me more nervous saying that."

A 5-foot-11 high school player was one phone call away from becoming a lottery pick. The Portland Trail Blazers were on the verge of taking a big gamble on a small kid, and not everyone in their draft room wanted to roll the dice.

○　○　○　○　○

The minute Adidas made Telfair as rich as he was famous, rumors spread throughout the league that a deal with an NBA team was in place. No way Adidas would have put itself out on a limb so long and wobbly, the thinking went. An NBA executive must have agreed to honor that investment in exchange for sponsorship dollars, luxury suite purchases, and billboards galore for a photogenic draft choice.

The Trail Blazers were fingered as the team most likely to have made that handshake deal.

The Blazers were in the market for a backup point guard who would be a viable replacement for Damon Stoudamire, headed for free agency in 2005. Dan Dickau wasn't the answer. Omar Cook, of all people, had earned a temporary home on the Blazers' roster, but nobody saw him as a keeper.

Nash was known to be smitten with Telfair; the GM thought the Lincoln point guard was already better than Stoudamire. And Adidas's corporate offices were around the bend from Portland's Rose Garden. Kevin Wulff, the Adidas executive who presided over the Telfair signing at the ESPN Zone, didn't do anything to quash the talk of a draft arrangement when he attended Telfair's workout in Portland on May 23rd.

Wulff had a good relationship with Blazers' team president Steve Patterson, who also held talks with David Bond, the Adidas executive who fell in love with Telfair after his performance at Pauley Pavilion. Nash would spend part of that May 23rd workout questioning Wulff on the extent of Adidas's background checks before it signed Telfair; Wulff would tell an associate he left the session "feeling probed."

But the more important development that day was Telfair's performance against Duke's Chris Duhon in drills observed by Nash and head coach Maurice Cheeks, among others.

"He did very well," Nash said that night. Miller offered to cancel Sebastian's remaining workouts if Nash would guarantee that he'd take the point guard at number 13, but Nash declined. "Andy has more to gain with a guarantee than we do," the GM said. "As far as the people we've brought in so far, Sebastian's been the most impressive. I like him better than Jameer."

In the Telfair-Duhon workout, Sebastian proved he was the quicker player and the superior passer; he also showed a surprisingly reliable shot from the outside. "Damon's contract has one year left on it," Nash said of Stoudamire. "Adidas is right here, and Andy told us he'd like him to get away from New York City if he can. But this is a crazy draft. People once thought Sebastian would be gone by 13, and now he might be available to us at 23."

Miller had no interest in waiting until 23, so he put on the full-court press at 13. The Blazers had to think long and hard before drafting a high school player so high. They'd just missed the play-offs for the first time in 22 years, this after using the 23rd pick of the 2003 draft to take Mississippi high school star Travis Outlaw, who would score all of 8 points in the 2003–04 season.

In fact, Outlaw, Ndudi Ebi, and Kendrick Perkins—the other three high schoolers taken in the first round of LeBron's draft—combined to score 43 points in their rookie seasons. James Lang, the Alabama high school star taken in the second round by the Hornets, was put on the injured list before he was cut without scoring a point.

But Portland had a strong support system in place in the event it drafted Telfair. Like many teams managing younger and younger rosters, the Blazers had hired staffers to help players find a home, open a bank account, order cable TV, install a phone, you name it. "Stuff parents help their 18-year-olds with," Nash said. "Because of their size and ability, we sometimes forget how young these players are. . . . The level of naivete is remarkable."

And sometimes sobering. Most teams asked their draft candidates to take psychological exams, and the Blazers hit Telfair with a 500-question test that he took over the 2 days he spent in Portland. A typical question read something like this:

If you're attending a party where all of your friends are drinking alcohol, what would you do?

A. Ask for a beer

B. Go home

C. Tell everyone drinking isn't cool

D. Just sit there and act cool

Nash wasn't looking for specific answers to certain questions; he just wanted the team psychologist to either identify potential problems or, in the GM's words, "find someone who knocks your socks off with competitive instinct."

Miller thought his client was that kind of competitor, but also knew Nash, Patterson, and their boss, billionaire Paul Allen, would eventually ask pointed questions about Telfair's family. With their players involved in a series of run-ins with the law, the Trail Blazers were universally ridiculed as the Jail Blazers. Patterson and Nash had come in with a new-sheriff-in-town management style, promising that their team would follow a strict code of conduct.

How would this new approach jibe with the drafting of a player whose brother was charged with attempted murder and whose father had been convicted of manslaughter?

The Blazers didn't push the issue, at least not in the early stages of the process, but Miller knew it was coming. Until then, the agent put out other fires. Two negative columns—one written by John Canzano of the *Oregonian*, the other by Peter Vecsey of the *New York Post*—left Miller in a tizzy. Canzano wrote that the Blazers should stay clear of the hyped-up New York prodigy and use the draft "to do what Telfair does best. That would be pass."

Vecsey wrote that "anonymous opponents from obscure colleges" had outplayed Telfair in workouts, and that Adidas's "comprehensive agreement" with the Blazers to buy corporate suites and extensively promote Telfair was in serious jeopardy. Miller believed Vaccaro was spreading false information to hurt him (for beating Vaccaro cronies Arn Tellem and Bill Duffy on Telfair), and to hurt Telfair (for aligning himself with Vaccaro's former employer, Adidas). Vaccaro denied Miller's claim, saying, "I can't stand Andy Miller, but I'd never do anything to hurt Sebastian."

On May 26th, 3 days after Telfair's workout in Portland, Vaccaro had told me, "Wulff and Portland have already made a deal. Adidas is going to do a lot of advertising and buy boxes and do a whole arena deal. You ought to ask how Wulff is at that workout. That's unbelievable. I heard Sebastian got his ass kicked by some unknown guard in that workout. Supposedly (Blazers scout) Tates Locke approached Nash and said, 'You can't do this Sebastian thing. At worst, we can get a guard as good as him at some other point.' I believe this is really political. I believe in my heart this deal's been done."

Nash had acknowledged that Adidas was a factor in the Blazers' considerations, only not one that would carry the day. He said he allowed Wulff to watch Sebastian's workout only as a courtesy to a sponsor and suite holder, and maintained that there was no signage deal with Adidas in place. "Sonny's got an ax to grind," Nash said. "He paid the rent and then didn't get the kid, and now he's apparently out to punish him and send a message to other kids that if you screw me, I'll screw you."

Adidas executives figured Vaccaro was acting out after promising Reebok he'd sign Sebastian, his own Iverson without tattoos. Whatever. Adidas was left to hope for the best possible landing place for its multi-million-dollar investment, and Miller thought the shoe company wanted Telfair in Portland. "Kevin Wulff wouldn't say that," the agent said, "but being so close, they could do a lot with Sebastian in that community. Kevin's into that stuff, and Portland would want to do business with Adidas."

Daren Kalish, the Adidas executive, wasn't so sure Portland was the right fit. "Ideally," he said, "you want Sebastian in one of the NBA's big markets. You don't want him in Toronto. But either way, he's the most marketable player in the draft. . . . All of our buyers are from New York, so if he's wearing a certain shoe they're going to buy more pairs."

Miller wasn't naive enough to bank on the prospect of Portland taking his client. He booked auditions around the country while working, as much as possible, around Telfair's schoolwork. Miller tried arranging all workouts between Friday and Monday to limit the damage in the classroom.

After his opening West Coast swing through the Clippers, Blazers, and Jazz, Telfair worked out for Golden State, Cleveland, Toronto, Boston, Miami, and Denver. Miller canceled Telfair's date with the Suns because of a slight groin strain, and he canceled one with the Hawks on the assumption that they wouldn't draft a point guard. The Lakers and Nets watched Telfair run through a session of his own design at the Hoop Zone in Englewood, New Jersey.

The Nets represented an interesting possibility. Telfair's good friend, Jay-Z, had purchased a stake in the franchise that the new owner, real estate developer Bruce Ratner, was planning to move to Telfair's hometown of Brooklyn. With the Nets needing a backup point guard and with Jason Kidd nearing the downslope of his career, Telfair was a player the team president, Rod Thorn, would have seriously considered at number 22.

"I think Sebastian's terrific," Thorn said. "He does all the things you think point guards should do, and he's going to get better as a shooter."

But with Ratner looking to cut costs while his team endured its lame-duck stay in Jersey, the Nets traded the 22nd pick to Portland for Eddie Gill and $3 million of Paul Allen's stash, giving the Blazers three first-round picks and back-to-back choices at numbers 22 and 23. "Do me a favor," Thorn told Nash. "If Sebastian falls to you at 22, wait until 23 to take him. I don't want to go down as the guy who traded the local hero."

The local Coney Island hero would take a Cyclone ride to draft night. Most of Telfair's workouts were met with positive reviews, although the Jazz wished he had shot the ball better. Marty Blake, the NBA's director of scouting, declined to include Telfair among the likely lottery picks who gathered at the Chicago predraft camp for physicals and news conference appearances. Blake's snub was taken as another sign that Telfair was on the plunge.

Danny Ainge continued raving about Telfair regardless, just like he had 5 months earlier at UCLA. At the Chicago camp, Ainge sat down with Nash and Cheeks and went on and on about the Lincoln point guard. After the Celtics executive left, Cheeks told Nash, "Wow, Danny really loves Telfair." To which Nash responded: "I just think Danny wants us to take him so he can use 15 to get who he really wants."

Ainge was hoping to draft Robert Swift, the very 7-foot high schooler from California whom he'd met with (and later ripped) at UCLA. Ainge's guarantee that he'd take Swift with one of his three first-round picks (15, 24, 25) allowed the California center to decline all NBA workout offers and stay home until his draft number was called. If Swift were gone by the time the Celtics picked, then Ainge would weigh Telfair against one or two other candidates.

Toronto was impressed with Telfair, but didn't think he was good enough to be picked at number 8. Cleveland and Golden State were interested at 10 and 11, but not interested enough. So Telfair's lottery shot came down to Portland at 13. Cheeks, himself a pro's pro at the point, had told the *Oregonian* that Telfair was a better prospect than Jameer Nelson and the one player who stood out among those the Blazers worked out. "That kid Telfair had something about him that I saw," Cheeks said. "It's there."

Miller was left to convince Portland's entire management team to see what its head coach saw, so he went to work on the teams that would pick right before the Blazers returned to the first-round plate at numbers 22 and 23. Miami's Pat Riley had interest at 19, and Miller was one of the few agents whose calls Riley returned. Denver had interest at 20. Utah was lukewarm at 21, but Orlando and Minnesota were interested in trading into that spot to get Telfair before Portland could.

"Kevin McHale really likes Sebastian," Miller said.

But not everyone in Portland did, which was more reason for Miller to create the leverage necessary to force Nash's hand at 13. Mark Warkentein, the Blazers' director of player personnel and a friend of Sonny Vaccaro's, shocked nobody within the organization when he led the anti-Sebastian brigade. Tates Locke, the scout, was another nonbeliever.

Neither had the juice to kill Telfair's chances. Paul Allen did.

Nash and Steve Patterson were Sebastian's biggest advocates, and the cofounder of Microsoft generally listened to both. Allen had hired Patterson the previous June, and Patterson's first major hire was Nash, a former executive with the Nets, the former Washington Bullets, and the Sixers. Their mission was to restore the severed bond between team and community, and their plan was to be far more accessible than their dismissed predecessor, Jail Blazer warden Bob Whitsitt.

The camera-shy Allen wasn't entirely comfortable with the fresh approach. But he knew his franchise was in desperate need of change, and he was willing to go along.

But would the owner go along with the selection of Sebastian Telfair at 13? Allen was a draft junkie. He enjoyed watching tapes of prospects as much as he enjoyed meeting them and talking to Nash and Patterson about them. Given the Blazers' long run of play-off appearances, Allen was new to the draft lottery. He wanted to savor this choice. He wanted to make sure his Blazers got it right.

So 3 days before the draft, Telfair returned to Portland to show off his new and improved shooting touch (he shot well despite being hobbled by a sore knee) and to meet with a Blazers contingent that included Allen, who hadn't attended Telfair's workout the previous month. Nash and Patterson asked most of the questions in the meeting, while Allen mostly observed in relative silence. Earlier that day, Allen watched as his $20 million-plus, three-seat rocket ship, SpaceShipOne, roared out of the California desert and into history, becoming the first privately financed manned spaceship to leave the atmosphere.

The Telfair meeting gave Allen a chance to come back to Earth.

"Paul has a real appreciation for someone like Sebastian because he's a self-made guy," Nash said. "It was good for Paul to see him in the flesh, because Sebastian comes across as a sincere, likable kid. I remember when I first talked to Paul about Sebastian, he said, 'I love those New York City point guards. I love those guys.'"

Allen had surprised Nash with his range of basketball and hip-hop interests. "I remember once I called him from the Rocky Mountain Revue summer league in Salt Lake," Nash said, "and there was this loud rap music in the background. I told Paul, 'Let me get to a different spot, this music is killing me.' And he said, 'What, you don't like rap music?' And then he starts rattling off all these different rappers he likes. Paul really is a street-hip guy."

Allen was street-hip enough to know that there was another high school star out there whom the Blazers needed to consider with the 13th pick. Al Jefferson was his name, and he would become one of the last hurdles Telfair had to clear.

Jefferson was a 6-foot-10, 265-pound forward from Mississippi who reminded some of a young Ben Wallace. He had delivered strong performances in the McDonald's All-American Game and in the Nike Hoop Summit, and no NBA executive or scout figured he could last long enough for Portland to get him at 22 or 23.

"Ideally," Nash said, "we'd like to come away with Jefferson and Telfair." He offered numbers 22 and 23, and number 23 and cash, to Atlanta (number 17) and other franchises drafting in the teens, but found no takers. The Blazers thought they could take Jefferson at 13, and then grab Telfair at, say, 17.

But when they couldn't find a trade partner, the Blazers realized they'd have to choose between the big man and little man. Nash was concerned that Jefferson's game was too similar to that of the Blazers' Zach Randolph. Warkentein was worried Telfair would go down as another over-hyped, Kenny Anderson-esque New York guard.

The Nash-Warkentein divide ran deeper than their differences over the 2004 draft. After 5 years as an assistant GM, Warkentein felt he deserved a promotion in the wake of Whitsitt's dismissal. Neither he nor Nash felt comfortable with each other's presence, and Nash spoke privately about his desire to bring in his own people to replace Warkentein and other members of the staff.

That was an issue for another day. On the night before the draft, Portland's management team met for dinner and made Telfair and Jefferson the only two items on the menu. "Paul really likes Sebastian," Nash said before that dinner, "but I think he slightly favors Jefferson."

Allen had seen Telfair on tape and found him to be an extraordinary passer, but the owner was concerned that a 5-foot-11 point guard would have trouble scoring around the basket. Nash shared that concern, but felt Telfair's extreme quickness would allow him to create enough space to score in transition.

"Sebastian was the fastest player we worked out," Nash said. "Put him and Jameer Nelson in a footrace with the ball, and Sebastian's going to beat him down the floor. He's a little jet. I don't think Jameer really even compares to him. From end line to end line, with a dribble, we timed Sebastian at 3.3 seconds. That's the same time it took Mickey Mantle to get from home to first base."

Nash needed a home run on the high school front. He failed to draft Kobe Bryant for Jersey in 1996 (he took Kerry Kittles), and failed to draft Kevin Garnett for Washington the year before (he took Rasheed

Wallace). Though Nash blamed Calipari and Abe Pollin for those choices, the GM faced no formidable opposition this time around.

In the predraft dinner, the pro-Telfair and pro-Jefferson officials engaged in spirited volleying. Warkentein and Locke simply didn't have the organizational clout to make a difference, and Allen didn't have a particularly strong preference for Jefferson. Something else was working in Nash's favor: Telfair had met Allen, and Jefferson had not. The Mississippi high school star had to cancel his scheduled workout in Portland when he injured his shoulder auditioning for the Sonics.

On the day of their dinner, the Blazers sent their psychologist to Mississippi to give Jefferson his exam. In the end, Sebastian's NBA fate might have rested on Jefferson's test.

Not that Sebastian scored an A-plus on his own psychological exam. The Blazers thought he fared fine, but their psychologist found contradictions and felt Telfair had been coached to answer some questions the way he felt the team wanted them answered.

"If our psychologist calls us and says Jefferson is one of the greatest competitive people he's ever tested," Nash said, "that could be the difference. Otherwise, it's just another factor to be considered. We don't know Jefferson that well, but our scouts really like him. People I trust tell me he's a man, and that if he's on the board, he'll be very hard to pass up."

Their dinner debate behind them, the Blazers rose on the morning of June 24, 2004, with a good feeling about whom they expected to draft. Nash wouldn't disclose the results of Jefferson's exam, but a source close to the team said Jefferson had arrived late for his meeting with its psychologist.

Nash and Patterson had one more test to administer. All along, they had a private investigator combing through Telfair's background, conducting interviews and checking everything from his academic progress to his motor vehicle records. This was standard operating procedure. In fact, the NBA had its own investigator working the halls at Lincoln High.

"He told us not to say anything about it," said Renan Ebeid, Lincoln athletic director, "but everyone gave a positive report."

"The NBA investigator was asking us if we'd ever seen Sebastian use drugs or anything like that," said Nyan Boateng. "The guy was like, 'Don't lie, because we'll find out one way or another.' But I told him Sebastian doesn't even drink."

The Blazers' investigator would hear much of the same. "We talked to Rick Pitino and everyone else around him," Nash said. "We only got glowing reports about Sebastian."

The Blazers were concerned about the criminal histories of Sebastian's brother and father. So with only hours to go before the draft began, Nash and Patterson were on a conference call with Miller, asking him why the Jail Blazer reform movement should welcome a young player with a turbulent family background.

Miller turned it around and declared that the Telfair family problems were the very reasons why the Blazers should take Sebastian. If Sebastian could emerge from that environment as a functional and likable kid, Miller reasoned, he would endure whatever adversity came his way.

The Blazers thanked the agent for his time and assembled in their draft room. Nash, Patterson, Allen, Warkentein, and Locke joined scout Philip "Chico" Averbuck, general counsel Mike Fennell, and staff members Allison Horn and Brad Weinrich. They gathered for a draft Nash called "one of the craziest I've seen. It might be the worst ever for immediate results, but also one of the best for 5 years down the road. You might get a better player at 20 than 4 in this draft. Who's to say that Shaun Livingston is going to be a better player than Sebastian Telfair? Livingston has the size, but does he have Telfair's cojones?"

Cojones? Telfair wasn't feeling so bold as his hour of reckoning approached. "I'm scared," he told Boateng.

He needed one phone call for that fear to strike out.

∘   ∘   ∘   ∘   ∘

"Sebastian," Andy Miller barked. "Do you want to go to the Garden if you're taken at 13?"

The Cavaliers had just picked Oregon's Luke Jackson at 10, and Nash had called to tell Miller the Blazers were preparing to take his point guard.

"Nah, fuck that," Telfair said. "I want to go see my family."

The Warriors picked Latvia's Andris Biedrins at 11, and Telfair clapped.

"Josh Smith and his agent aren't too happy now," Miller said through a laugh. "They're fucked."

Telfair dropped his head into his hands.

"Stephon called me four times today," Miller said. "He's mad I haven't called him back. On his last message he said, 'Call me back!'"

The Sonics took Robert Swift at 12, and suddenly the room stopped. Even Tiny Morton grew still. Miller had already told Telfair the Blazers were 75 percent there, even though John Nash had actually told the agent their decision was more or less set in stone. More or less. Miller had been around long enough to know that counting unhatched chickens at the draft was a dangerous game to play.

No, Miller needed that official call as much as Telfair did. In Portland, Nash did one final check with his people in the draft room, then rang Miller's phone.

"John," the agent said. "Okay, thanks."

Miller turned to Telfair. It was 8:43 P.M., June 24, 2004, when the agent pointed to the 5-foot-11 point guard out of Abraham Lincoln High School and pronounced him an NBA lottery pick. "You're a Trail Blazer," Miller said.

Telfair couldn't even smile as he pointed toward the TV. "Hell no," Telfair said. "I've got to hear it out of his mouth."

David Stern approached the mike at 8:45 P.M. At the dining table, Telfair slid up to the edge of his seat and braced his 168-pound body as if he were expecting a punch in the gut.

"With the 13th pick of the 2004 NBA draft," Stern said on TV, "the Portland Trail Blazers select Se-bas. . . ."

Telfair exploded out of his chair and began wildly pumping his fists, this as Stern finished his name and just stood there at the podium, all alone for the world to see. Morton, Bubba, Samantha, Miller, Brantley, and the driver converged around Telfair. On the TV, ESPN cameras showed New Yorkers standing and cheering in the Garden's Theater crowd. "Fuck that," Sebastian shouted. Jameer Nelson was among the five players invited to the draft who were still sitting there, still waiting for their names to be called.

ESPN's Jay Bilas and Stephen A. Smith started pounding the Blazers for making this choice, and Miller told his client, "I'm glad we're not there. You don't need that." Miller's cell rang. "Hey John, congratulations," the agent said to Nash. "I know you're going to be very proud of this decision."

Miller handed the cell to Telfair. Nash and Maurice Cheeks were on the line, soon to be followed by Allen. "Hello," said Telfair, his voice quaking with glee. "How are you doing? I'll do that forever. Thanks a lot. I appreciate everything. A lot of hard work, a lot of hard work. Thanks so much. I'm so excited."

Telfair would speak to Mike Hanson, Portland's PR guy, to set up a conference call later that night with the Blazers' media. After hanging up, Telfair got on his own cell. "Where's Mommy?" he said. "I'm coming right now."

Still wearing his Adidas headband, Telfair slid into a black Armani suit and readied Bubba and Samantha for the ride to Jay-Z's 40/40 club.

"When it became apparent Sebastian wouldn't get to us at 22 and 23," Nash said, "we made a tough decision. . . . We had Telfair and Jefferson rated pretty evenly, but if Jefferson became the player we thought he'd be, either he or Zach Randolph would have to be traded.

"We think people will look back on this someday as a great pick for us."

Telfair wasn't looking back as he hopped into a Trump Tower elevator with Samantha and Bubba and Desmond the driver and sped off to see the family members barred from his suite. Telfair had just landed another $5.1 million over 3 years, giving him a total guarantee of some $24 million in NBA and marketing wages.

High on his point guard's stunning selection and feeling the buzz of a few Amstel Lights, Morton jumped into my cab as we headed south to

40/40. The last thing on Morton's mind was that Department of Education investigation that appeared to be as lifeless as those experts who had predicted gloom and doom for Telfair's draft.

"Fuck everyone now," the Lincoln coach shouted. "Fuck Sonny. Fuck Ziggy. Both of them should retire. Out of business. Tell Sonny, 'Ha ha.' You just don't understand how many people attacked me over how I handled this kid. Well, how do I look now? People were trying to expose me in the paper, but this proves I did it the right way. Amazing. There were so many doubters. And things with Sebastian's family over the last 3 years. People don't know what I went through.

"Now I can't wait for the next challenge. Win a city title without Bassy. Oh yeah, I'm coming back to Lincoln. We're going to win four in a row."

The 40/40 club had that dark and unmarked appearance of an after-hours place. We beat Telfair to the club by a few minutes, then waited near the front door for him to arrive. Telfair pulled up, moved briskly through the door, and headed upstairs and past some silver curtains to the two rooms reserved for dozens upon dozens of family members and friends.

Telfair was engulfed in cheers as he embraced his mother, Erica. Sebastian began to sob. Someone poured a bottle of Cristal over his head, and Telfair staggered across the hallway and into an anteroom, wincing from the sting of champagne.

He began to sob some more. As his son settled into a seat, Otis started toweling him off as if he were a trainer working over his fighter in the corner.

"Thirteen," Otis said, brushing his white towel back and forth. "They can't take that from you. You upset the world right now."

The walls in this room were covered with LeBron, Jordan, and Mariano Rivera jerseys. Kenny Anderson would make an appearance. So would Josh Smith, finally taken by the Hawks at 17, and Kevin Wulff, the Adidas man.

Half of Coney Island was jammed into this small corner of Jay-Z's extra-large world. Telfair was telling people about the best phone call of his life—"and I've gotten a lot of calls," he said. Bubba, the sidekick Miller called "the underboss of the operation" and "the MVP of the predraft process" for his reliability, said his long-awaited Crossfire was due to roll in the following week.

Jamel Thomas worked the room and told people that the moment he first hugged Sebastian Telfair, lottery pick, "it felt like I'd gotten drafted." Wearing his white cap and dark shades while sitting stoically on the club's Hugh Hefner–size bed, Otis said he and his wife were ready to move out of the Surfside Gardens projects. "But there's no rush," he added. "I mean, this was perfect. A dream come true. We're going to enjoy this first."

Otis and Erica both had kind words for Miller, the agent they never wanted in Sebastian's life. "Thanks for taking care of my son," Otis told him. "You're an angel sent down by God," Erica added. She later said, "We were wrong about Andy. We judged him too harshly."

Thomas was heard to say that Telfair still should have been a top 10 pick, talk that Miller ignored. In the end, Telfair might have gone to Boston at 15 or Miami at 19 had the Blazers taken a pass. In the end, the point guard couldn't have cared less.

"It turned out the right way for me," Telfair said to a group of reporters and cameramen that had cornered him. "My mother don't have to count no more."

Telfair would shoot pool and drink bottled water. Miller would share stories about the immense pressure he felt to do right by his client, pressure that produced his best body of work. He would talk of the difficulty in fighting off Sonny Vaccaro before he slipped away from the club, crossed the Hudson, and returned to his New Jersey home.

It was 2:30 A.M. when Miller's 3-year-old daughter, Emma, rose from her slumber to sit on her father's lap. SportsCenter's draft highlights threw flickering light across the black night. Miller's pregnant wife, Ilene, joined her family while fighting a losing battle with heartburn.

Ilene put her head on Miller's shoulder, and husband, wife, and child watched in silence as Telfair got picked all over again on ESPN.

The agent couldn't savor the moment. He was already dreaming up methods of attack for Telfair's second contract negotiation in 2008, and reminding himself that he had to get up in a few hours to find a team for his undrafted client out of Gulf Coast (Florida) Community College, Sani Ibrahim.

Across the river, Bubba and Sebastian were back in their Trump Tower suite. They talked about the late-night appearance of Jay-Z and Beyonce at 40/40. They talked about traveling the NBA circuit together, and living the American dream that remains a foreign concept to so many Coney Island boys.

"Is this really happening?" Sebastian asked Bubba.

"You made it happen," Bubba told his best friend.

They agreed to fall asleep. Ten hours later, Sebastian Telfair stepped into Jay-Z's Mercedes limousine and headed off to graduate from Abraham Lincoln High.

EPILOGUE

Sylvester Telfair was freed from prison in late October 2004 when a judge dismissed the attempted murder charges against him after the victim said he couldn't identify Telfair as his assailant. In the final stages of his case, Sylvester was represented by Barry Krinsky, the lawyer who had represented Sylvester's father, Otis, in his manslaughter case.

Eugene Lawrence earned the major Division I scholarship he was shooting for when he transferred from Canarsie to Lincoln; he signed with St. John's. Yuriy Matsakov enrolled at Brooklyn's Kingsborough Community College in the hope of playing basketball and attracting the eye of a Division I or II recruiter. Antonio Pena transferred to St. Thomas More, the Connecticut prep school, in an effort to improve his academic standing. Nyan Boateng, the all-American wide receiver, broke his ankle in football camp but planned on recovering in time to play at least part of his final basketball season at Lincoln.

Corinne Heslin retired as Lincoln's principal. In the fall of 2004, Renan Ebeid said the school still hadn't heard from the Department of Education regarding its endless investigation of Tiny Morton. Brooklyn USA's Ziggy Sicignano declared Morton the winner of the street war Ziggy had declared on the Lincoln coach.

Ziggy hadn't heard back from the NCAA. "Tiny beat the system," he said. "He more than survived; he used the system and won. Case closed. He beat everybody."

Morton said Sebastian Telfair had offered to pay off his student loans as a show of appreciation.

Evan Pickman of the Clippers won four dinners from fellow NBA team officials who had bet him that Telfair wouldn't get picked in the lottery.

Jim Boeheim called Telfair's decision to go pro one that no college coach could question. "You can't even come close to second-guessing it," Boeheim said. "It was a great move. If he'd gone to Louisville for a year or two, it wouldn't have worked out any better."

Rick Pitino was back at Sonny Vaccaro's ABCD camp in July of 2004, standing in the same courtside spot where he watched Telfair face Darius Washington in 2003, and looking ready to have his heart broken all over again. Vaccaro claimed he was thrilled that Telfair went as high in the draft as he did. "The kid deserves everything he got," Vaccaro said. "He got a lot of money and my ex-friends at Adidas had to give it to him, so I'm happy about that."

Vaccaro signed Shaun Livingston for Reebok, giving him a deal worth $1 million annually. Kevin Wulff, the Adidas executive who signed Telfair and fellow high school draftees Dwight Howard, Josh Smith, and J. R. Smith, stepped down in a company shake-up.

Omar Cook was released by Portland to make room for Telfair, who entered the draft against the warning of those who feared he'd become another Omar Cook. Cook was later signed by the Charlotte Bobcats. Mark Warkentein, the Portland executive who was in the anti-Telfair camp, resigned just days after the draft.

Danny Turner ran his first summer tournament through Telfair's deal with Adidas. Bubba Barker said he would travel with his best friend during his rookie season with the Blazers. Jamel Thomas played for Portland's summer league team, on Telfair's recommendation, but wasn't invited to the Blazers' training camp. Jamel signed with a team in Italy.

Otis proudly drove the streets of Coney Island in his Infiniti QX56. "We're going to get a new home," Otis said, "but we're not in any big rush." Erica said she felt the neighborhood was starting to grow more dangerous. "Kids are dropping like flies out here now," she said. "It's getting to be like it was in the '80s. It's like the OK Corral." Three weeks after Stephon Marbury returned from Greece with an Olympic bronze medal, a cousin on his father's side,

Yusuf McEaddy, was shot dead two blocks from the Telfair home.

Sebastian Telfair was given his Lincoln number, 31, by the Blazers. He impressed Blazers coaches with his quickness and passing during summer league and preseason play. Sebastian moved into a 3,900-square-foot, multilevel house in the Portland area, complete with skylights and a sauna.